0196356655
748.29
FLO

W9-AVM-126

JUL 1 9 2011

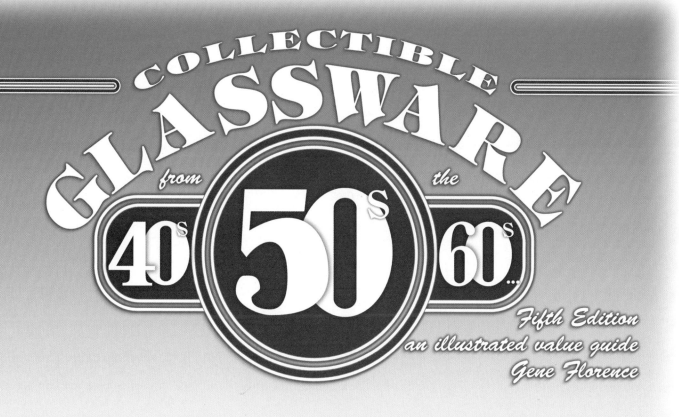

COLLECTIBLE GLASSWARE from the 40s 50s 60s...

Fifth Edition
an illustrated value guide
Gene Florence

MISSISSIPPI VALLEY
LIBRARY DISTRICT
408 WEST MAIN ST.
COLLINSVILLE, IL 62234

COLLECTOR BOOKS
A Division of Schroeder Publishing Co., Inc.

ABOUT THE AUTHOR

Gene Florence, Jr., born in Lexington in 1944, graduated from the University of Kentucky where he held a double major in mathematics and English. He taught nine years in Kentucky at the junior high and high school levels before his glass collecting "hobby" became his full-time job.

Mr. Florence has been interested in collecting since childhood, beginning with baseball cards and progressing through comic books, coins, bottles and finally, glassware. He first became interested in Depression glassware after purchasing an entire set of Sharon dinnerware for $5.00 at a garage sale.

He has written numerous books on collectibles: *The Collector's Encyclopedia of Depression Glass*, in its fourteenth edition; *Kitchen Glassware of the Depression Years*, in its fifth edition with updated values; *Elegant Glassware of the Depression Era*, in its eighth edition; *The Collector's Encyclopedia of Akro Agate, The Collector's Encyclopedia of Occupied Japan, Volumes I, II, III, IV, V* and *Price Guide Update Series 1–5; Very Rare Glassware of the Depression Years, Volumes I, II, III, IV, V, VI; Glassware Pattern Identification Guide; Stemware Identification; Anchor Hocking's Fire-King & More;* and the *Pocket Guide to Depression Glass*, now in its eleventh edition. A new book to be released this year is *Glass Candleholders of the Depression Era*. He also authored six editions of a baseball book that is now out of print as well as a book on Degenhart for that museum.

His Grannie Bear Antique Shop in Lexington, KY, closed in 1993, due to the death of his beloved mother, "Grannie Bear," who oversaw that store. However, Mr. Florence continues to sell glassware at Depression glass shows throughout the country as well as via mail order or his web page (http://www.geneflorence.com). Currently, substantial time is spent in Florida where writing is easier without the phone ringing every five minutes — and fishing is just out the office door!

If you know of unlisted or unusual pieces of glassware in the **patterns shown in this book,** you may write him at Box 22186, Lexington, KY 40522, or at Box 64, Astatula, FL 34705. If you expect a reply, you must enclose a SASE (self-addressed, stamped envelope) — and be patient. Very little mail is answered between Christmas and the middle of May due to his writing, research, and travel schedule. This often causes a backlog of the hundreds of letters he receives weekly. He appreciates your interest and input and spends many hours answering letters when time and circumstances permit which is often on plane trips or in motel rooms across the country. Remember that SASE! He does not open mail. Most letters without a SASE are never seen by him!

On The Cover

Front: Royal Ruby two-tier set, $50.00; Early American green water goblet, $35.00; Big Top peanut butter water tumbler (pattern not featured in this edition), $20.00 with original lid and contents; Panel Grape banana stand, $160.00.

Back: Fire-King "Shell" platter, $20.00; Fire-King "Shell" cream and sugar, $30.00 set; Early American Prescut individual shakers, $75.00 pair.

Cover Design: Beth Summers
Book Design: Beth Ray

The current values in this book should be used only as a guide. They are not intended to set prices, which vary from one section of the country to another. Auction prices as well as dealer prices vary greatly and are affected by condition as well as demand. Neither the author nor the publisher assumes responsibility for any losses that might be incurred as a result of consulting this guide.

COLLECTOR BOOKS
P.O. Box 3009
Paducah, Kentucky 42002-3009

or

GENE FLORENCE

P.O. Box 22186   or   P.O. Box 64
Lexington, KY 40522   Astatula, FL 34705

Copyright © 2000 by Gene Florence

All rights reserved. No part of this book may be reproduced, stored in any retrieval system, or transmitted in any form, or by any means including but not limited to electronic, mechanical, photocopy, recording, or otherwise, without the written consent of the author and publisher.

Printed in the U. S. A.

CONTENTS

ACKNOWLEDGMENTS

Thanks to all the friends, readers, collectors, and dealers who have contributed extensive data on patterns for this book. There are an additional seven patterns in this fifth edition of the *Collectible Glassware from the 40s, 50s, 60s...* and the book is now fifty percent larger than it was when started in 1992. Were it not for you, it could not have grown the way it has.

Thanks, particularly, to Cathy, my wife, who works long hours as my chief editor and critic. She adjusts my words to tell you what I thought I said! It doesn't seem as if half of our lives have been involved in this publishing world; but they have. There are sixty-six books out there as a legacy to our efforts. I hope they have enriched you in some way.

Thanks, too, to Cathy's mom and dad, Sibyl and Charles, who helped us sort, pack and repack glass for days on end. A new system has cut this job to weeks instead of months; but it expanded our sorting routine at the annual, week-long photo session. Charles, Sibyl, and Marc kept everything under control in Kentucky while we traveled. Marc is overseeing my web page (http://www.geneflorence.com) along with his computer teaching job. Chad has faithfully been around to load and unload photography and show boxes when needed. Revising books every two years necessitates all hands on deck pitching in time and effort.

A special thanks to Barbara Wolfe and Marianne Jackson at Anchor Hocking for their wonderful help and information. Glass, brochures, catalogs, and pricing information were furnished by collectors and dealers from all over the country. Among these delightful people are the following: from Illinois, Dick and Pat Spencer, and Floyd Craft; from Tennessee, Jimmy Gilbreath; from Washington, Carrie Domitz; and from New Jersey, René Fry. Additional information came from various readers across the U.S.A., Canada, England, Puerto Rico, Australia and New Zealand! Please know I appreciate your efforts; and just lately, I've had a number of collectors specifically tell me to convey their thanks to all who help. Even data given that I cannot yet use is much treasured — and, even better, recorded.

Photographs for the book were taken by Richard Walker of New York, and Charles R. Lynch of Kentucky, both of whom went above and beyond. Most photographs were taken during one six-day session; additional photographs were taken as needed by Charley at Collector Books. We did a marathon five books last year; that's too many. I decided to cut back this year to three!

Unwrapping, sorting, arranging, carting, and repacking glass for our photography session were handled by Cathy Florence, Dick and Pat Spencer, Jane White, Zibby Walker, and the guys from the shipping department at Collector Books. My supervisory position was a strain! Glassware brought in by collector friends filled an extra twelve tables of glass! Assembling all these photographs in the time available is an enormous task, particularly since we have two photographers working four different photography stations. We photograph large groups, small groups, shelf shots, and individual shots all in the same large room at nearly the same time. You have to see it to believe it! Richard explained that he took four or five photos in a day on the jobs he had "BGF" (Before Gene Florence). We have him up to thirty or more on good days.

Thanks for all the photographs and information that confirm new discoveries (or point out omissions) that you readers have sent! It really takes a picture to validate new pieces. If you have trouble photographing glass, take it outside in natural light, place the glass on a neutral surface, and forget the camera has a flash attachment. A bright cloudy day works best. If you wish photos returned, please enclose a large, self addressed, stamped envelope. It has to be large enough to return your pictures. You would not believe the number of smaller-than-the-picture envelopes I get.

Thanks, also, to Beth Ray in the Editorial Department at Collector Books who did design and layout for this book. It's great to see all the work become reality in a few short months. I have enough trouble keeping up with new software updates without having to learn designing skills! If I've omitted the name of anyone who contributed, please forgive me; know that I, as well as all readers, thank you for your contributions.

PREFACE

Collectible Glassware of the 40s, 50s, 60s... has gone through a transformation from the initial concept; primarily, the book encompasses glassware made after the Depression era that is now being bought by glass collectors. Patterns after 1940 (e.g., Holiday and Moonstone) were removed from *The Collector's Encyclopedia of Depression Glass* except for a few that overlapped both time periods. This permitted me to research newer glass being collected and also to augment patterns in *The Collector's Encyclopedia of Depression Glass*.

Preparations took over five years before launching the 50s book; but it has been so well received that some Depression glass clubs and show promoters have had to revise contracts to make allowances for glassware made during this time span. Many club contracts were written twenty (or more) years ago and times and collecting habits have changed. One club sent a contract out in early summer that said glass was acceptable made up until 1970. Two weeks before the show, that contract was voided, saying Fire-King made after 1958 was not allowed. There were many disappointed collectors searching for last year's hottest commodity and not seeing it. Collecting patterns change! Everyone in the collecting business needs to keep up. Twenty-nine years ago, when I first started writing about glass, Depression glass was found regularly at garage, estate, and rummage sales. Now, glassware made during the 40s, 50s and 60s is being discovered in those same haunts. Before this book, there was little information available for collectors on this generation of glassware. Now, there are dozens of books; so, you have to even be selective about what books to buy.

Both mass-produced and handmade glassware from this 50s era are included in this book inasmuch as both classifications are being collected. A few handmade glassware patterns included were begun near the end of 1930, but their predominate production was during the 1940s, 1950s, or even later.

Anniversary and Fire-King patterns have been considered Depression glass, but neither was introduced until after 1940. I have spent considerable time compiling available information on Fire-King lines. All that work led to a new book last year called *Anchor Hocking's Fire-King & More*. I can honestly say that when I wrote this foreword two years ago, that was the furthest thing from my mind; but before that fourth edition was released, my publisher had convinced me to write the Fire-King book. That book has helped straighten up Fire-King listings in this book. You should check them out for new information.

Fenton made few dinnerware lines before 1940. I have included several of their lines made since then.

I will continue to add company catalog pages of various patterns when available. With actual catalog pages, many pieces are precisely identified for collectors. Many of the Fire-King catalog pages have been transferred to that book. That allowed me to add more patterns and information to this book. I hope the trade is beneficial to you.

Anchor Hocking's Early American Prescut was included as one of the new patterns in the last book. What a change is being seen in collecting that pattern! I recognize that I am only scratching the surface of this era, but it is a start! Eventually, this book may be divided into some arrangement of Elegant and mass-produced glassware, but not yet.

If you have a collection that you would be willing to lend for photography purposes or copies of glass company advertisements listing pieces which you received with your sets, let me hear from you. Requests and collecting trends will determine the direction this book will take in the future. I hope you are finding the education enjoyable! Keep me apprised of your discoveries! I will try to pass your information along to other collectors.

PRICING
All prices in this book are retail prices for mint condition glassware. This book is intended to be only a guide to prices since there are some regional price differences which cannot reasonably be dealt with herein.

You may expect dealers to pay from 40% to 50% less than the prices quoted. Glass that is in less than mint condition, i.e., chipped, cracked, scratched, or poorly molded, will bring only a small percentage of the price of glass that is in mint condition. Since this book covers glassware made from 1940 onward, you may expect that dealers and collectors will be **less** tolerant of wear marks or imperfections than in glass made earlier.

Prices are now fairly standardized due to national advertising of glassware and dealers who market it at numerous glass shows held from coast to coast. I have attended shows in Florida, Houston, and Chicago in the last month to study price trends. Still, there are **some regional differences in prices** due partly to glass being more readily available in some areas than in others. Many companies charged more initially for wares shipped to the West Coast, and companies distributed certain pieces in some areas that they did not in others. This happens today, also. It's called "test marketing."

Prices tend to increase exponentially on rare items. In general, prices increase due to **demand** from additional collectors entering the field and from people becoming more aware of the worth of this 1950s glass.

One of the most important aspects of this book is the attempt to illustrate as well as realistically price those items that are in demand. My desire is to give you the most realistic guide to collectible glass patterns available.

MEASUREMENTS
All measurements are taken from company catalogs or by actually measuring each piece if no catalog lists are available. Capacities of tumblers, stemware, and pitchers are always measured to the very top edge **until nothing more can be added.** Heights are measured **perpendicular** to the bottom of the piece, not up a slanted side. In company catalogs, plate measurements were usually rounded to the nearest inch or half inch, across the widest point; this creates problems today, when we demand exactness!

ANNIVERSARY JEANNETTE GLASS COMPANY, 1947 – 1949; late 1960s – mid 1970s

Colors: pink, crystal, iridescent, and Shell Pink

Collecting all 1950s memorabilia is now the rage; glassware made in that era has suddenly been noticed by collectors who never sought glassware previously! Many basements and rec rooms have added 1950s glassware to the juke boxes, bars and chrome sets as accoutrements. Some of this has to do with availability. 1950s glassware is naturally more available than that made in the 1920s and 1930s. Changing collecting trends launched this book in 1992; and as the millennium approaches, this fifth edition is being published with yet an additional seven patterns never shown in earlier editions! Some of these added patterns are very 50s... yes, a bit avant-garde, a little "out there" as befits the Sputnik era. As collecting trends change, I try to keep up!

It is definitely more exciting to collect a pattern that you can have some hope of acquiring than to search for pieces of a pattern with limited distribution or that time has simply decimated the supply. Some of the patterns within this book had years of production and were marketed nationally, while others were distributed only regionally. The good news is that almost every pattern represented in this book can still be collected — with time and persistence.

Anniversary is a pattern formerly collected by Depression glass collectors, which was never actually produced during that Depression era time frame. Many "older" collectors still think Anniversary is Depression glass – but it truly is not! Pink Anniversary was only included in Jeannette catalogs from 1947 until 1949; but crystal and iridescent could be acquired in boxed sets in "dish barn" outlets as late as 1975. You will find crystal trimmed with both silver (platinum) and gold; so far, these trims do not add to the price.

Iridescent Anniversary can be seen at flea markets and antique malls; but often it is excluded from many Depression era glass shows since it was made in the 1970s. Iridescent is collectible and prices are actually surpassing those of crystal in some areas. Iridescent Anniversary is not "carnival glass;" don't be fooled by those pricing it as such. A snack plate with a cup indent has just been spotted in

Iridescent; watch for those. There is a growing trend for collecting snack plates, so add iridescent Anniversary's as a new one to attain. The soup bowl with the metal lady base seems to have been a popular merchandising ploy since they abound using glassware from several different companies.

A groove is found on the crystal cake plate. That aluminum lid pictured fits into this groove. There seem to be an endless array of decals on these cake covers.

The pink Anniversary butter dish, pin-up vase, wine glass, and sandwich plate are troublesome to find. Both the wine and pin-up vase are reasonably priced considering how few of them are exhibited at shows.

The 1947 Jeannette catalog lists the open, three-legged candy as a comport and that is how I list it. Jeannette chose to use the older term "comport" rather than "compote." Terminology has simply changed over time.

	Crystal	Pink	Iridescent
Bowl, 4⅞", berry	3.50	8.00	4.00
Bowl, 7⅜", soup	9.00	18.00	6.50
Bowl, 9", fruit	12.00	25.00	12.00
Butter dish bottom	14.00	30.00	
Butter dish top	13.50	30.00	
Butter dish and cover	27.50	60.00	
Candy jar and cover	22.50	45.00	
*Cake plate, 12½"	10.00	20.00	
Cake plate w/metal cover, round	17.50		
Cake plate, 12⅜" **square** w/metal cover	25.00		
Candlestick, 4⅞" pr.	17.50		25.00
Comport, open, 3-legged	5.00	15.00	5.00
Comport, ruffled, 3-legged	6.00		
Creamer, footed	5.00	10.00	6.00

	Crystal	Pink	Iridescent
Cup	4.50	8.00	4.00
Pickle dish, 9"	6.00	15.00	7.00
Plate, 6¼", sherbet	1.75	3.00	2.00
Plate, 9", dinner	5.00	15.00	6.00
Plate, 12½", sandwich server	6.50	15.00	8.00
Relish dish, 8"	5.00	14.00	6.50
Relish, 4-part on metal base	20.00		
Saucer	1.00	2.00	1.00
Sherbet, ftd.	3.50	10.00	
Sugar	4.50	9.00	5.00
Sugar cover	6.00	11.00	3.00
Tidbit, berry & fruit bowls w/metal hndl.	13.00		
Vase, 6½"	13.00	30.00	
**Vase, wall pin-up	15.00	35.00	
Wine glass, 2½ oz.	10.00	20.00	

*Shell Pink $225.00
**Shell Pink $200.00

"BEADED EDGE" (PATTERN #22 MILK GLASS), WESTMORELAND GLASS COMPANY, late 1930s – 1950s

I have always been told by Westmoreland collectors that "Beaded Edge" is only a collector's name for Westmoreland's Pattern #22 milk glass. If you will look at the catalog sheet depicted on page 13, you will note that Westmoreland, as a matter of fact, referred to this pattern as Beaded Edge. There are additional catalog pages shown in earlier editions of this book; however, space limitations do not allow me to repeat them.

I have been unable to acquire several items with fruit decorations. The three-part relish, oval celery, and platter may be more difficult to find than I had previously thought. In fact, I have only seen a few of those particular pieces, but they were without decorations! One of the fun things about being an author is searching for items that I do not have pictured. Decorations of fruits, flowers, and birds appear in sets of eight designs. I finally found dinner plates in eight fruit patterns and tumblers in eight flower decorations. It took quite a few years and miles to accomplish that task, but I enjoy the pursuit!

Most bird decorations are still flying out of my grasp! You may also find an occasional Christmas decoration; I have had reports of them, and have now seen one red poinsettia plate.

Illustrated on page 9 are "Strawberries" and varied purple fruits including "Plums," "Raspberries," and "Grapes." and on page 11 are "Apples," "Cherries," "Peaches," and "Pears." The 15" torte should be found with each fruit, although I haven't seen all of them. Apples, pears, and peaches are seemingly prevalent in the mid-America areas I have been searching. Dinner plates, crimped bowls, and sherbets can be hard to find; buy them when you can! Actually, only the luncheon plates, cups, saucers, and tumblers are considered easy to find. I am particularly fond of those pastel, bordered plates shown on the bottom of page 9. I assume these can only be found on plates. Let me know if you see any other pieces.

The creamer and covered sugar shown with cherries at the bottom of page 11 have grapes pictured on the opposite side. That sugar and creamer is Westmoreland's Pattern #108 and not "Beaded Edge." If you collect either one of these fruit patterns, I recommend you find a set of these Pattern #108 instead of the normally found footed ones, shown beside them. Westmoreland, like most glass companies, issued numbers to "patterns" and not the names which collectors are so accustomed to using.

The reverse side of the 15" plate is pictured at the bottom of page 12 showing twelve zodiac symbols. The opaque white color hides this surprise until the plate is turned over!

	Plain	Red Edge	Decorated
Creamer, ftd.	11.00	13.00	17.50
Creamer, ftd. w/lid #108	18.00	25.00	35.00
Cup	5.00	7.00	12.00
Nappy, 5"	4.50	6.50	16.00
Nappy, 6", crimped, oval	7.00	10.00	20.00
Plate, 6", bread and butter	5.00	7.00	9.00
Plate, 7", salad	7.00	10.00	12.00
Plate, 8½", luncheon	7.00	10.00	12.00
Plate, 10½", dinner	15.00	22.00	35.00
Plate, 15", torte	25.00	40.00	65.00
Platter, 12", oval w/tab hndls.	30.00	45.00	95.00
Relish, 3-part	25.00	40.00	95.00
Salt and pepper, pr.	30.00	35.00	60.00
Saucer	2.00	3.00	4.00
Sherbet, ftd.	9.00	12.00	18.00
Sugar, ftd.	12.50	15.00	17.50
Sugar, ftd. w/lid #108	18.00	25.00	35.00
Tumbler, 8 oz., ftd.	8.00	12.00	18.00

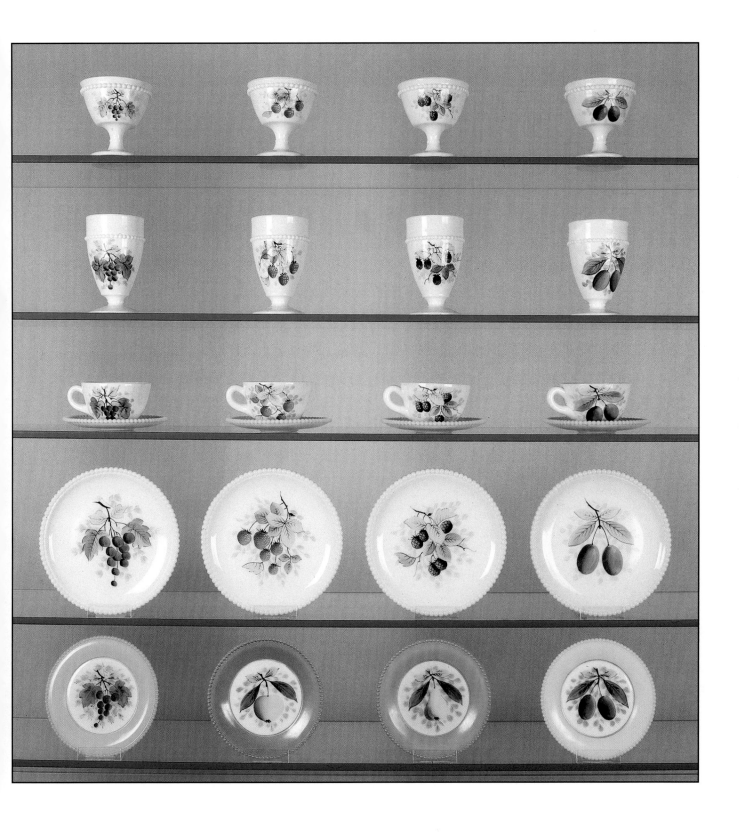

Westmoreland Handmade, Hand Painted Milk Glass Dinner Sets

Top Row: No. 22/6"/64-2. Oval crimped Nappy, "Beaded Edge." Note: all items are available in a set of eight different hand painted fruit decorations: Grape, Cherry, Pear, Plum, Apple, Blackberry, Strawberry and Peach, or in any fruit decoration specified above.
No. 22/64-2. Salt and Pepper.
No. 22/64-2. Cream and Sugar.
No. 22/64-2. Cup and Saucer.
No. 22/64-2. Sherbet, low foot.
No. 22/64-2. Tumbler, footed.

Second Row: No. 22/64-2. Celery Dish, oval.
No. 22/5"/64-2. Nappy, round.
No. 22/15"/64-2. Plate, torte.
No. 22/3part/64-2. Plate, relish, 3-part.

Third Row: 22/64-2. Dish, vegetable.
No. 22/12"/64-2. Platter, oval.

Fourth Row: 22/10½"/64-2. Plate, dinner.
No. 22/8½"/64-2. Plate, luncheon.
No. 22/1/8½"/64-2. Plate, luncheon, coupe shape.
No. 22/1/7"/64-2. Plate, salad, coupe shape.
No. 22/6"/64-2. Plate, bread and butter.

Fifth Row: No. 22/A-28. Cream and Sugar, coral red "Beaded Edge" pattern.
No. 22/A-28. Cup and Saucer.
No. 22/A-28. Tumbler, footed.
No. 22/6"/A-28. Nappy, oval, crimped.
No. 22/5"/A-28. Nappy, round.

No. 22/A-28. Salt and Pepper.
No. 77. Egg Cup, "American Hobnail" with coral red decoration.

Bottom Row: No. 22/10½"/A-28. Plate, dinner.
No. 22/8½"/A-28. Plate, luncheon.
No. 22/1/8½"/A-28. Plate, luncheon, coupe shape.
No. 22/1/7"/A-28. Plate, salad, coupe shape.
No. 22/6"/A-28. Plate, bread and butter.

(The "Red-Beaded Edge" pattern is also available in torte plate, platter, relish, vegetable dish and celery.)

"BUBBLE," "BULLSEYE," PROVINCIAL, ANCHOR HOCKING GLASS COMPANY, 1940 – 1965

Colors: pink, Sapphire blue, Forest Green, Royal Ruby, crystal, and any known Hocking color

Neophyte collectors love Anchor Hocking's "Bubble" because it's one of the patterns they can easily recognize. The simple, circular design mixes easily with present day decor and the vast supply of blue and crystal cups, saucers, and dinner plates makes this pattern appear easily obtainable. However, gathering a complete set is not quite so simple! Despite bountiful basic pieces in blue and crystal, other pieces are in smaller supply. A collector at a New York show who bought our "Bubble" creamer said she'd been looking for it for five years! Blue creamers have always been scarce, and the 9" flanged bowl has essentially left the collecting arena. Not only is that bowl hard to find, but it has now been found in two distinct styles. Both forms are shown in my book, *Anchor Hocking's Fire-King & More*. You will search long and hard for blue grill plates and 4" berry bowls without inner rim damage. Grill plates are customarily divided into three sections and were used in many of the restaurants of the 1940s and 1950s. They kept the food separated and allowed smaller servings to fill the plate.

Original labels on crystal "Bubble" on page 16 read "Heat Proof." A 1942 ad guaranteed this Fire-King tableware to be "heat-proof," indeed a "tableware that can be used in the oven, on the table, in the refrigerator." In all probability, since this ad is dated 1942, it refers to the Sapphire blue color. This added dimension is distinctive to Fire-King since earlier Depression glass patterns do not permit sudden changes in temperature without breaking! Forest Green or Royal Ruby "Bubble" original stickers do not expound these corresponding heat-proof capabilities, however, so be advised!

Forest Green (dark) and Royal Ruby (red) "Bubble" dinner plates have both become difficult to find in mint condition (without scratches or knife marks on the surface). There are two styles of green and crystal dinner plates. The first plate measures ⅛" larger than the normally found dinner plate. The center of this plate is smaller and there are four rows of bubbles outside the center. The normally found dinner plate has three rows of bubbles. The plates with four rows seem to be in shorter supply than those with three rows. I point this out because there are precisionists who will not accept the smaller centered plate in their collection. You have to decide which style you like. A collector recently told me that she remembered the larger diameter, smaller centered crystal plates were a flour premium and marketed as a cake plate.

Many collectors use red and green "Bubble" for Christmas tables. Green and red water goblets were frequently used for advertising. Usually, collectors buying these pieces are intrigued by a representation of their home town or organization. There are a few pieces of amber and iridescent "Bubble" found. I have yet to meet a collector of either color!

Pink is hard to find except for the 8⅜" bowl that sells in the $10.00 to $12.00 range. That 8⅜" berry bowl can be found in almost any color that Anchor Hocking made (including all the opaque and iridescent colors common to Hocking). Due to a recent surge in demand for Jade-ite, that particular Jade-ite "Bubble" bowl has jumped to selling for $20.00. Milk White was listed only in the 1959 – 60 catalog but many of them still exist today. The inside depths of these bowls vary. Price all other colors of "Bubble" as you would crystal. I have found no new information on the plastic "Bubble" bowls pictured in the last edition. Those four colors were made by S & K.

According to one Anchor Hocking catalog, "Bubble" stemware was originally called "Early American" line. The other stemware line sold along with "Bubble," now known as "Boopie," was actually named Berwick. Both of these stemware lines were manufactured after production of blue "Bubble" had ceased; thus, there are no blue "Bubble" stems to be found.

Royal Ruby Berwick is priced in the same range as Royal Ruby "Bubble" stemware; but the Forest Green Berwick is selling for somewhat less than the Forest Green "Bubble" stemware. The catalog lists an iced tea in Berwick with a capacity of 15 oz. All I can find measure 14 oz.! Measurements for capacity are done by filling to the top rim (spilling-out-point) of the object to be measured.

	Crystal	Forest Green	Light Blue	Royal Ruby		Crystal	Forest Green	Light Blue	Royal Ruby
Bowl, 4", berry	4.00		17.50		***Stem, 4 oz., juice	4.50	10.00		10.00
Bowl, 4½", fruit	4.50	9.00	11.00	8.00	Stem, 4½ oz., cocktail	4.00	12.50		12.50
Bowl, 5¼", cereal	8.00	20.00	12.50		Stem, 5½ oz., juice	5.00	12.50		12.50
Bowl, 7¾", flat soup	10.00		15.00		***Stem, 6 oz., sherbet	3.00	8.00		7.00
Bowl, 8⅜", large berry					Stem, 6 oz., sherbet	3.50	9.00		9.00
(Pink-$8.00)	8.00	20.00	16.50	20.00	***Stem, 9 oz., goblet	7.00	12.00		12.50
Bowl, 9", flanged			395.00		Stem, 10¾ oz., goblet	7.00	14.00		13.00
Candlesticks, pr.	16.00	60.00			***Stem, 14 oz., iced tea	9.00	18.00		
Creamer	6.00	15.00	35.00		Sugar	6.00	15.00	25.00	
*Cup	3.50	7.00	5.00	8.00	Tidbit, 2 tier				65.00
Lamp, 3 Styles	40.00				Tumbler, 5 oz., juice	3.50			8.00
Pitcher, 64 oz., ice lip	80.00			60.00	Tumbler, 8 oz., 3¼", old fashioned	10.00			16.00
Plate, 6¾", bread and butter	3.00	18.00	3.00		Tumbler, 9 oz., water	5.00			9.00
Plate, 9⅜", grill			22.50		Tumbler, 12 oz., 4½", iced tea	12.00			12.50
Plate, 9⅜", dinner	7.00	25.00	7.00	24.00	Tumbler, 16 oz., 5⅞", lemonade	14.00			16.00
Platter, 12", oval	12.00		16.00						
**Saucer	1.00	4.00	1.50	4.00					
***Stem, 3½ oz., cocktail	4.00	10.00		10.00					

*Pink - $125.00   **Pink - $40.00   ***Berwick

BUTTERCUP, ETCHING #340, FOSTORIA GLASS COMPANY, 1941 – 1960

Color: crystal

    Buttercup, a small, yellow, cupped flower was a term of endearment made famous in Hollywood movies. No doubt it was thus a natural choice as a name for Fostoria's bridal crystal. Buttercup was produced for twenty years; consequently, there were many brides who chose Buttercup as their crystal pattern. A few of these sets are now reaching the market due to retirement or death. Often, as families reduce or disburse their estate, glassware is either sold into the collectible market or split up within the family and either situation may create new collectors.

    I mentioned in the last edition that I had just obtained a small set of Buttercup from a seller who asked me if I knew who made that pretty pattern! That dealer has since approached me to tell me she'd read about herself in the book and to tell me that she certainly knew what Buttercup was now! In fact, she was looking for it for a customer and did I have any left?

    Vases are difficult to find in almost all Fostoria crystal patterns. The smaller vase, pictured on the right of the photo, is the 6" footed #6021. The larger is the 7½" footed #4143. The small pieces in front are an individual ash tray and a cigarette holder which can also be found in Holly pattern (a newly included Fostoria pattern in this book). That cigarette holder might make a better toothpick holder today. Stemware, salad, and luncheon plates were in catalog listings as late as 1960 and that may be why those items are easier to find today than many of the other Buttercup listings. After 1960, Buttercup disappeared from Fostoria's catalog and became a "searched for" collectible! Buttercup also had a corresponding Gorham silver pattern.

	Crystal		Crystal
Ash tray, #2364, 2⅝", individual	22.00	Plate, #2337, 8½"	17.50
Bottle, #2083, salad dressing	250.00	Plate, #2337, 9½"	40.00
Bowl, #2364, 6", baked apple	20.00	Plate, #2364, 6¾", mayonnaise	7.50
Bowl, #2364, 9", salad	50.00	Plate, #2364, 7¼" x 4½", crescent salad	45.00
Bowl, #2364, 10½", salad	55.00	Plate, #2364, 11¼", cracker	30.00
Bowl, #2364, 11", salad	55.00	Plate, #2364, 11", sandwich	35.00
Bowl, #2364, 12", flared	60.00	Plate, #2364, 14", torte	50.00
Bowl, #2364, 12", lily pond	55.00	Plate, #2364, 16", torte	90.00
Bowl, #2364, 13", fruit	65.00	Relish, #2364, 6½" x 5", 2-part	25.00
Bowl, #2594, 10", 2 hndl.	55.00	Relish, #2364, 10" x 7¼", 3-part	33.00
Candlestick, #2324, 4"	17.50	Saucer, #2350	5.00
Candlestick, #2324, 6"	32.50	Shaker, #2364, 2⅝"	32.50
Candlestick, #2594, 5½"	30.00	Stem, #6030, 3¾", 4 oz., oyster cocktail	18.00
Candlestick, #2594, 8", trindle	55.00	Stem, #6030, 3⅞", 1 oz., cordial	40.00
Candlestick, #6023, 5½", duo	40.00	Stem, #6030, 4⅜", 6 oz., low sherbet	17.50
Candy w/cover, #2364, 3¾" diameter	115.00	Stem, #6030, 5¼", 3½ oz., cocktail	22.50
Celery, #2350, 11"	27.50	Stem, #6030, 5⅝", 6 oz., high sherbet	20.00
Cheese stand, #2364, 5¾" x 2⅞"	20.00	Stem, #6030, 6", 3½ oz., claret-wine	32.50
Cigarette holder, #2364, 2" high	35.00	Stem, #6030, 6⅜", 10 oz., low goblet	22.50
Coaster	15.00	Stem, #6030, 7⅞", 10 oz., water goblet	27.50
Comport, # 2364, 8"	40.00	Sugar, #2350½, 3⅛", ftd.	15.00
Comport, #6030, 5"	35.00	Syrup, #2586, sani-cut	295.00
Creamer, #2350½, 3¼", ftd.	16.00	Tray, #2364, 11¼", center handled	32.50
Cup, #2350½, ftd.	15.00	Tumbler, #6030, 4⅝", 5 oz., ftd. juice	22.00
Mayonnaise, #2364, 5"	25.00	Tumbler, #6030, 6", 12 oz., ftd. iced tea	30.00
Pickle, #2350, 8"	25.00	Vase, 6", ftd., #4143	95.00
Pitcher, #6011, 8⅞", 53 oz.	285.00	Vase, 6", ftd., #6021	95.00
Plate, #2337, 6"	7.00	Vase, 7½", ftd., #4143	135.00
Plate, #2337, 7½"	12.00	Vase, 10", #2614	150.00

CABOCHON, A.H. HEISEY & COMPANY, 1950 – 1957

Colors: amber, crystal, and Dawn

Cabochon is mostly found in crystal. The simplicity of the pattern holds tremendous appeal for certain collectors; but by the same token, that same, uncomplicated shape is ignored by others. The name itself means a gem cut in a convex curve with no facets! Obviously, the original designers of the Cabochon pattern intended the design to stand alone... as a "gem" of glassware!

Amber and Dawn colors are rarely seen unless you go to a major Heisey or glass show. The amber plate pictured is one of the few pieces that I have seen in that color. Dawn can be found, but you will pay a dear price for the privilege of owning it. Prices overall remain moderate for this pattern manufactured in those last years before the closing of the Heisey plant in 1957. This listing is copied from a 1953 catalog. Most patterns made in the declining years of the factory are more difficult to find than those manufactured during the renown years from the 1930s into the early 1950s.

The 6¼" Dawn candy dish in the top row is very seldom seen in this Heisey color. You will find a few other pieces of Cabochon that are cut or etched, but finding Orchid and Rose etchings on Cabochon fascinates a majority of Heisey collectors. The cordial pictured below has Heisey's Debutante cut. For me, that cutting adds a lot to this pattern!

	Crystal
Bon bon, 6¼", hndl.,	
(sides sloped w/squared hndl.) #1951	24.00
Bottle, oil, w/#101 stopper #1951	30.00
Bowl, 4½", dessert #1951	4.00
Bowl, 5", dessert #1951	5.00
Bowl, 7", cereal #1951	6.00
Bowl, 13", floral or salad #1951	18.00
Bowl, 13", gardenia	
(low w/edge cupped irregularly) #1951	18.00
Butter dish, ¼ lb. #1951	25.00
Cake salver, ftd. #1951	65.00
Candle holder, 2 lite, ground bottom, pr. #1951	165.00
Candlette, 1 lite (like bowl), pr. #1951	38.00
Candy, 6¼", w/lid (bowl w/lid) #1951	38.00
Cheese, 5¾", ftd., compote for cracker plate	17.50
Cream #1951	9.00
Creamer, cereal, 12 oz. #1951	30.00
Cup #1951	6.00
Jelly, 6", hndl., (sides and hndl. rounded) #1951	24.00
Mayonnaise, 3-pc. (plate, bowl, ladle) #1951	27.50
Mint, 5¾", ftd., (sides slanted) #1951	22.50
Pickle tray, 8½" #1951	20.00
Plate, 8", salad #1951	6.00
Plate, 13", center hndl. #1951	42.00
Plate, 14", cracker w/center ring #1951	18.00
Plate, 14", party (edge cupped irregularly) #1951	18.00
Plate, 14", sandwich #1951	18.00
Relish, 9", three-part, oblong #1951	22.00
Relish, 9", three-part, square #1951	20.00
Salt and pepper, square, w/#60 silver	
plated tops, pr. #1951	13.00
Saucer #1951	1.50
Sherbet, 6 oz. #1951 (pressed)	4.00

	Crystal
Sherbet, 6 oz. #6092 (blown)	4.00
Stemware, 1 oz., cordial #6091	22.50
Stemware, 3 oz., oyster cocktail #6091	4.00
Stemware, 3 oz., wine #6091	8.00
Stemware, 4 oz., cocktail #6091	4.00
Stemware, 5½ oz., sherbet #6091	4.00
Stemware, 10 oz., goblet #6091	8.00
Sugar, w/cover #1951	14.00
Tidbit, 7½" (bowl w/sloped outsides) #1951	12.50
Tray, 9", for cream and sugar #1951	45.00
Tumbler, 5 oz. #1951 (pressed)	7.00
Tumbler, 5 oz., juice, flat bottomed #6092 (blown)	7.00
Tumbler, 5 oz., juice, ftd. #6091	7.00
Tumbler, 10 oz., beverage #6092 (blown)	8.00
Tumbler, 10 oz., tumbler #6092 (blown)	8.00
Tumbler, 12 oz. #1951 (pressed)	12.50
Tumbler, 12 oz., iced tea #6092 (blown)	12.50
Tumbler, 12 oz., iced tea, ftd. #6091	8.00
Tumbler, 14 oz., soda #6092 (blown)	11.00
Vase, 3½", flared #1951	20.00

CAMELLIA, JEANNETTE GLASS COMPANY, 1950s

Colors: crystal, crystal with gold trim, iridized, flashed red and blue

Camellia is a small Jeannette Glass pattern that can be used alone or as accessory pieces for patterns needing serving pieces. The punch bowl set features a 9⅜" bowl which is 4¼" deep, set upon a wire rack with extended metal protrusions surrounding the bowl to hang the eight cup handles. I have seen several styles besides this wrought iron one that is pictured. A gold tone metal stand looks best with the gold trimmed bowl and cups. All pieces seem to come with or without the gold trim. Personally, the gold trim seems to add to the charm of this pattern. That trim could wear off easily with use.

You may find additional pieces of Camellia; let me know what you find. The luncheon plate surrounded by aluminum with an attached handle makes a great floral or fruit holder. I believe the creamers and sugars come both with and without the embossed flower. So far, I've only found those without the embossing. The two-handled tray and the relish have been the hardest to find items. I have seen the punch bowl iridized. It should sell at about double the crystal bowl.

	Crystal
Bowl, 5"	4.00
Bowl, 1-hndl., nappy	8.00
Bowl, 8⅞", vegetable	10.00
Bowl, 9⅜", 4¼" deep, punch	18.00
Bowl, 10⅛", 3½" deep, salad	15.00
Candleholder	10.00
Creamer, ftd.	5.00
Cup	1.00
Plate 8" luncheon	8.00
Plate, 12" sandwich	12.00
Relish, 6¾" x 11¾"	10.00
Saucer	.50
Sugar, ftd.	5.00
Tray, two-handled	15.00

CAMELLIA Plate Etching #344, FOSTORIA GLASS COMPANY, 1952 – 1976

Color: crystal

Fostoria's Camellia is often confused by beginning dealers and collectors with Heisey's Rose Pattern. Experience has shown me that novice dealers nearly always **believe** that they find the more expensive (desirable) patterns as soon as they start out, instead of a lesser collected pattern. I had a piece brought to me at a glass show over the weekend that had been misrepresented as Heisey Rose. The collector was upset because she paid a Heisey Rose price for a cup and saucer that should have been considerably less expensive. She bought it at an antique mall. Have you noticed that almost all antique malls have signs posted — "No Refunds or Returns?" You need to know **what you are buying** and from whom! If you buy it, and it is not what it was supposed to be, then it is **your fault** alone! There are no warranties when buying in an antique mall!

Many collectors refer to this pattern as "Camellia Rose." Camellia was a contemporary of Heisey's Rose, Cambridge's Rose Point, and Tiffin's Cherokee Rose. Fostoria's Camellia production outlasted all the other companies' rose patterns time wise; but it never reached the collecting status of those of the Heisey or Cambridge rose patterns.

All pieces in the listing below that have no line number shown are made on Fostoria's #2630 blank, better known as Century. You probably will find additional pieces in this pattern that are not listed. Let me know what you observe and I'll endeavor to get it listed!

Basket, 10¼" x 6½", wicker hndl.	85.00
Bowl, 4½", hndl.	15.00
Bowl, 5", fruit	16.00
Bowl, 6", cereal	25.00
Bowl, 6¼", snack, ftd.	20.00
Bowl, 7¼", bonbon, 3-ftd.	25.00
Bowl, 7⅛", 3-ftd., triangular	18.00
Bowl, 8", flared	35.00
Bowl, 8½", salad	40.00
Bowl, 9", lily pond	37.50
Bowl, 9½", hndl., serving bowl	45.00
Bowl, 9½", oval, serving bowl	45.00
Bowl, 10", oval, hndl.	45.00
Bowl, 10½", salad	47.50
Bowl, 10¾", ftd., flared	50.00
Bowl, 11, ftd., rolled edge	55.00
Bowl, 11¼", lily pond	45.00
Bowl, 12", flared	52.50
Butter, w/cover, ¼ lb.	50.00
Candlestick, 4½"	22.50
Candlestick, 7", double	45.00
Candlestick, 7¾", triple	65.00
Candy, w/cover, 7"	55.00
Comport, 2¾", cheese	20.00
Comport, 4⅜"	25.00
Cracker plate, 10¾"	30.00
Creamer, 4¼"	15.00
Creamer, individual	12.00
Cup, 6 oz., ftd.	17.00
Ice bucket	75.00
Mayonnaise, 3-pc.	37.50
Mayonnaise, 4-pc., div. w/2 ladles	42.50
Mustard, w/spoon, cover	35.00
Oil, w/stopper, 5 oz.	60.00
Pickle, 8¾"	25.00
Pitcher, 6⅛", 16 oz.	85.00
Pitcher, 7⅛", 48 oz.	165.00
Plate, 6½", bread/butter	7.00
Plate, 7½", crescent salad	45.00
Plate, 7½", salad	10.00
Plate, 8", party, w/indent for cup	27.50
Plate, 8½", luncheon	15.00
Plate, 9½", small dinner	30.00
Plate, 10", hndl., cake	30.00
Plate, 10¼", dinner	45.00
Plate, 10½", snack, small center	30.00
Plate, 14", torte	50.00
Plate, 16", torte	75.00
Platter, 12"	47.50
Preserve, w/cover, 6"	65.00
Relish, 7⅜", 2-part	18.00
Relish, 11⅛", 3-part	45.00
Salt and pepper, 3⅛", pr.	45.00
Salver, 12¼", ftd. (like cake stand)	75.00
Saucer	4.00
Stem, #6036, 3¼", 1 oz., cordial	40.00
Stem, #6036, 3¾", 4 oz., oyster cocktail	17.50
Stem, #6036, 4⅛", 3½ oz., cocktail	22.00
Stem, #6036, 4⅛", 6 oz., low sherbet	10.00
Stem, #6036, 4¾", 3¼ oz., claret-wine	30.00
Stem, #6036, 4¾", 6 oz., high sherbet	15.00
Stem, #6036, 5⅞", 5½ oz., parfait	25.00
Stem, #6036, 6⅞", 9½ oz., water	25.00
Sugar, 4", ftd.	14.00
Sugar, individual	10.00
Tidbit, 8⅛", 3 ftd., upturned edge	30.00
Tidbit, 10¼", 2 tier, metal hndl.	45.00
Tray, 4¼", for ind. salt/pepper	17.50
Tray, 7⅛", for ind. sugar/creamer	20.00
Tray, 9½", hndl., muffin	32.50
Tray, 9⅛", hndl., utility	30.00
Tray, 11½", center hndl.	38.00
Tumbler, #6036, 4⅝", 5 oz., ftd. juice	20.00
Tumbler, #6306, 6⅛", 12 oz., ftd. iced tea	25.00
Vase, 5", #4121	60.00
Vase, 6", bud	30.00
Vase, 6", ftd., #4143	85.00
Vase, 6", ftd., #6021	65.00
Vase, 7½", hndl.	85.00
Vase, 8", flip, #2660	85.00
Vase, 8", ftd., #5092	75.00
Vase, 8½", oval	85.00
Vase, 10", ftd., #2470	115.00
Vase, 10½", ftd., #2657	115.00

CAPRI, "SEASHELL," "SWIRL COLONIAL," "COLONIAL," "ALPINE"

HAZEL WARE, DIVISION OF CONTINENTAL CAN, 1960s

Color: Azure blue

We have discovered that the "Capri" designation referred to the blue color of this ware rather than an actual pattern name. I have tried to organize the various Capri designs into some form of reference to make it easier to identify differing patterns and shapes within this Hazel Atlas color. I will restate this terminology for those who skipped buying the last edition of this book and will be lost trying to understand what I am describing. Knowing distinctions will help when discussing the pattern with dealers or other collectors.

The top of page 26 show the designs known as "Seashell" and "Tulip." The "Seashell" (swirled) pattern is the most commonly found design in Capri and "Tulip" (petal edged with circular dotted center) the most sparsely distributed. The ash trays in the top photo all are the same moulds as Moroccan Amethyst. That embossed floral ash tray seems to be rare in both Capri and Moroccan. The round ash tray and the coaster are Capri, but not of any particular design. That tumbler has five rounded protrusions that remind you of the bases on Duncan's Canterbury flat tumblers. Even though these designs are different, they could be used together if you were so inclined.

Pictured on the bottom of page 26 are Colony, "Square," "Hexagonal," and "Octagonal." The Colony name comes from actual labels on the square based items; "square," "hexagonal," and "octagonal" are descriptions coming from the shapes on which Capri was made. Being a former mathematics teacher, shape names seemed the only way to describe these. The Moroccan tumbler is the only square based item that will fit the indented plate. I couldn't find a tumbler in Capri, so we used what we had available. There may be a square based cup, but I haven't seen one.

Pentagonal flat tumblers, hexagonal stems, and octagonal dinnerware items make for some interesting geometric settings! **Only Capri labels have been found on these pieces so far.**

On the top of page 27 in the foreground are Colony pieces with a distinct twist to them which will be called "Colony Swirl." The "Swirl" is my added name for this pattern. Notice that the bases of both patterns are square or rectangular. Until someone finds a piece of the swirled with a pattern name, it will remain "Colony Swirl." That sounds great except I do have a crystal Colony shaped bowl sent me by a reader that has a label "Simplicity." The "Dots" pattern on the left are Skol Swedish-style glasses according to a boxed set I have. The three sized tumblers in this boxed set were priced 12¢, 15¢, and 18¢. Maybe the whole design is Skol, but I can only say the glasses were named that for sure! That box was shown in the last edition! The "Hobnails" design is shown on the right. The cup, creamer, and sugar have the hobs on the base of those respective pieces.

The bottom of page 27 shows "Pentagonal" Capri, flat bottomed tumblers and an assortment of other colors and pieces that you can decide to collect with Capri. Some are definitely Hazel Atlas in other colors and you can use these to blend in or ignore them completely. The choice is yours! For a rainbow effect, they might add interest.

	Blue		Blue		Blue
Ash tray, 3¼", triangular	6.00	Creamer, round	12.00	Sugar, round	8.00
Ash tray, 3¼", round	6.00	Cup, octagonal	6.00	Sugar lid	12.00
Ash tray, 3½", square, embossed		Cup, round, "Hobnails"	5.00	Tidbit, 3-tier (round 9⅞" plate,	
flower	17.50	Cup, round, swirled	5.00	7⅛" plate, 6" saucer)	22.50
Ash tray, 5", round	8.00	Cup, round, Tulip	8.00	Tumbler, 2¾", 4 oz., "Colony Swirl"	7.00
Ash tray, 6⅞", triangular	12.00	Plate, 5¾", bread and butter,		Tumbler, 3", 4 oz., fruit "Dots"	5.00
Bowl, 4¾", octagonal	7.50	octagonal	5.00	Tumbler, 3", 5 oz., pentagonal bottom	7.00
Bowl, 4¾", swirled	6.00	Plate, 7", salad, round, "Colony Swirl"	7.00	Tumbler, 3 1/16", Colony or	
Bowl, 4⅞", round, "Dots"	7.00	Plate, 7⅛", round, salad, "Colony		"Colony Swirl"	8.00
Bowl, 5⅜", salad, round, "Hobnails"	8.00	Swirl"	7.00	Tumbler, 3⅛", 5 oz., pentagonal	8.00
Bowl, 5⅝", "Colony Swirl"	9.00	Plate, 7¼", salad, "Hobnails"	6.50	Tumbler, 3¼", 8 oz., old fashioned,	
Bowl, 5¾", square, deep, Colony	10.00	Plate, 7¼", salad, octagonal	7.00	"Dots"	7.50
Bowl, 6", round, Tulip	12.00	Plate, 8", square	9.00	Tumbler, 3⅝", 3 oz., "Dots"	6.00
Bowl, 6", round, "Dots"	8.00	Plate, 8", square, w/square cup rest	8.00	Tumbler, 4", "Dots"	5.00
Bowl, 6", round, sq. bottom, Colony	8.00	Plate, 8⅞", square	10.00	Tumbler, 4¼", 9 oz., "Colony Swirl"	7.50
Bowl, 6 1/16", round, "Colony Swirl"	8.00	Plate, 8⅞", square, w/round cup rest	9.00	Tumbler, 4¼", 9 oz., water, pentagonal	
Bowl, 7¾", oval, Colony	15.00	Plate, 9½", round, snack w/cup rest,		bottom	7.50
Bowl, 7¾", rectangular, Colony	14.00	Tulip	9.50	Tumbler, 5", 12 oz., "Colony Swirl"	10.00
Bowl, 8¾", swirled	12.00	Plate, 9¾", dinner, octagonal	10.00	Tumbler, 5", 12 oz., tea, pentagonal	
Bowl, 9⅛" x 3" high	25.00	Plate, 9⅞", dinner, round, "Hobnails"	9.00	bottom	10.00
Bowl, 9½" x 2⅞" high	22.00	Plate, 10", snack, fan shaped w/cup rest	8.50	Tumbler, 5¼", "Dots"	6.00
Bowl, 9½" oval 1½" high	9.00	Saucer, 5½" square	1.50	Tumbler, 5½", 12 oz., tea, swirl	10.00
Bowl, 10¾", salad, Colony	26.00	Saucer, 6", round, "Hobnails"	1.00	Tumbler, 6", 10 oz., "Dots"	8.00
Candy jar, w/cover, ftd.	32.00	Saucer, octagonal	1.50	Vase, 8", "Dots"	20.00
Chip and dip, 2 swirled bowls		Stem, 4½", sherbet	7.50	Vase, 8½", ruffled	35.00
(8¾" and 4¾" on metal rack)	28.00	Stem, 5½", water	9.00		

CASCADE, 4000 LINE CAMBRIDGE GLASS COMPANY, 1950s

Colors: crystal, Emerald Green, Mandarin Gold, and Milk White

No one has ever been able to explain to me why there are two styles of stems on the water goblets — something to notice if you are just beginning to buy this pattern. One is turned upside down from the other. Pick the style you like or whichever you can find might make more sense.

That Cascade 8" ash tray had multiple purposes. Besides the lamp base and its normal use, it also served as the punch bowl base when turned upside down. Then, too, it rested atop the 21" plate to make a buffet set. That 21" plate also became the punch bowl liner in the punch set. It was a judicious use of expensive moulds at a time when Cambridge was headed toward liquidation.

	Crystal	Green	Yellow
Ash tray, 4½"	6.00		
Ash tray, 6"	10.00		
Ash tray, 8"	20.00		
Bowl, 4½", fruit	7.00		
Bowl, 6½", relish	13.00		
Bowl, 6½", relish, 2-pt.	13.00		
Bowl, 6", 4-ftd. bonbon	11.00		
Bowl, 7", 2 hndl., ftd., bonbon	13.00		
Bowl, 10", 3-pt., celery	20.00		
Bowl, 10", 4-ftd., flared	30.00		
Bowl, 10½", 4-ftd., shallow	30.00		
Bowl, 12", 4-ftd., oval	33.00		
Bowl, 12½", 4-ftd., flared	35.00		
Bowl, 13", 4-ftd., shallow	35.00		
Buffet set (21" plate w/8" ash tray)	70.00		
Candlestick, 5"	17.50	35.00	35.00
Candlestick, 6", 2-lite	27.50		
Candy box, w/cover	35.00	75.00	75.00
Cigarette box w/cover	22.50		
Comport, 5½"	17.50		
Creamer	8.50	20.00	20.00
Cup	8.00		
Ice tub, tab hndl.	32.50		
Mayonnaise spoon	7.50		
Mayonnaise, w/liner	17.50	60.00	60.00

	Crystal	Green	Yellow
Plate, 6½", bread & butter	5.50		
Plate, 8½", salad	9.00		
Plate, 8", 2 hndl., ftd. bonbon	12.50		
Plate, 11½", 4-ftd.	17.50		
Plate, 14", 4-ftd. torte	22.50		
Plate, 21"	50.00		
Punch base (same as 8" ash tray)	20.00		
Punch bowl liner, 21"	55.00		
Punch bowl, 15"	125.00		
Punch cup	7.50		
Saucer	2.50		
Shaker, pr.	20.00		
Stem, cocktail	11.00		
Stem, sherbet	10.00		
Stem, water goblet	14.00		
Sugar	8.00	20.00	20.00
Tumbler, 5 oz., flat	10.00		
Tumbler, 5 oz., ftd.	10.00		
Tumbler, 12 oz., ftd.	13.00		
Tumbler, 12 oz., flat	12.00		
*Vase 9½"	35.00	75.00	75.00
Vase, 9½", oval	40.00		

*Milk White $45.00

Footed Bowl

Mayonnaise Set

Ash Tray

CASCADE
By CAMBRIDGE

Like a stream of pure light tumbling rhythmically into sun-splashed pools, Cascade brings you one of the most fascinating, brilliant *new* crystal designs to be seen in years. It is hand-made *modern* crystal in a variety of pieces . . . substantial, practical . . . ideal for formal or informal occasions.

You will fall in love with Cascade for yourself and willingly share its beauty in gifts to others. Be sure to see this fine American crystal now . . . at good stores, priced moderately.

THE CAMBRIDGE GLASS COMPANY • CAMBRIDGE, OHIO

CENTURY LINE #2630, FOSTORIA GLASS COMPANY, 1950 – 1982

Color: crystal, rare in pink

Century was the Fostoria **blank** used for many of their etched patterns made after 1950, just as the Fairfax **blank** was used for etching earlier patterns. Heather and Camellia are the two etched patterns most commonly found on this #2630 shape. You can look at the pictures for those patterns to see additional pieces in this line.

Prices for Century have stabilized after a couple of years of spiraling upward. Prices for wines, water goblets, and footed iced tea have leveled as more collectors have turned to etched Century blanks instead of the pattern itself. Nationally, prices are fairly consistent. Prices asked for elegant glassware in general are more reasonable in the western states than are the prices for Depression glassware. Dealers at the moment are having a troublesome time replenishing fundamental patterns in Depression ware, and serving pieces are fetching whatever the market will uphold. Using that parameter, it's very possible that comparable scarcities will consequently occur in a few years in the 40s, 50s, and 60s glassware. Give it some thought.

Fostoria catalog listings for Century plates conflict with the actual measurements by up to ½ inch. I have tried to use actual measurements for Fostoria patterns in this book. I recognize that this has been a profound problem for people ordering through the mail or via the Internet. Glassware is certainly alive and well on the Internet! You can view my books and glass listings at http://www.geneflorence.com.

Two sizes of dinner plates can be found in Century (as occurs in most of Fostoria's patterns). The larger plates (usually listed as a service plate) are harder to find. They were priced higher initially, and many consumers did without the service plates. With any use, abrasions and scuffs are inevitable with Century pieces. Since all the items are very plain in the center section, they show scratches easily than those patterns having center designs. The bottom rims (usually ground flat on elegant patterns) of stacked plates are frequently the culprit since they rub the surface of the underneath plate. Consider using paper plates between your glass plates — and do not serve guests foods that require cutting.

The ice bucket has button "tabs" for attaching a metal handle. One is pictured in the bottom row. The 8½" oval vase is shaped like the ice bucket but without those tabs. A few damaged ice buckets (sans handles) have changed hands as vases. Pay attention to the glass you buy! You can see where the tabs used to be upon close examination. Buying mint condition glassware will pay dividends in the future. Damaged glassware will always be damaged (or repaired) and nothing can change that!

	Crystal		Crystal
Ash tray, 2¾"	10.00	Pitcher, 7⅛", 48 oz.	110.00
Basket, 10¼" x 6½", wicker hndl.	70.00	Plate, 6½", bread/butter	6.00
Bowl, 4½", hndl.	12.00	Plate, 7½", salad	8.00
Bowl, 5", fruit	14.00	Plate, 7½", crescent salad	35.00
Bowl, 6", cereal	22.50	Plate, 8", party, w/indent for cup	25.00
Bowl, 6¼", snack, ftd.	14.00	Plate, 8½", luncheon	12.50
Bowl, 7⅛", 3-ftd., triangular	15.00	Plate, 9½", small dinner	25.00
Bowl, 7¼", bonbon, 3-ftd.	20.00	Plate, 10", hndl., cake	22.00
Bowl, 8", flared	25.00	Plate, 10½", dinner	32.00
Bowl, 8½", salad	25.00	Plate, 14", torte	30.00
Bowl, 9", lily pond	30.00	Platter, 12"	47.50
Bowl, 9½", hndl., serving bowl	35.00	Preserve, w/cover, 6"	35.00
Bowl, 9½", oval, serving bowl	32.50	Relish, 7⅜", 2-part	15.00
Bowl, 10", oval, hndl.	32.50	Relish, 11⅛", 3-part	25.00
Bowl, 10½", salad	30.00	Salt and pepper, 2⅜", (individual), pr.	15.00
Bowl, 10¾", ftd., flared	40.00	Salt and pepper, 3⅛", pr.	20.00
Bowl, 11, ftd., rolled edge	40.00	Salver, 12¼", ftd. (like cake stand)	55.00
Bowl, 11¼", lily pond	32.50	Saucer	3.50
Bowl, 12", flared	37.50	Stem, 3½ oz., cocktail, 4⅛"	20.00
Butter, w/cover, ¼ lb.	35.00	Stem, 3½ oz., wine, 4½"	30.00
Candy, w/cover, 7"	37.50	Stem, 4½ oz., oyster cocktail, 3¾"	20.00
Candlestick, 4½"	17.50	Stem, 5½" oz., sherbet, 4½"	12.00
Candlestick, 7", double	30.00	Stem, 10 oz., goblet, 5¾"	22.50
Candlestick, 7¾", triple	40.00	Sugar, 4", ftd.	9.00
Comport, 2¾", cheese	15.00	Sugar, individual	9.00
Comport, 4⅜"	20.00	Tidbit, 8⅛", 3-ftd., upturned edge	18.00
Cracker plate, 10¾"	30.00	Tidbit, 10¼", 2 tier, metal hndl.	25.00
Creamer, 4¼"	9.00	Tray, 4¼", for ind. salt/pepper	14.00
Creamer, individual	9.00	Tray, 7⅛", for ind. sugar/creamer	14.00
Cup, 6 oz., ftd.	13.00	Tray, 9⅛", hndl., utility	25.00
Ice bucket	65.00	Tray, 9½", hndl., muffin	30.00
Mayonnaise, 3-pc.	30.00	Tray, 11½", center hndl.	30.00
Mayonnaise, 4-pc., div. w/2 ladles	35.00	Tumbler, 5 oz., ftd., juice, 4¾"	22.50
Mustard, w/spoon, cover	27.50	Tumbler, 12 oz., ftd., tea, 5⅞"	27.50
Oil, w/stopper, 5 oz.	45.00	Vase, 6", bud	18.00
Pickle, 8¾"	15.00	Vase, 7½", hndl.	70.00
Pitcher, 6⅛", 16 oz.	60.00	Vase, 8½", oval	67.50

Color: crystal

Fostoria's Chintz pattern was switched to this 50s book because its production years better fit the era encompassed by this book than those of the *Elegant Glassware of the Depression Era*. As with Century pattern, Chintz has now been removed from the Elegant book and is only found in this book.

Several evasive pieces of Chintz are driving diehard collectors of this pattern to distraction. Most notable are the syrup pitcher and the oil bottle. There are other pieces not easily uncovered including the footed 9¼" bowl, cream soup, finger bowl, oval vegetable, and any of the vases. All these pieces are considered to be scarce.

An advanced collector told me that the 11" celery on the #2496 (Baroque) blank did not exist; so I have removed that from my listing. I have found that any advanced collector who specializes in only one or two patterns always knows more about those patterns than I do. Considering that my books cover hundreds of patterns, it's difficult keeping up with all the idiosyncrasies of each pattern; but I surely do try! For novice collectors, a fleur-de-lis in relief is the design for the Baroque blank.

As is the case of most elegant patterns of this time, Chintz stemware is abundant. Apparently, people in the 1950s acquired stemware whether they ordered the serving pieces or not. Almost any serving piece is elusive as anyone collecting Chintz will attest.

Unlike many Fostoria patterns, only one size dinner plate exists in Chintz. There was no service plate as in earlier patterns. You will have to settle for a 9½" plate. Scuffed and worn plates are a nemesis and unfortunately, the rule; select your merchandise prudently. Prices below are for mint condition plates and not ones with so-called "light" surface damage! If it has any damage, then the price should be less!

The drip cut syrup with metal lid was listed as Sani-cut in sales brochures. Evidently, this was not a significant item then since they are so scarce today. The 8" oval bowl was called a sauce dish by Fostoria. These came divided or not. Many collectors refer to them as gravy boats. The oval sauce boat liner came with both, but a brochure listed it as a tray instead of liner.

	Crystal		Crystal
Bell, dinner	125.00	Plate, #2496, 9½", dinner	55.00
Bowl, #869, 4½", finger	65.00	Plate, #2496, 10½", hndl., cake	45.00
Bowl, #2496, 4⅝", tri-cornered	22.50	Plate, #2496, 11", cracker	42.00
Bowl, #2496, cream soup	85.00	Plate, #2496, 14", upturned edge	55.00
Bowl, #2496, 5", fruit	30.00	Plate, #2496, 16", torte, plain edge	125.00
Bowl, #2496, 5", hndl.	25.00	Plate, 17½", upturned edge	175.00
Bowl, #2496, 7⅝", bon bon	32.50	Platter, #2496, 12"	100.00
Bowl, #2496, 8½", hndl.	65.00	Relish, #2496, 6", 2 part, square	33.00
Bowl, #2496, 9¼" ftd.	300.00	Relish, #2496, 10" x 7½", 3 part	40.00
Bowl, #2496, 9½", oval vegetable	195.00	Relish, #2419, 5 part	40.00
Bowl, #2496, 9½", vegetable	75.00	Salad dressing bottle, #2083, 6½"	395.00
Bowl, #2484, 10", hndl.	65.00	Salt and pepper, #2496, 2¾", flat, pr.	95.00
Bowl, #2496, 10½", hndl.	70.00	Sauce boat, #2496, oval	65.00
Bowl, #2496, 11½", flared	65.00	Sauce boat, #2496, oval, divided	65.00
Bowl, #6023, ftd.	50.00	Sauce boat liner, #2496, oblong, 8"	30.00
Candlestick, #2496, 3½", double	32.00	Saucer, #2496	5.00
Candlestick, #2496, 4"	20.00	Stem, #6026, 1 oz., cordial, 3⅞"	47.50
Candlestick, #2496, 5½"	35.00	Stem, #6026, 4 oz., cocktail, 5"	24.00
Candlestick, #2496, 6", triple	55.00	Stem, #6026, 4 oz., oyster cocktail, 3⅜"	27.50
Candlestick, #6023, double	50.00	Stem, #6026, 4½ oz., claret-wine, 5⅜"	40.00
Candy, w/cover, #2496, 3-part	140.00	Stem, #6026, 6 oz., low sherbet, 4⅜"	20.00
Comport, #2496, 3¼", cheese	35.00	Stem, #6026, 6 oz., saucer champagne, 5½"	22.00
Comport, #2496, 4¾"	32.50	Stem, #6026, 9 oz., water goblet, 7⅝"	33.00
Comport, #2496, 5½"	37.50	Sugar, #2496, 3½", ftd.	16.00
Creamer, #2496, 3¾", ftd.	17.50	Sugar, #2496½, individual	21.00
Creamer, #2496½, individual	22.50	Syrup, #2586, Sani-cut	425.00
Cup, #2496, ftd.	21.00	Tidbit, #2496, 8¼", 3 ftd., upturned edge	26.00
Ice bucket, #2496	130.00	Tray, #2496½, 6½", for ind. sugar/creamer	22.00
Jelly, w/cover, #2496, 7½"	85.00	Tray, #2375, 11", center hndl.	40.00
Mayonnaise, #2496½, 3-piece	60.00	Tumbler, #6026, 5 oz., juice, ftd.	27.50
Oil, w/stopper, #2496, 3½ oz.	110.00	Tumbler, #6026, 9 oz., water or low goblet	27.50
Pickle, #2496, 8"	32.00	Tumbler, #6026, 13 oz., tea, ftd.	32.50
Pitcher, #5000, 48 oz., ftd.	395.00	Vase, #4108, 5"	95.00
Plate, #2496, 6", bread/butter	10.00	Vase, #4128, 5"	95.00
Plate, #2496, 7½", salad	15.00	Vase, #4143, 6", ftd.	110.00
Plate, #2496, 8½", luncheon	21.00	Vase, #4143, 7½", ftd.	195.00

"CHRISTMAS CANDY," NO. 624, INDIANA GLASS COMPANY, 1937 – EARLY 1950s

Colors: Terrace Green (teal) and crystal

"Christmas Candy" is Indiana's #624 line. Prices for teal Terrace Green, as it was named by the company, finally slowed their ascent, but not before reaching some unbelievable heights. Crystal prices have changed very little over the last two years. Hopefully, you found all the pieces you wanted before the price surge, because there is very little Terrace Green found today — at any price! (Of course, pricing is relative. Years from now, we may think these were very fair prices for uncommon items!)

Many times, "Christmas Candy" is found in sets rather than a piece here and there. Glassware made in the 1950s is regularly found in sets — having been carefully or haphazardly stored in someone's attic, garage, or basement. Lots of "superfluous" gifts were never used — or were saved for later use. Nearly all the teal colored pieces I have acquired over the years came from my trips through Indiana. I used to see groupings in Florida, but that hasn't been true in the last couple of years. Teal "Christmas Candy" may have been locally distributed. Dunkirk, the home of Indiana Glass, is not far from Indianapolis where I used to frequent a couple of Depression glass shows each year. Crystal is seen **nationally,** but not so the teal.

One good thing about buying glassware in Florida, is that "snow birds" (Northerners in the local vernacular) yearly bring glass to sell from all over the country. You never know what will show up! Retirees bring glassware south with them, and as they downsize or leave this world, much of that glass comes into the market place!

The round vegetable bowl pictured on the right in the top photo on the next page continues to be the only one known! It has created quite a commotion among "Christmas Candy" collectors. I mentioned that it was going to a new home and it now has. It only took a little over a year to find its hiding place among my many boxes of glass used for photography. The collector was willing to wait, and I believe she felt it was worth it! I sincerely doubt Indiana made only **one** bowl! So, keep looking for others!

The bowl atop the crystal tidbit measures 5¾". That bowl is difficult to find and has never been seen in Terrace Green. Crystal "Christmas Candy" has attracted few collectors, but it is a pattern that can still be found at reasonable prices.

I received a copy of a letter from a lady who had written Indiana Glass Company about this pattern. They told her it was made in the late 1930s and the 1950s. I will repeat information found on the only known boxed set. On a 15-piece set was the following: "15 pc. Luncheon set (Terrace Green) To F W Newburger & Co. New Albany Ind Dept M 1346; From Pitman Dretzer Dunkirk Ind 4-3-52." This was valuable dating information because this color had been attributed only to a much earlier production schedule in other published material.

	Crystal	Teal
Bowl, 5¾"	4.50	
Bowl, 7⅜", soup	7.00	47.50
Bowl, 9½", vegetable		550.00
Creamer	9.00	32.50
Cup	5.00	32.50
Mayonnaise, w/ladle, liner	22.00	
Plate, 6", bread and butter	3.50	12.50
Plate, 8¼", luncheon	7.00	25.00
Plate, 9⅝", dinner	11.00	47.50
Plate, 11¼", sandwich	16.00	65.00
Saucer	2.00	10.00
Sugar	9.00	32.50
Tidbit, 2-tier	17.50	

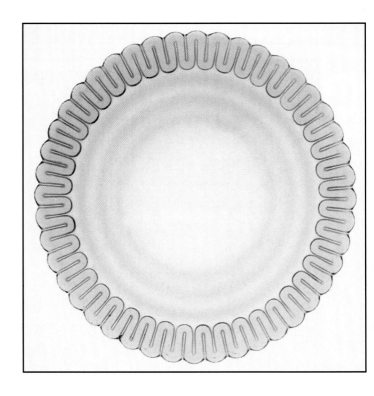

Colors: amber, blue, crystal, green, Olive, and red

Fostoria's Coin Glass continues to sell, albeit more slowly. The reproductions that Lancaster Colony (who now owns the Fostoria moulds), began remaking have put a noticeable dip in sales of this pattern. The collectors of the past continue to buy, but they are looking for rarely seen items and bargains. It is the lack of beginning collectors that puts a dent in sales of commonly found items! I originally included Coin in this book because it was becoming an increasingly desirable collectible — so desirable, in fact, that it was remade! I do not mean they merely moulded a few pieces, but produced a whole line in many of the original colors! These colors deviate slightly from the cherished collectibles in amber, blue, and green; but there is virtually no way for new collectors to verify the red or crystal made yesterday from that made in the 1950s and 1960s. Most collectors and novice dealers are unaware that Coin is still being produced today. It will be your decision alone to buy!

I have put an asterisk (*) by all pieces that have been recently (last six years) made. Recognize that even that could possibly change by the time this book becomes available. Obviously, this has caused chaos in pricing. Because the newly made pieces are priced so expensively, dealers are raising the prices on the older pieces. Who can blame them? Why sell an older piece for $50.00 when the newer item sells for $40.00? The older piece is going to be raised to $60.00 or even $75.00. This has happened in other collectibles, oak furniture for an example. The quandary I now have is how to handle it. If you collect Fostoria Coin, never has the following been truer. **Know your dealer!** Ask him if he can date the piece and keep the dated information with the piece; remember, if the price sounds too good to be true, it probably is! Buying in an antique mall or over the Internet may not be so great an idea unless the piece is guaranteed by the dealer. Then, too, phone calls, postage, and aggravation can all be costly!

The amber lamp (electric patio) in the bottom picture on page 39 has the shade sitting beside it. It was too tall for the photo with the shade on it! The blue lamp is the handled, courting lamp. (It must have been difficult courting holding onto that lamp!) The decanters, lamps, and pitchers sold very fast when we put them out after the photography was finished!

Olive Green is sometimes referred to as avocado, but Olive was the official name. The green most desired is often called "emerald" by collectors. This color is represented by the handled jelly in the bottom photo on page 39. All other green pieces in that photo are Olive!

If you enjoy this pattern, by all means, collect it. Just be aware that future selling may be somewhat endangered by the remaking of older colors. Buy accordingly.

	Amber	Blue	Crystal	Green	Olive	Ruby
Ash tray, 5" #1372/123	17.50	25.00	18.00	30.00	17.50	22.50
Ash tray, 7½", center coin #1372/119	20.00		25.00	35.00		25.00
Ash tray, 7½", round #1372/114	25.00	40.00	25.00	45.00	30.00	20.00
Ash tray, 10" #1372/124	30.00	50.00	25.00	65.00	30.00	
Ash tray, oblong #1372/115	15.00	20.00	10.00	25.00	25.00	
Ash tray/cover, 3" #1372/110	20.00	25.00	25.00	30.00		
Bowl, 8", round #1372/179	30.00	50.00	25.00	70.00	25.00	45.00
Bowl, 8½", ftd. #1372/199	60.00	90.00	50.00	125.00	55.00	75.00
Bowl, 8½", ftd. w/cover #1372/212	100.00	175.00	85.00	225.00		
*Bowl, 9", oval #1372/189	30.00	55.00	30.00	70.00	30.00	50.00
*Bowl, wedding w/cover #1372/162	70.00	90.00	55.00	150.00	55.00	85.00
Candle holder, 4½", pr. #1372/316	30.00	50.00	40.00	50.00	30.00	50.00
Candle holder, 8", pr. #1372/326	60.00		50.00		50.00	125.00
Candy box w/cover, 4⅛" #1372/354	30.00	60.00	30.00	100.00	30.00	60.00
*Candy jar w/cover, 6⁵⁄₁₆" #1372/347	25.00	50.00	25.00	125.00	25.00	50.00
*Cigarette box w/cover, 5¾" x 4½" #1372/374	50.00	80.00	40.00	115.00		
Cigarette holder w/ash tray cover #1372/372	50.00	75.00	45.00	90.00		
Cigarette urn, 3⅜", ftd. #1372/381	25.00	45.00	20.00	50.00	20.00	40.00
Condiment set, 4 pc. (tray, 2 shakers and cruet) #1372/737	210.00	325.00	135.00		225.00	
Condiment tray, 9⅝", #1372/738	60.00	75.00	40.00		75.00	
*Creamer #1372/680	11.00	16.00	10.00	30.00	15.00	16.00
Cruet, 7 oz. w/stopper #1372/531	65.00	165.00	55.00	200.00	80.00	
*Decanter w/stopper, pint, 10³⁄₁₆" #1372/400	125.00	250.00	95.00	350.00	165.00	
*Jelly #1372/448	17.50	25.00	15.00	35.00	15.00	25.00
Lamp chimney, coach or patio #1372/461	50.00	60.00	40.00			
Lamp chimney, hndl., courting #1372/292	45.00	65.00				
Lamp, 9¾", hndl., courting, oil #1372/310	110.00	170.00				
Lamp, 10⅛", hndl., courting, electric #1372/311	110.00	200.00				
Lamp, 13½", coach, electric #1372/321	135.00	225.00	95.00			
Lamp, 13½", coach, oil #1372/320	135.00	225.00	95.00			

COIN GLASS #1372

	Amber	Blue	Crystal	Green	Olive	Ruby
Lamp, 16⅝", patio, electric #1372/466	160.00	275.00	135.00			
Lamp, 16⅝", patio, oil #1372/459	160.00	275.00	135.00			
Nappy, 4½" #1372/495			22.00			
*Nappy, 5⅜", w/hndl. #1372/499	20.00	30.00	15.00	40.00	18.00	30.00
Pitcher, 32 oz., 6³⁄₁₆" #1372/453	55.00	135.00	55.00	175.00	55.00	150.00
Plate, 8", #1372/550			20.00		20.00	40.00
Punch bowl base #1372/602			165.00			
Punch bowl, 14", 1½ gal., #1372/600			165.00			
Punch cup #1372/615			35.00			
*Salver, ftd., 6½" tall #1372/630	110.00	225.00	90.00	295.00	125.00	
Shaker, 3¼", pr. w/chrome top #1372/652	30.00	65.00	25.00	90.00	30.00	65.00
Stem, 4", 5 oz. wine #1372/26			35.00		50.00	95.00
Stem, 5¼", 9 oz., sherbet, #1372/7			25.00		45.00	70.00
Stem, 10½ oz., goblet #1372/2			38.00		50.00	95.00
*Sugar w/cover #1372/673	35.00	45.00	25.00	65.00	35.00	45.00
Tumbler, 3⅝", 9 oz. juice/old fashioned #1372/81			30.00			
Tumbler, 4¼", 9 oz. water, scotch & soda #1372/73			30.00			
Tumbler, 5⅛", 12 oz. iced tea/highball #1372/64			37.50			
Tumbler, 5⅜", 10 oz. double old fashioned #1372/23			30.00			
Tumbler, 5³⁄₁₆", 14 oz. iced tea #1372/58			38.00		40.00	75.00
*Urn, 12¾", ftd., w/cover #1372/829	80.00	125.00	75.00	200.00	80.00	100.00
Vase, 8", bud #1372/799	22.00	40.00	20.00	60.00	25.00	45.00
Vase, 10", ftd. #1372/818			45.00			

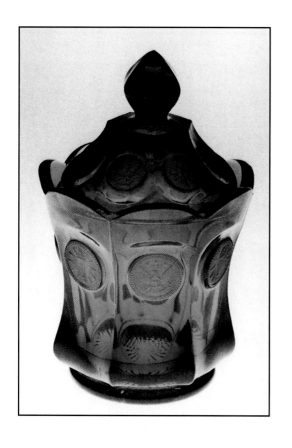

CORSAGE Plate Etching #325, FOSTORIA GLASS COMPANY, 1935 – 1960

Color: crystal

    Corsage is one of a small number of Fostoria dinnerware lines found on **several** distinct **blanks.** There are three lines depicted in the picture on the right. The creamer and sugar shown are #2440, or Lafayette blank, as are the cup and saucer and a few other serving pieces. The individual creamer and sugar (not pictured) are found on #2496 that is known as Baroque. I can't think of any other Fostoria pattern that has different lines for two sizes of sugar and creamers. The ice bucket is on the Baroque blank. Oddly enough, the basic plates are from the #2337 line that has plain, round plates like those found in Buttercup. The larger cake plate and the 13" torte plate are found on the Lafayette line.

    I found all these different lines highly entertaining as I scrutinized this pattern for the book. It's almost as if they were etching surplus inventory! Maybe you'll spot another line that I missed!

	Crystal		Crystal
Bowl, #869, finger	25.00	Plate, 10", hndl., cake, #2496	35.00
Bowl, 4", #4119, ftd.	22.00	Plate, 11", cracker, #2496	35.00
Bowl, 4⅝", 3-corner, #2496	20.00	Plate, 13", torte, #2440	50.00
Bowl, 7⅜" 3-ftd., bon bon, #2496	20.00	Plate, 16", #2364	85.00
Bowl, 9", hndl., #2536	65.00	Relish, 2-part, #2440	27.50
Bowl, 9½", ftd., #2537	145.00	Relish, 2-part, #2496	22.50
Bowl, 10", hndl., #2484	60.00	Relish, 3-part, #2440	35.00
Bowl, 12", flared, #2496	55.00	Relish, 3-part, #2496	32.50
Bowl, 12½", oval, #2545, "Flame"	45.00	Relish, 4-part, #2419	42.50
Candelabra, 2 light w/prisms, #2527	95.00	Relish, 4-part, #2496	37.50
Candlestick, 5½", #2496	30.00	Relish, 5-part, #2419	57.50
Candlestick, 5½", #2535	35.00	Sauce bowl, 6½", oval, #2440	75.00
Candlestick, 6¾", duo, #2545, "Flame"	50.00	Sauce tray, 8½", oval, #2440	35.00
Candlestick, duo, #2496	45.00	Saucer, #2440	5.00
Candlestick, trindle, #2496	55.00	Stem, #6014, 3¾", 1 oz., cordial	45.00
Candy, w/lid, 3-part, #2496	100.00	Stem, #6014, 3¾", 4 oz., oyster cocktail	17.50
Celery, #2440	32.00	Stem, #6014, 4½", 5½ oz., low sherbet	16.00
Comport, 3¼", cheese	20.00	Stem, #6014, 5¼", 3 oz., wine	30.00
Comport, 5½", #2496	25.00	Stem, #6014, 5⅜", 5½ oz., high sherbet	22.00
Creamer, #2440	17.50	Stem, #6014, 5", 3½ oz., cocktail	22.00
Creamer, ind., #2496	12.50	Stem, #6014, 7⅜", 9 oz., water	27.50
Cup, #2440	18.00	Stem, #6014, 7⅞", 4 oz., claret	35.00
Ice bucket, #2496	75.00	Sugar, #2440	17.50
Mayonnaise, 2-part, #2440	25.00	Sugar, ind., #2496	12.50
Mayonnaise, 3-pc., #2496½	47.50	Tidbit, 3-footed, #2496	15.00
Pickle, #2440	25.00	Tray, 6½", ind. sug/cr., #2496½	12.50
Pitcher	265.00	Tumbler, #6014, 4¾", 5 oz., ftd. juice	20.00
Plate, 6½", #2337	8.00	Tumbler, #6014, 5½", 9 oz., ftd. water	22.00
Plate, 7½", #2337	10.00	Tumbler, #6014, 6", 12 oz., ftd. iced tea	28.00
Plate, 8½",	12.50	Vase, 8", bud, #5092	60.00
Plate, 9½", #2337	37.50	Vase, 10", ftd., #2470	135.00
Plate, 10½", cake, hndl., #2440	32.50		

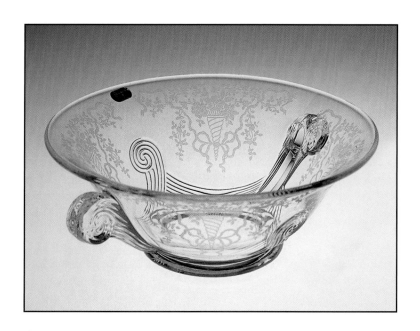

CROCHETED CRYSTAL, IMPERIAL GLASS COMPANY, 1943 – EARLY 1950S

Color: crystal

Crocheted Crystal was made by Imperial exclusively for Sears, Roebuck and Company. It was listed in Sears catalogs for years; if you have any old catalogs, you can check it out. I have been unable to find a complete run of these, but the listing below is from the fall 1943 Sears catalog with additional pieces listed that were not in that particular inventory. In order to show you the stemware in this pattern, I have included an ad showing them (page 46). I want one of each size for photography, but I have been unable to locate any of them myself. The difficulty lies with the fact that no one seems to recognize these as Crocheted Crystal. Besides those stems, the cake stand, 12" basket, and narcissus bowl are not readily found.

You can see the 12" basket on the bottom of page 45 alongside the rare style creamer and sugar. The normally found creamer and sugar have the open lace work of the other pieces. A reader sent me a copy of a catalog page last summer which showed this other set. I read the letter while at a show in White Plains, New York. Cathy and I had seen that creamer and sugar set at an antique mall on the previous Thursday. She asked if it were Pretzel when she saw it, and I said no. (I did not know what it was at the time!) We drove back on Monday after the show and were waiting when the mall opened. Someone else must have liked the $9.00 price on the set because it was gone. Several months later, Cathy found another set; and now, you can see it too!

I first started looking at this pattern because the shapes and styles reminded me of Laced Edge, also made by Imperial. Some of the pieces I have pictured are not in the listing below, although they have all the characteristics of the pattern. You will find a number of go-with pieces in this pattern. Not only did Imperial make a multitude of similar designs, but so did other companies.

The punch bowl also came with closed handle cups, although the catalog ad shows open-handled ones. Cups came both ways, and I suspect the earlier cups had the open handles. Consumer complaints of "punch drenching" may have inspired a design change on this cup! There is no punch liner listed, but the 14" or 17" plate could serve as such if you so desire. The single candleholder next to the double one is shaped like the Narcissus bowl. Even though the candle is not listed in the catalogs I have, there is no doubt that this is Crocheted Crystal. That double candleholder is the most commonly found piece of Crocheted Crystal.

The really astounding thing I encountered while trying to buy pieces of this pattern was the disparity of prices. No one seemed to know what the **pattern** was, but they all had proud prices because it was "pretty good glass" or "elegant looking glass." One individual swore that the epergne set was Heisey. She said it was pictured in the Heisey book and she could let it go for a special dealer price of $395.00! I suspect she still owns it!

Contrary to what I see on dealers' price labels of mysterious glass, Heisey and Cambridge did not make every elegant looking piece of glass in the country!

	Crystal		Crystal
Basket, 6"	30.00	Mayonnaise ladle	5.00
Basket, 9"	40.00	Mayonnaise plate, 7½"	7.50
Basket, 12"	70.00	Plate, 8", salad	7.50
Bowl, 7", Narcissus	40.00	Plate, 9½"	12.50
Bowl, 10½", salad	30.00	Plate, 13", salad bowl liner	22.50
Bowl, 11", console	30.00	Plate, 14"	25.00
Bowl, 12", console	32.50	Plate, 17"	40.00
Buffet set, 14" plate, ftd. sauce bowl, ladle	45.00	Punch bowl, 14"	65.00
Cake stand, 12", ftd.	40.00	Punch cup, closed hndl.	4.00
Candleholder, 4½" high, double	15.00	Punch cup, open hndl.	7.50
Candleholder, 6" wide, single	20.00	Relish, 11½", 3 pt.	25.00
Candleholder (Narcissus bowl shape)	32.50	Stem, 4½", 3½ oz., cocktail	12.50
Celery, 10", oval	25.00	Stem, 5½", 4½ oz., wine	17.50
Cheese & cracker, 12" plate, ftd. dish	40.00	Stem, 5", 6 oz., sherbet	10.00
Creamer, flat	25.00	Stem, 7⅛", 9 oz., water goblet	14.00
Creamer, ftd.	20.00	Sugar, flat	25.00
Epergne, 11", ftd. bowl, center vase	130.00	Sugar, ftd.	20.00
Hors d'oeuvre dish, 10½", 4-pt., round	30.00	Tumbler, 6", 6 oz., ftd. fruit juice	10.00
Lamp, 11", hurricane	50.00	Tumbler, 7⅛", 12 oz., ftd. iced tea	15.00
Mayonnaise bowl, 5¼"	12.50	Vase, 5", 4-ftd.	35.00
		Vase, 8"	35.00

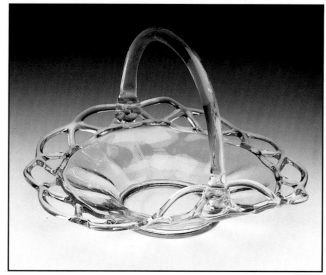

Our choice and yours ... Harmony House *Crocheted Crystal*

Your table deserves fine hand-made crystal, and this is it. Harmony House Crocheted Crystal ... unusually elegant, unusually low priced ... exclusive with Sears. You'll want it for yourself, and you'll choose it for impressive gifts. All pieces (except stemware) have graceful "crocheted" openwork edges.

4-piece Salad Set

[A] With this set you'll add sparkle to salads, flatter your dining table. Bowl, 10½-in. diam.; plate, 13-in. diam.; glass serving fork, spoon.
35 E 01732—Shpg. wt., 7 lbs...4-piece set **$2.65**

Charming Epergne Centerpiece

[B] Filled with colorful fruit or flowers, this beautiful epergne will brighten your living room or add a graceful touch to your dining table or buffet. Sparkling, footed crystal glass bowl, 11 inches in diameter, with removable vase. Overall height, 11 inches. Shipping weight, 7 pounds.
35 E 01727 ....Complete centerpiece **$2.89**

Graceful Cake Stand

[C] This beautiful cake stand will even do justice to your prize cakes—and it's equally good for holding smaller tid-bits like cookies, candies, and fruit. Overall diam., 12 in. Height, 4 in.
35 E 1729—Shipping weight, 5 pounds ..Each **$1.49**

Lovely 3-piece Console Set

[D] Glittering crystal and glowing candle-light add charm and glamour to any occasion. Here is a 3-piece console set, consisting of two exquisitely styled crystal glass twin candle-holders, each about 4½ inches high, and a lovely crystal glass bowl, about 11 inches in diameter. Candles not incl.
35 E 01739—Shpg. wt., 6 lbs......3-piece set **$1.45**

Matched Crocheted Stemware

[E] Start your collection of crocheted crystal with this 12-piece set, which includes the most popular, most-used pieces. All have strikingly beautiful shapes and decorated stems. Set of four goblets, four sherbets and four 8-inch salad plates. Makes a romantic gift any bride would treasure.
35 E 01751—Shpg. wt., 10 lbs...12-piece set **$5.79**

Add more stemware from time to time from open stock

35 E 1750—State pieces.	Height	Shpg. wt.,	Each	Six for
Goblet......Size 9 oz	7⅛ in	.1 lb	.55c	$3.25
Sherbet.....Size 6 oz	.5 in	1 lb	.55c	3.25
Wine......Size 4½ oz	.5½ in	.1 lb	.55c	3.25
Iced Tea ...Size 12 oz	7⅛ in	1 lb	.55c	3.25
Salad Plate .Size 8-in. diam.		2 lbs	.38c	2.19

Narcissus Bowl

[F] Just the thing for growing narcissus or other bulbs; you'll like it, too, for candies, preserves and salted nuts. Deep bowl. 4½-in. high, 7 in. diam.
35 E 1714—Shipping weight, 3 pounds 8 ounces **85c**

14-piece Punch Set

[G] If you're one who plays hostess often, this set will prove practical—really invaluable. It adds a festive touch to any occasion, and is wonderful for holiday entertaining. Cups hook over the edge of the bowl, which can also be used for salads. 4-qt. bowl. 14 in. in diam.; 12 six-ounce cups; glass ladle.
35 E 01719—Shpg. wt., 18 lbs......14-piece set **$5.75**
35 E 1720—Set of 12 cups only. Shpg. wt., 8 lbs. **$2.89**

3-Piece Mayonnaise Set

[H] Bowl 5¼-in. diam.; plate 7½-in. diam.; ladle.
35 E 1705—Shipping weight, 3 lbs. 8 oz ...Set **89c**

Exquisite Crocheted Plates

[J] Use the 9½-inch size for place plates; 14-inch size plate for cake; 17-inch size for sandwiches.
35 E 01701—9½-in. Shpg. wt., 9 lbs...Set of six **$2.59**
35 E 01703—14-in. Shpg. wt., 5 lbs.........Each 1.25
35 E 01704—17-in. Shpg. wt., 8 lbs.........Each 3.45

3-piece Buffet Set

[K] Ideal for serving snacks that require sauces. 14-in. serving plate, removable bowl for sauce, and ladle.
35 E 01736—Shipping weight, 6 pounds......Set **$1.65**

Hors d'oeuvre Dish

[L] Useful relish dish with four handy partitions.
35 E 1716—Diam. 10½ in. Shpg. wt., 3 lbs. **98c**

Crocheted Crystal can be added to your Easy Terms order . . . see inside back cover

"DAISY," NUMBER 620, INDIANA GLASS COMPANY

Colors: crystal, 1933 – 1940; fired-on red, late 30s; amber, 1940s; dark green and milk glass, 1960s, 1970s, 1980s.

"Daisy" is one of the few patterns that fits the boundary of both *Collector's Encyclopedia of Depression Glass* and *Collectible Glassware of the 40s, 50s, 60s* .... Since there are more collectors searching for amber or green "Daisy," I determined that it best fit this book. Realize that crystal was made in 1930s, but there are only a few collectors looking for it today, pretty though it may be.

Avocado colored "Daisy" was marketed by Indiana as "Heritage" in the 1960s through 1980s and not under the name "Daisy" or No. 620 as it was called when it was first produced in the late 1930s. This causes confusion because Federal Glass Company also made a "Heritage" pattern that is **rare in green** (see page 102). Federal's green is the brighter, normally found Depression glass color and not the avocado colored green shown here. Anytime you see avocado colored glassware, think late 1960s or early 1970s. A rumor persists that harvest gold and avocado green are coming back into vogue!

Amber "Daisy" has its admirers and prices have advanced. The indented grill plate, 12 oz. footed tea, relish dish, 9⅜" berry, and cereal bowls are all uncommon, not scarce. Perfect (without inner rim roughness) cereal bowls have become the most perplexing pieces to find, taking that honor away from the iced tea. It's amazing how many teas jumped out of the woodwork when the price reached $40.00!

We have mixed colors in some of our pictures this time. For example, you can see a green cream soup on the amber grill plate. It's all part of the rainbow idea of collecting. The pattern shown below is an indented grill plate in green. Note how large that ring is. It is much larger than the base of a cup, but fits the base of the cream soup exactly. I never have figured out how the grill plate/cream soup combination came about. If anyone knows why this combo, let me know!

There are a few pieces of fired-on red "Daisy" being discovered. A reader's letter a few years back said that her family had a red set that was acquired in 1935. That helps date this production. There is a pitcher in a fired-on red being found with the No. 618 (Pineapple and Floral) tumblers. This pitcher does not belong to either pattern per se, but was sold with both of these Indiana patterns. Thus, it's a legitimate go-with pitcher. It has a squared base, if you spot one. Most of the red pieces are dull and not a bright red color.

	Crystal	Green	Red, Amber
Bowl, 4½", berry	4.50	6.00	9.00
Bowl, 4½", cream soup	4.50	6.00	12.00
Bowl, 6", cereal	10.00	12.00	33.00
Bowl, 7⅜", deep berry	7.50	9.00	15.00
Bowl, 9⅜", deep berry	13.00	16.00	35.00
Bowl, 10", oval vegetable	10.00	11.00	18.00
Creamer, footed	6.00	5.00	8.00
Cup	4.00	4.00	6.00
Plate, 6", sherbet	2.00	2.00	3.00
Plate, 7⅜", salad	3.50	3.50	7.00
Plate, 8⅜", luncheon	4.00	4.50	6.00
Plate, 10⅜", grill	5.50	7.50	10.00
Plate, 9⅜", dinner	5.50	6.50	9.00
Plate, 10⅜", grill w/indent for cream soup		16.00	30.00
Plate, 11½", cake or sandwich	6.50	7.50	15.00
Platter, 10¾"	7.50	8.50	17.50
Relish dish, 8⅜", 3-part	12.50		35.00
Saucer	1.50	1.50	2.00
Sherbet, ftd.	5.00	5.50	9.00
Sugar, ftd.	6.00	5.00	8.00
Tumbler, 9 oz., ftd.	10.00	9.50	20.00
Tumbler, 12 oz., ftd.	20.00	22.00	40.00

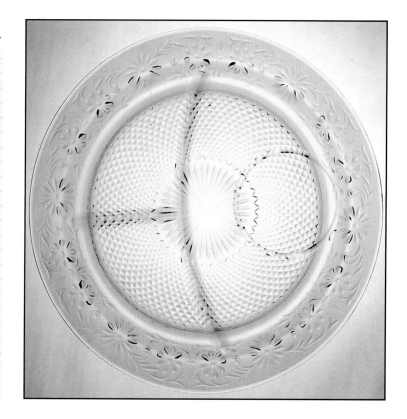

Colors: crystal and iridized

There has been a wave of new collectors looking for Dewdrop recently. Both tumblers are difficult to find, but the iced tea is virtually impossible. I have included a photo of the iced tea tumbler below. I haven't found a smaller tumbler but collectors tell me it is easily located! Unfortunately, many of the shows I attend have few dealers who stock Dewdrop. I think they are making a mistake!

Dewdrop pitchers have caused a stir. There are two styles showing up and I have probably pictured the wrong one previously. The footed one may be a "go-with" type while the flat, iridized one pictured on bottom of page 50 may be the true Dewdrop pitcher. These are also found in crystal, but I was astonished to find one iridized! Notice how the top edge matches the top edge of the creamer while the footed one has a non-scalloped edge. Since I have no catalog listing for this pattern, I will list both styles.

Many collectors in the past bought the Lazy Susan in Dewdrop to obtain the missing ball bearings for their Shell Pink Lazy Susan! The ball bearings are interchangeable in every Jeannette pattern that has Lazy Susans. The boxed Lazy Susan below is an original. The Shell Pink Lazy Susan came in the same decorated floral box, but with pink flowers.

The snack sets were sold in sets of four. I have seen several boxed sets of these in my travels. TV tray sets of various types were something of a phenomenon in the mid 1950s.

Dewdrop will not break your bank account, so buy it now. Besides, nearly all crystal patterns make marvelous table settings.

	Crystal		Crystal
Bowl, 4¾"	5.00	Plate, 11½"	17.50
Bowl, 8½"	12.00	Plate, snack, w/indent for cup	4.00
Bowl, 10⅜"	17.50	Punch bowl base	10.00
Butter, w/cover	27.50	Punch bowl, 6 qt.	30.00
Candy dish, w/cover, 7", round	22.00	Relish, leaf shape w/hndl.	8.00
Creamer	8.00	Sugar, w/cover	13.00
Cup, punch or snack	4.00	Tray, 13", Lazy Susan, complete	45.00
Pitcher, ½ gallon, ftd.	22.00	Tumbler, 9 oz., water, 2 pc. w/ ball bearing ring	16.00
Pitcher, flat	50.00	Tumbler, 12 oz., iced tea, 6"	20.00

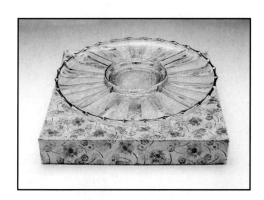

EARLY AMERICAN PRESCUT, ANCHOR HOCKING GLASS CORPORATION, 1960 – 1999

Colors: crystal, some amber, blue green, red, and black; some with painted designs

All Early American Prescut (designated EAPC) pieces are designated as the 700 line in Hocking's catalogs. There were other Prescut patterns made at Anchor Hocking, and I'm trying to help solve this confusion by addressing that problem on page 55. To be EAPC, there has to be the star in the design with two exceptions. The double candle has a knob in place of the star. That star was **pictured** in the catalog where the knob is attached; so probably the mould makers changed the design to better release the piece from the mould. That was a common battle at glass factories — glass designers against mould makers! From what I have seen, mould makers won out! Also, the cup used with punch or snack sets does not have the star. It was borrowed from the "Oatmeal" line rather than having to make a new cup mould!

Four pieces of EAPC were introduced by Anchor Hocking in the 1960 – 1961 catalog. Most pieces were discontinued by 1978, but the creamer, sugar, cruet, and shakers with plastic tops were made as late as 1997. The only piece I can find currently listed is the 8½" vase which is being sold to the floral industry.

The creamer, sugar, oil bottle, regular shakers, and 13½" plate are difficult to sell. Actually, these pieces can sometimes still be found on the shelves of dish barns and close-out stores. I saw a whole display in a dish barn outside Lexington last fall. It was gathering dust among the Fiesta close-outs! The ever-present punch bowl can still be seen at prices ranging from $20.00 to $75.00. For me, they sell slowly at $30.00 and I have been able to move them more quickly at $25.00. I have seen red ash trays and a blue sugar bowl and lid. You can also find pieces in dark green and amber. Colored pieces are uncommon and some are deceiving, having sprayed-on colors.

Some items were only made for a year or two. The most difficult, but desirable pieces to own are the oil lamp, individual shakers, and 11¾" paneled bowl! Additionally, the EAPC 40 ounce (square) pitcher, **smooth rim** 4¼" bowls, 6¾" plates with or wo/ring, 10" 4-part plate, and 13½" five-part relish are missing from many collections. According to dealers, the following items are **becoming** hard to find: iced tea tumblers, Lazy Susans with a wire rack, and the frosted lamp shade.

There are four and five inch round powder jars with a crinolated locking system that look like EAPC. They sell in the $20.00 – 25.00 range. These are **not** EAPC. If you look around the center of each piece, the word "Italy" will be embossed. There is also a heart dish marked Italy!

For more detailed information on EAPC, check out my book, *Anchor Hocking's Fire-King & More.*

	Crystal		Crystal
Ash tray, 4", #700/690	5.00	Oil lamp	295.00
Ash tray, 5"	10.00	Pitcher, 18 oz., #744	10.00
Ash tray, 7¾", #718-G	15.00	Pitcher, 40 oz., square	55.00
Bowl, 4¼", #726 (scalloped rim)	7.00	Pictcher, 60 oz., #791	17.00
Bowl, 4¼", #726 (smooth rim)	22.00	Plate, 6¾", no ring, salad w/indent	55.00
Bowl, 5¼", #775 (scalloped rim)	7.00	Plate, 6¾", w/ring for 6 oz. cup	40.00
Bowl, 6¾", three-toed, #768	4.50	Plate, 10", snack, #780	10.00
Bowl, 7¼", (scalloped rim)	20.00	Plate, 11", 4-part w/swirl dividers	95.00
Bowl, 7¼", round, #767	6.00	Plate, 11"	12.00
Bowl, 8¾", #787	9.00	Plate, 11¾", deviled egg/relish, #750	42.00
Bowl, 9", console, #797	15.00	Plate, 13½", serving, #790	12.50
Bowl, 9", oval, #776	7.00	Punch set, 15-pc.	35.00
Bowl, 9⅜", gondola dish, #752	4.00	Relish, 8½", oval, 3-part, #778	5.00
Bowl, 10¾", salad, #788	12.00	Relish, 10", divided, tab hndl., #770	7.00
Bowl, 11¾", paneled, #794	195.00	Relish, 13½", 5-part	40.00
Bowl, dessert, 5⅜", #765	2.50	Server, 12 oz. (syrup), #707	20.00
Butter, bottom w/metal handle and knife	15.00	Shakers, pr., metal tops, #700/699	8.00
Butter, w/cover, ¼ lb., #705	6.00	Shakers, pr., plastic tops, #725	8.00
Cake plate, 13½", ftd., #706	25.00	Shakers, pr., 2¼", individual, #700/736	75.00
Candlestick, 7" x 5⅝", double, #784	30.00	Sherbet, 3½", 6 oz., ftd.	100.00
Candy, w/lid, 5¼", #744	10.00	Sugar, w/lid, #753	4.00
Candy, w/cover, 7¼" x 5½", #792	12.00	Tray, 6½" x 12", hostess, #750	12.50
Chip & dip, 10¾" bowl, 5¼",		Tray, cr/sug, #700/671	3.00
brass finish holder, #700/733	25.00	Tumbler, 5 oz., 4", juice, #730	5.00
Coaster, #700/702	2.00	Tumbler, 10 oz., 4½" tumbler, #731	6.00
Cocktail shaker, 9", 30 oz.	350.00	Tumbler, 15 oz., 6", iced tea, #732	20.00
Creamer, #754	3.00	Vase, 5", ftd., bud	300.00
Cruet, w/stopper, 7¾", #711	6.00	Vase, 6 x 4½", basket/block, #704/205	16.00
Cup, punch or snack, 6 oz. (no star)	2.50	Vase, 8½", #741	7.00
Lazy Susan, 9-pc., #700/713	55.00	Vase, 10", #742	12.50

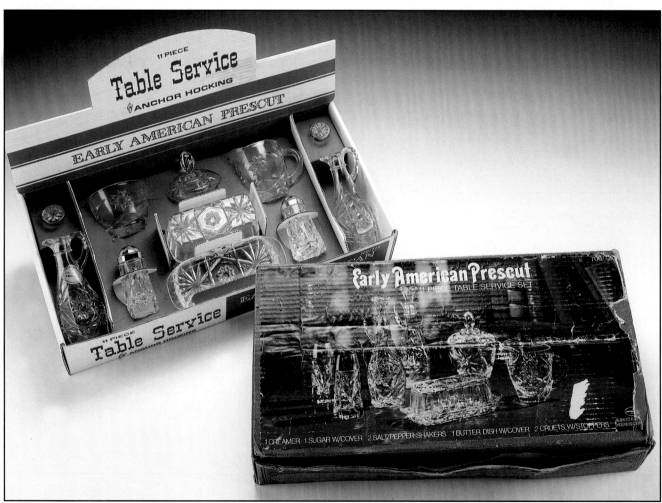

PRESCUT: "OATMEAL" & "PINEAPPLE," ANCHOR HOCKING GLASS CORPORATION, 1941 – 1970s

There has been confusion among collectors as to what constitutes EAPC and what does not. Read page 51 on EAPC. "Oatmeal" is presently defined as EAPC pieces without the "star." The "Oatmeal" name comes the fact that seven of these pieces were premiums in boxes of Crystal Wedding Oats. The soap dish may have not been in the oatmeal boxes but is the same pattern. You can tell by its price that it is not as common as the others. Like the five pieces of Forest Green sandwich that were packed in oatmeal, these items are **plentiful** today.

The other pattern often mistakenly identified as EAPC has been called "Pineapple" by collectors. It was first shown in the 1941 catalog, twenty years before the birth of EAPC. This can be found mostly in crystal with an occasional piece in white. You might even find white items decorated with painted flowers. The crystal cigarette box can be found with a Royal Ruby lid.

"OATMEAL"	Crystal
Bowl, 4¼", berry	2.00
Cup	2.50
Saucer, 4⅜"	1.50
Sherbet, 5 oz.	1.50
Soap dish, 5¼" x 3¾"	15.00
Tumbler, 4 oz., juice	2.00
Tumbler, 7 oz., old fashioned	2.50
Tumbler, 9 oz., water	2.00

"PINEAPPLE"	Crystal	White
Box, 4¾", cigarette or dresser	15.00	12.50
Box, 4¾", w/Royal Ruby lid	25.00	
Butter, round	15.00	
Marmalade, w/Royal Ruby lid	18.00	
Pitcher, 12 oz., milk	8.00	10.00
Sugar w/lid, handled	12.00	
Sugar w/lid, no handles	10.00	
Syrup pitcher	12.00	
Tumbler, 10 oz., iced tea	6.00	8.00

EMERALD CREST, FENTON ART GLASS COMPANY, 1949 – 1955

Color: white with green edge

Emerald Crest was listed in Fenton catalogs from 1949 until January 1955. I had a recent letter from a lady who was married in 1957 and received several wedding gifts of Emerald Crest. Although production would have ended by 1956 since it was not in that year's catalog, that doesn't mean inventories in stores were exhausted, just that the stores could not reorder that pattern.

This popular line succeeded the Aqua Crest (blue trimmed) started in 1941, and Silver Crest (crystal trimmed) started in 1943. Since Aqua Crest is not in this book, you will find prices for Aqua Crest fall between those of Emerald Crest and Silver Crest (priced on pages 221 and 223). I had arranged for Aqua Crest to be pictured in an earlier book, but a divorce sent the glass farther west than I wished to pursue it for a picture!

I do not buy or sell a lot of Fenton; consequently, I appreciate the help from Fenton collectors and dealers as well as readers who have aided with listings of Fenton patterns in this book. I value their time and guidance in acquiring price listings for Emerald and Silver Crest.

Emerald Crest mayonnaise sets are commonly found with crystal spoons, but a green spoon was made. It is occasionally found in mayos and mustards, and the green spoons alone sell for $30.00 – 35.00. You can see two green spoons in the mustards. The green stopper for the oil bottle is also difficult to locate. Most stoppers were crystal. Personally, I feel the green adds to the pattern presentation.

Certain pieces of Emerald Crest have two different line numbers. Originally, this line was #680, and all pieces carried that designation. In July 1952, Fenton began issuing a Ware Number for each piece; that is why you see two separate numbers for the different sized plates and vases in my listing.

	White w/Green		White w/Green
Basket, 5" #7236	77.50	Mayonnaise set, 3-pc. w/gr. ladle #7203	95.00
Basket, 7" #7237	110.00	Mustard, w/lid and spoon	85.00
Bowl, 5", finger or deep dessert #7221	22.50	Oil bottle, w/green stopper #680, 7269	125.00
Bowl, 5½", soup #680, 7230	37.50	Pitcher, 6" hndl., beaded melon #7116	55.00
Bowl, 8½", flared #680	45.00	Plate, 5½" #680, 7218	15.00
Bowl, 9½" #682	57.50	Plate, 6½" #680, 7219	16.00
Bowl, 10" salad #7220	72.50	Plate, 8½" #680, 7217	22.50
Bowl, dessert, shallow #7222	20.00	Plate, 10" #680, 7210	40.00
Bowl, ftd., tall, square #7330	225.00	Plate, 12" #680, 7212	47.50
Cake plate, 13" high ftd. #680, 7213	120.00	Plate, 12" #682	47.50
Cake plate, low ftd. #5813	100.00	Plate, 16", torte #7216	65.00
Candle holder, flat saucer base, pr. #680	75.00	Saucer #7208	15.00
Comport, 6", ftd., flared #206	37.50	Sherbet, ftd. #7226	22.50
Comport, ftd., double crimped	37.50	Sugar, clear reeded hndls. #7231	35.00
Creamer, clear reeded hndls. #7231	35.00	Tidbit, 2-tier bowls, 5½" & 8½"	65.00
Cup #7208	55.00	Tidbit, 2-tier bowls, 8½" & 10"	85.00
Flower pot w/attached saucer #7299	67.50	Tidbit, 2-tier plates #7297	57.50
Mayonnaise bowl, #7203	32.50	Tidbit, 3-tier plates #7298	77.50
Mayonnaise ladle, crystal #7203	5.00	Vase, 4½", fan #36, #7355	30.00
Mayonnaise ladle, green, #7203	35.00	Vase, 6¼", fan #36, #7357	35.00
Mayonnaise liner, #7203	12.00	Vase, 8", bulbous base #186	65.00
Mayonnaise set, 3-pc. w/crys. ladle #7203	60.00		

EMERALD GLO, PADEN CITY AND FENTON ART GLASS COMPANY, 1940s – 1950s

Color: Emerald green

Emerald Glo was primarily made by Paden City Glass Company for Rubel; however, the pattern was also made by Fenton Art Glass Company in the later years of its production. Labeled pieces have been found which state "Cavalier Emerald-Glo Hand-Made." All "star cut" pieces were made by Paden City, but uncut pieces were made by both companies. Normally, the Fenton manufactured pieces are a slightly darker green color. Fenton pieces are most often found with cast-iron accoutrements as opposed to the gold toned ones pictured on the right. The picture below shows all Fenton pieces. Fenton also made other colors from these moulds, so be on the lookout for them.

	Emerald Green
Candleholders, pr., ball with metal cups	35.00
Casserole w/metal cover	40.00
Cheese dish w/metal top and handle	65.00
Condiment set (2 jars, metal lids, spoons & tray)	60.00
Condiment set (3 jars, metal lids, spoons & tray)	75.00
Creamer	20.00
Creamer/sugar, individual (metal) w/metal lid, on metal tray	32.50
Creamer/sugar, individual w/metal lid, on metal tray	35.00
Cruet	30.00
Ice bucket, metal holder & tongs	65.00
Marmalade w/metal lid & spoon	25.00
Mayonnaise, divided w/metal underliner & spoons	35.00
Oil bottle	30.00
Relish, 9" divided w/metal handle	30.00
Relish, 9", tab hndl. w/metal handle	35.00
Relish, heart shaped	25.00
Salad bowl w/metal base, fork and spoon	55.00
Salad bowl, 10"	30.00
Server, 5-part w/metal covered center	65.00
Sugar	20.00
Sugar w/metal lid & liner	25.00
Syrup w/metal lid & liner	45.00
Tidbit, 2-tier (bowls, 6" & 8")	50.00

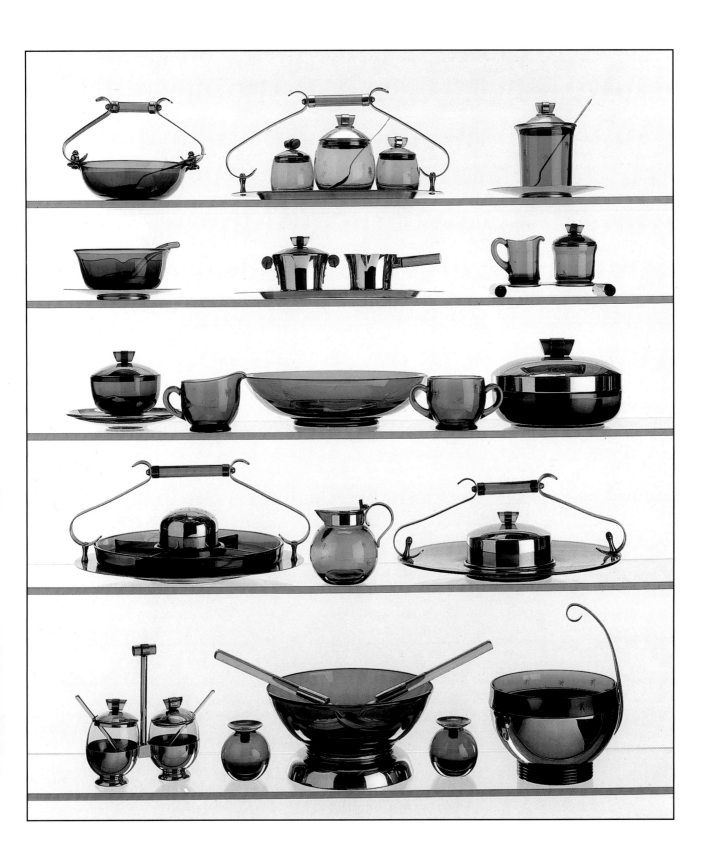

ENGLISH HOBNAIL Line No. 555, WESTMORELAND GLASS COMPANY, 1920s – 1983

Colors: amber, crystal, and crystal with various color treatments and white

    English Hobnail was listed in my first Depression glass book in 1972; but crystal and amber English Hobnail were being made until Westmoreland closed in 1983. As a result, I am listing amber and crystal in this book. I recognize that crystal, crystal with amber or black feet, and some tints of amber were made before 1940. Pricing is relatively the same for all crystal and amber no matter when made. Milk glass English Hobnail was only made in this book's time frame. It sells for about the same price as crystal or a little lower. You can double the price listed for any **decorated** milk glass English Hobnail. Ruby flashed English Hobnail is difficult to sell at regular crystal prices. There is a strong clientele for crystal English Hobnail, but collectors actively soliciting amber are few and far between.

    The 8" compote on the bottom row was called a sweetmeat by Westmoreland. The ice bucket pictured there can also be a large candy or a covered ice bucket when a lid is present. The same lid that fits the three-footed candy fits that bucket. The two tiered tidbit could be original, but many of these (in numerous patterns) were made in the early 1970s by a dealer in St. Louis. Even if old hardware were used, there is no way to tell how old these are. Remember that a tidbit carries the cost of two drilled plates plus the cost of the hardware. An original tidbit could be rare, but who can tell the difference between a newly made one and one that is forty years old?

	Amber/Crystal		Amber/Crystal		Amber/Crystal
Ash tray, 3"	5.00	Bowl, 11", bell	35.00	Cup, demitasse	18.00
Ash tray, 4½"	7.00	Bowl, 11", rolled edge	22.00	Decanter, 20 oz.	55.00
Ash tray, 4½", sq.	7.50	Bowl, 12", celery	20.00	Egg cup	14.00
Basket, 5", hndl.	20.00	Bowl, 12", flange or console	30.00	Hat, high	18.00
Basket, 6", tall, hndl.	40.00	Bowl, 12", flared	35.00	Hat, low	15.00
Bon bon, 6½", hndl.	12.50	Bowl, 12", oval crimped	40.00	Ice tub, 4"	20.00
Bottle, toilet, 5 oz.	22.00	Bowl, cream soup	15.00	Ice tub, 5½"	40.00
Bowl, 4", rose	16.00	Candelabra, 2-lite	25.00	Icer, sq. base,	
Bowl, 4½", finger	7.50	Candlestick, 3½", rnd. base	10.00	w/patterned insert	50.00
Bowl, 4½", round nappy	7.00	Candlestick, 5½", sq. base	15.00	Lamp, 6½", electric	32.00
Bowl, 4½", sq. ftd., finger	9.00	Candlestick, 9", rnd. base	25.00	Lamp, 9½", electric	45.00
Bowl, 4½", sq. nappy	7.00	Candy dish, 3-ftd.	30.00	Lamp, candlestick	
Bowl, 5", round nappy	9.50	Candy, ½ lb. and cover,		(several types)	30.00
Bowl, 5½", bell nappy	11.50	cone shaped	25.00	Lampshade, 17"	175.00
Bowl, 6", crimped dish	12.50	Chandelier, 17" shade		Marmalade w/cover	22.00
Bowl, 6", rose	17.50	w/200+ prisms	395.00	Mayonnaise, 6"	10.00
Bowl, 6", round nappy	10.00	Cheese w/cover, 6"	35.00	Mustard, sq. ftd., w/lid	20.00
Bowl, 6", sq. nappy	10.00	Cheese w/cover, 8¾"	55.00	Nut, individual, ftd.	6.00
Bowl, 6½", grapefruit	11.00	Cigarette box and cover,		Oil bottle, 2 oz., hndl.	20.00
Bowl, 6½", round nappy	12.00	4½"x2½"	20.00	Oil bottle, 6 oz., hndl.	30.00
Bowl, 6½", sq. nappy	12.50	Cigarette jar w/cover, rnd.	15.00	Oil-vinegar combination, 6 oz.	37.50
Bowl, 7", 6 pt.	25.00	Cigarette lighter		Parfait, rnd. ftd.	15.00
Bowl, 7", oblong spoon	17.50	(milk glass only)	14.00	Pitcher, 23 oz., rounded	50.00
Bowl, 7", preserve	15.00	Coaster, 3"	5.00	Pitcher, 32 oz., straight side	55.00
Bowl, 7", round nappy	15.00	Compote, 5", round, rnd. ftd.	12.00	Pitcher, 38 oz., rounded	65.00
Bowl, 7½", bell nappy	16.00	Compote, 5", sq. ftd., round	12.50	Pitcher, 60 oz., rounded	70.00
Bowl, 8", 6 pt.	25.00	Compote, 5½", ball stem,		Pitcher, 64 oz., straight side	80.00
Bowl, 8", cupped, nappy	25.00	sweetmeat	30.00	Plate, 5½", rnd.	4.50
Bowl, 8", ftd.	30.00	Compote, 5½", bell	15.00	Plate, 6", sq.	5.00
Bowl, 8", hexagonal ftd.,		Compote, 5½", sq. ftd., bell	18.00	Plate, 6", sq. finger bowl liner	5.00
2-hndl.	40.00	Compote, 6", honey, rnd. ftd.	18.00	Plate, 6½", depressed center, rnd.	6.00
Bowl, 8", pickle	15.00	Compote, 6", sq. ftd., honey	18.00	Plate, 6½", round.	6.00
Bowl, 8", round nappy	27.50	Compote, 8", ball stem,		Plate, 6½, rnd. finger bowl liner	6.50
Bowl, 9", bell nappy	32.50	sweetmeat	35.00	Plate, 8", rnd.	7.50
Bowl, 9", celery	17.50	Creamer, hexagonal, ftd.	9.00	Plate, 8", rnd., 3-ftd.	15.00
Bowl, 9½", round crimped	32.00	Creamer, low, flat	7.50	Plate, 8½", plain edge	8.00
Bowl, 10", flared	35.00	Creamer, sq. ftd.	8.50	Plate, 8½", rnd.	8.00
Bowl, 10", oval crimped	40.00	Cup	6.00	Plate, 8¾", sq.	8.00

ENGLISH HOBNAIL

	Amber/Crystal		Amber/Crystal		Amber/Crystal
Plate, 10½", grill, rnd	15.00	Stem, 5 oz., rnd. claret	12.50	Tumbler, 7 oz., sq. ftd., juice	9.00
Plate, 10", rnd.	15.00	Stem, 5 oz., sq. ftd., oyster cocktail	9.00	Tumbler, 8 oz., rnd., ball, water	10.00
Plate, 10", sq.	15.00	Stem, 8 oz., rnd. water goblet	10.00	Tumbler, 8 oz., water	10.00
Plate, 12", sq.	22.00	Stem, 8 oz., sq. ftd., water goblet	10.00	Tumbler, 9 oz., rnd., ball, water	10.00
Plate, 15", sq.	35.00	Stem, sherbet, low, one ball, rnd. ftd.	6.00	Tumbler, 9 oz., rnd., ftd. water	10.00
Plate, 14", rnd., torte	30.00	Stem, sherbet, rnd. low foot	7.00	Tumbler, 9 oz., sq. ftd., water	10.00
Plate, 20½", rnd., torte	55.00	Stem, sherbet, sq. ftd., low	7.00	Tumbler, 10 oz., iced tea	12.00
Plate, cream soup liner, rnd.	5.00	Stem. champagne, two ball, rnd. ftd.	8.00	Tumbler, 11 oz., rnd., ball, iced tea	10.00
Puff box, w/ cover, 6", rnd.	20.00	Stem. sherbet, high, two ball, rnd. ftd.	9.00	Tumbler, 11 oz., sq. ftd., iced tea	12.00
Punch bowl	200.00	Stem. sherbet, rnd. high foot	9.00	Tumbler, 12 oz., iced tea	12.50
Punch bowl stand	70.00	Stem. sherbet, sq. ftd., high	9.00	Tumbler, 12½ oz., rnd. ftd. iced tea	10.00
Punch cup	6.50	Sugar, hexagonal, ftd.	8.50	Urn, 11", w/cover	50.00
Punch set (bowl, stand, 12 cups, ladle)	365.00	Sugar, low, flat	7.50	Vase, 6½", ivy bowl, sq., ftd., crimp top	30.00
Relish, 8", 3-part	15.00	Sugar, sq. ftd.	8.50	Vase, 6½", sq., ftd., flower holder	25.00
Saucer, demitasse, rnd.	10.00	Tidbit, 2-tier	22.50	Vase, 7½", flip	30.00
Saucer, demitasse, sq.	10.00	Tumbler, 1½ oz., whiskey	11.00	Vase, 7½", flip jar w/cover	60.00
Saucer, rnd.	2.00	Tumbler, 3 oz., whiskey	10.00	Vase, 8", sq. ftd.	35.00
Saucer, sq.	2.00	Tumbler, 5 oz., ginger ale	8.00	Vase, 8½", flared top	37.50
Shaker, pr., rnd. ftd.	20.00	Tumbler, 5 oz., old fashioned cocktail	11.00	Vase, 10" (straw jar)	65.00
Shaker, pr., sq. ftd.	20.00	Tumbler, 5 oz., rnd. ftd., ginger ale	8.00		
Stem, 1 oz., rnd. ftd., cordial	16.00	Tumbler, 5 oz., sq. ftd., ginger ale	8.00		
Stem, 1 oz., rnd., ball, cordial	18.00	Tumbler, 7 oz., rnd. ftd. juice	9.00		
Stem, 1 oz., sq. ftd., cordial	16.00				
Stem, 2 oz., rnd. ftd., wine	10.00				
Stem, 2 oz., sq. ftd., wine	10.00				
Stem, 2¼ oz., rnd. ball, wine	9.00				
Stem, 3 oz., rnd. cocktail	8.00				
Stem, 3 oz., sq. ftd., cocktail	8.00				
Stem, 3½ oz., rnd. ball, cocktail	7.00				

Westmoreland's Handmade "English Hobnail" Crystal—Line No. 555

WESTMORELAND'S "English Hobnail" Crystal Pattern is handmade in one hundred and thirty-seven open stock items. It is fashioned in three Line Numbers: Line 555 with round foot; Line No. 555/2 has square plates and all stemware items are made with square foot. Line No. 555/3 stemware is barrel-shape, with ball stem and round foot. All three versions are identical in pattern, except for difference in foot as illustrated on the following pages. The various items of all three Lines intermix charmingly, and provide a wide choice for complete luncheon or dinner service.

555/12½ oz. Ice Tea, ftd. | 555/9 oz. Tumbler, ftd. | 555/7 oz. Tumbler, ftd. | 555 Parfait | 555 Sherbet High foot. | 555 Sherbet Low foot. | 555/3 oz. Cocktail | 555/8 oz. Goblet

555/5 oz. Claret | 555/2 oz. Wine | 555 Cordial | 555 Old Fashioned Cocktail | 1½ oz. Whiskey. Also 3 oz. | 555/5 oz. Ginger Ale | 555/8 oz. Tumbler | 555/10 oz. Ice Tea | 555/12 oz. Ice Tea

555/2 oz. Oil | 555/6 oz. Oil | 555/6 oz. Oil-Vinegar Comb. | 555/20 oz. Decanter | 555/1 qt. Jug Also in ½ Gal. | 555/38 oz. Jug. Also 23 oz., 60 oz.

555 Sugar & Cream Set, footed. | 555 Sugar & Cream Set, Low. | 555 Salt and Pepper | 555/5½ Bell Compote

Westmoreland's Handmade "English Hobnail" Crystal—Line No. 555

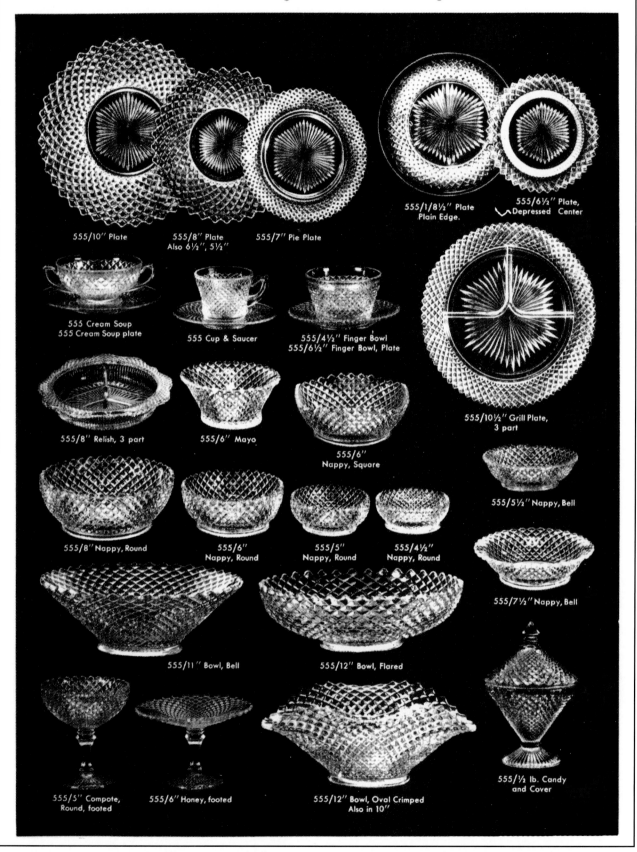

555/10" Plate

555/8" Plate
Also 6½", 5½"

555/7" Pie Plate

555/1/8½" Plate
Plain Edge.

555/6½" Plate,
Depressed Center

555 Cream Soup
555 Cream Soup plate

555 Cup & Saucer

555/4½" Finger Bowl
555/6½" Finger Bowl, Plate

555/10½" Grill Plate,
3 part

555/8" Relish, 3 part

555/6" Mayo

555/6"
Nappy, Square

555/5½" Nappy, Bell

555/8" Nappy, Round

555/6"
Nappy, Round

555/5"
Nappy, Round

555/4½"
Nappy, Round

555/7½" Nappy, Bell

555/11" Bowl, Bell

555/12" Bowl, Flared

555/½ lb. Candy
and Cover

555/5" Compote,
Round, footed

555/6" Honey, footed

555/12" Bowl, Oval Crimped
Also in 10"

Westmoreland's Handmade "English Hobnail" Crystal—Line No. 555

555/4½x2½" Cigarette Box & Cover

High Hat

Low Hat

555/4½" Ash Tray.

555 Ind. Nut, ftd.

3" Ash Tray

555 3" Coaster

555/6½" Grapefruit

555/6½" Bon Bon, H'ld.

555/8" Pickle

555/6" Crimped Dish

555/6" Rose Bowl

4" Rose Bowl

555/8"/6 Pt. Bowl. Also in 7"

555/2-Lite Candelabra

555/6" Basket, Tall Handled.

555/6" Three-Footed Covered Dish

555 Marmalade and Cover

555/3½" Candlestick

555/9½" Bowl, Round, Crimped

555/12" Celery, Also 9"

555/14" Torte Plate, Also in 20½"

555/15 Piece Punch Set

Westmoreland's Handmade "English Hobnail" Crystal—Line No. 555/2

555/2/11 oz. Ice Tea, ftd.

555/2/9 oz. Tumbler, ftd.

555/2/7 oz. Tumbler, ftd.

555/2/5 oz. Ginger Ale

555/2/8 oz. Goblet

555/2/3 oz. Cocktail

555/2 Sherbet, Low

555/2 Sherbet, High

555/2/2 oz. Wine

555/2 Cordial

555/2 Oyster Cocktail

555/2 Mustard

555/2 Salt and Pepper

555/2 Cream and Sugar, footed

555/2/5" Compote, Round

555/2/5½" Compote, Bell

555/2/6" Honey, ftd.

555/2/5½" Candlestick

555/2/4½" Nappy, Sq.

555/2 Finger Bowl, footed

555/2/10" Square Plate

555/2 Cup and Saucer

555/2/4½" Ash Tray, Sq.

555 Finger Bowl 555/2/6" Sq. Plate

555/2/6" Cheese and Cover. Also 8¾"

555/2/8¾" Square Plate

555/2/6" Square Plate

555/2/6½" Flower Holder, footed

555/2/6½" Ivy Ball, Crimp Top, ftd.

FIRE-KING "ALICE," ANCHOR HOCKING GLASS CORPORATION, EARLY 1940s

Colors: Jade-ite, Vitrock w/trims of blue or red

"Alice" is available in plain Vitrock, Vitrock trimmed in red or blue, or Jade-ite. Some of the red-trimmed pieces fade to pink, and there are two shades of blue-trimmed pieces being found. Unfortunately, my three pieces of red trimmed Alice are still among the departed. Everything eventually turns up, doesn't it? Shifting the volume of glassware we do, I guess we manage fairly well.

As I prepared for the Fire-King book, I became aware that I need to point out that the white "Alice" is Vitrock. There are two distinct shades of Vitrock as illustrated in the photograph. These do not coexist very well; so you need to decide whether you like the beige/gray shade.

Dinner plates are the pieces to possess in this minuscule "Alice" pattern. Evidently, few people bought the plates to go with those cups and saucers that were packed in oatmeal boxes. Plates were too big for boxes; if they were give-aways, it was not in oatmeal. The amount of dinner plates I see in the Missouri area between St. Louis and Joplin make me believe they were given away in that area. Lucky you, if you live in that area because you should be able to find them more easily than the rest of us.

	Jade-ite	Vitrock/Blue trim	Vitrock/Red trim	Vitrock
Cup	7.00	12.00	25.00	5.00
Plate, 9½"	30.00	35.00	50.00	25.00
Saucer	3.00	5.00	10.00	2.00

FIRE-KING BLUE MOSAIC, ANCHOR HOCKING GLASS CORPORATION, 1966 – LATE 1969

Blue Mosaic **should** be the first snack set that collectors of those items find! There is an abundance of these available and surely Florida was a main distribution area. I see at least one Blue Mosaic snack set every time I go shopping here. The snack tray in this pattern is oval and not rectangular as are most Fire-King patterns.

The sugar, creamer, and cup have solid blue exteriors without little blue squares which make up the Mosaic on all the other pieces. The sugar is a cup with no handles plus a white lid; the creamer is a cup with a spout. Note the sugar lid is white, but a different style than found on most Fire-King patterns. The same cup was used for both the saucer and the snack tray unlike other snack cups in Fire-King patterns. Most have a smaller cup for the snack tray! This briefly-made Anchor Hocking pattern was illustrated only in a 1966 – 1967 catalog.

	Blue Mosaic		Blue Mosaic
Bowl, 4⅝", dessert	8.00	Plate, 10", dinner	10.00
Bowl, 6⅝", soup plate	14.00	Platter, 9" x 12"	20.00
Bowl, 8¼", vegetable	20.00	Saucer, 5¾"	2.00
Creamer	8.00	Sugar	8.00
Cup, 7½ oz.	4.50	Sugar cover	5.00
Plate, 7⅜", salad	6.00	Tray, 10" x 7½", oval, snack	6.00

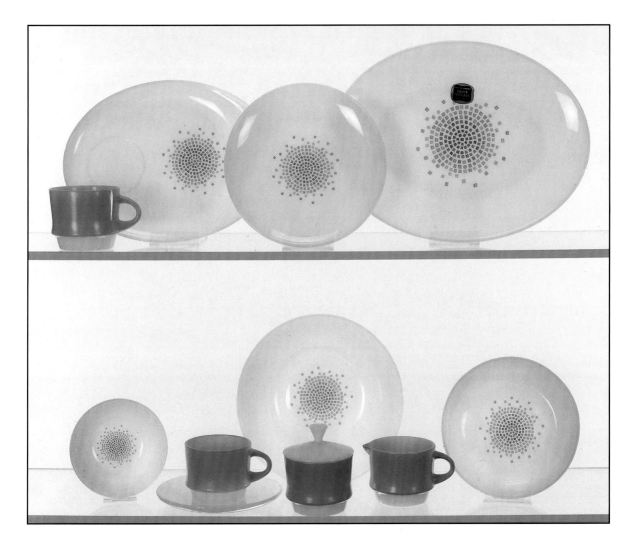

FIRE-KING CHARM, ANCHOR HOCKING GLASS CORPORATION, 1950 – 1954

Colors: Azur-ite, Forest Green, Ivory, Jade-ite, Milk White, pink, and Royal Ruby

It is difficult to please all readers. I received letters asking me to price Forest Green and Royal Ruby Charm under Charm and not under Forest Green and Royal Ruby. I did, and then registered about a dozen complaints asking why I didn't price square Royal Ruby and Forest Green square. Charm was the original designation for the square dishes made by Anchor Hocking from 1950 through 1954. Jade-ite and Azur-ite colors were advertised alongside Forest Green and Royal Ruby; however, the color names of Forest Green and Royal Ruby predominated on the red and green instead of Charm.

That ash tray pictured on top of page 71 does not belong; please disregard that as a piece of Charm! It is priced under Forest Green where it should be. There are only five pieces of Royal Ruby Charm. You will note a huge price jump on the large berry bowl which has turned out to be in short supply.

This squared shape Charm is the most burdensome Jade-ite to find. At present, the platter and dinner plates in Jade-ite are very elusive and Jade-ite Charm prices continue to soar. There seems to be an adequate supply of Azur-ite except for soups, platters, and dinner plates.

	Azur-ite	Forest Green	Jade-ite	Royal Ruby
Bowl, 4¾", dessert	8.00	7.00	15.00	8.00
Bowl, 6", soup	18.00	20.00	45.00	
Bowl, 7⅜", salad	20.00	15.00	50.00	75.00
Creamer	12.00	7.50	20.00	
Cup	4.00	5.00	12.00	6.00
Plate, 6⅝", salad	9.00	10.00	22.00	
Plate, 8⅜", luncheon	10.00	8.00	28.00	10.00
Plate, 9¼", dinner	22.00	32.00	50.00	
Platter, 11" x 8"	22.00	23.00	65.00	
Saucer, 5⅜"	1.50	1.50	3.00	2.50
Sugar	12.00	7.50	20.00	

FIRE-KING FLEURETTE AND HONEYSUCKLE
ANCHOR HOCKING GLASS CORPORATION, 1958 – 1960

Color: white w/decal

Fleurette first appeared in Anchor Hocking's 1959 – 1960 catalog printed in April 1958, with Honeysuckle showing up the following year. Both patterns seem to have given way to Primrose by the 1960 – 1961 catalog. Both Fleurette and Honeysuckle are in shorter supply than Primrose.

There were three sizes of tumblers listed for Honeysuckle, but I have seen only one size in Fleurette. The only worn decals in all the Fire-King patterns seem to occur on Fleurette. Maybe that problem was corrected for later patterns.

All Fire-King sugar lids are interchangeable though they all don't have the same type knob handle. They are plain white without a pattern. Be sure to check these out. Sometimes you may find an American sweetheart lid that has been misplaced. It happened at a farmer's market in Plant City, Florida, not long ago!

	Fleurette	Honeysuckle		Fleurette	Honeysuckle
Bowl, 4⅝", dessert	3.00	4.00	Platter, 9" x 12"	14.00	20.00
Bowl, 6⅝", soup plate	12.00	9.00	Saucer, 5¾"	1.00	1.50
Bowl, 8¼", vegetable	12.00	20.00	Sugar	5.00	5.00
Creamer	5.00	5.00	Sugar cover	5.00	5.00
Cup, 5 oz., snack	3.00		Tumbler, 5 oz., juice		18.00
Cup, 8 oz.	4.00	4.00	Tumbler, 9 oz., water	75.00	15.00
Plate, 6¼", bread and butter	15.00	15.00	Tumbler, 12 oz., iced tea		15.00
Plate, 7⅜", salad	10.00	7.00	Tray, 11"x 6", snack	4.00	
Plate, 9⅛", dinner	5.00	7.00			

FIRE-KING "GAME BIRD," ANCHOR HOCKING GLASS CORPORATION, 1959 – 1962

Color: white w/decal decoration

Anchor Hocking called these both "Wild Bird" and "Game Bird," but the "Game Bird" seemed more apropos when I was first writing *Collectible Glassware from the 40s, 50s, 60s....* You will find the following birds on this pattern: Canada Goose, Ringed-Necked Pheasant, Ruffled Grouse, and Mallard Duck. I have catalog sheets of mugs, cereals, and ash trays listed for 1960 – 1961; but as you can see below, there are many more pieces available than those.

Had I to do it over, I would have chosen the Wild Birds name because corralling some of the pieces for this set has been a really wild time! I now have everything except three juice glasses. I have a Mallard juice; but the other juices are flying past me. Note the new listing of a water tumbler. So far, it has only been seen with a Pheasant, but who knows?

That Ringed-Neck Pheasant is the only game in town if you are looking for serving pieces. The sugar, creamer, 8¼" vegetable, and platter only have been found with Pheasants. It is possible to collect an entire set of Pheasant decorated dinnerware, but no other bird can be collected in a full set as far as I can ascertain.

Our excursions to Tulsa, Oklahoma, for Depression glass shows and the first Fire-King show convinced me that a bird hunting trip to southwestern Missouri and Oklahoma would be the way to go if you are looking for this pattern. Promotional sales or give-aways make this area a haven for coveys of "Game Birds." I did see dozens of mugs and tumblers on my last trip!

Prices on this little pattern have steadily grown due to the abundance of collectors searching for these fowl! Serving pieces are becoming more than a problem for the many collectors looking for them. Mugs and tumblers can be found with some work, and many of these are being used. Mugs are microwaveable and great for coffee, tea or hot chocolate! In fact, mug collecting per se, is catching on, especially in Fire-King circles. It's amazing how many different types there are!

	White w/decals		White w/decals
Ash tray, 5¼"	18.00	Plate, 9⅛", dinner	6.50
Bowl, 4⅝", dessert	5.00	Platter, 12" x 9"	50.00
Bowl, 5", soup or cereal	8.00	Sugar	15.00
Bowl, 8¼", vegetable	50.00	Sugar cover	5.00
Creamer	15.00	Tumbler, 5oz., juice	50.00
Mug, 8 oz.	8.00	Tumbler, 11 oz., iced tea	12.00
Plate, 6¼", bread & butter	12.00		

FIRE-KING GRAY LAUREL, ANCHOR HOCKING GLASS CORPORATION, 1952 – 1963

A laurel leaf design was made into Gray Laurel in 1953. That 1953 catalog is the only time that Gray Laurel is mentioned in Anchor Hocking records! Gray has turned out to be scarce when compared to the quantity of Peach Lustre ("laurel leaf" design) found.

The 11" serving plate and 8¼" vegetable bowl are hard to find, particularly with good color. That is the major detraction for Gray Laurel — the color wears through and shows white streaks. Dishwashers and harsh detergents are deadly on this color, as well as many other glassware patterns of this era. With the advent of the dishwasher, glass companies had to learn to combat the heated abuse suddenly heaped upon their dishes! There was much testing of color thereafter to get it to stay put.

Three sizes of tumblers were made to go with Gray Laurel. These tumblers are "complementary decorated" with gray and maroon bands. There is a 5 ounce juice, a 9 ounce water, and a 13 ounce iced tea. To date, I have not spotted any of these. Do you have any? I need only one of each!

Crystal stemware like the Early American Line shown under "Bubble" were also engraved with a "Laurel" cutting to go with this pattern.

A few pieces of Ivory and white Laurel are being seen, especially creamers and sugars; watch for them!

	Gray Laurel			Gray Laurel
Bowl, 4⅞", dessert	8.00		Plate, 7⅜", salad	10.00
Bowl, 7⅝", soup plate	17.50		Plate, 9⅛", dinner	12.00
Bowl, 8¼", vegetable	30.00		Plate, 11", serving	22.50
Creamer, ftd.	6.00		Saucer, 5¾"	3.00
Cup, 8 oz.	4.00		Sugar, ftd.	6.00

FIRE-KING "JANE RAY" ANCHOR HOCKING GLASS CORPORATION, 1945 – 1963

Colors: Ivory, Jade-ite, Peach Lustre, crystal, amber, white, and white trimmed in gold

"Jane Ray" is a name that collectors have given this pattern. This ribbed Fire-King pattern is the most commonly found Jade-ite. It is also the most collected Anchor Hocking pattern from the 1950s. "Jane Ray" was listed in catalogs for almost 20 years. A Jade-ite set is still possible to attain in this dinnerware, though price is beginning to make a difference for many collectors. A few years ago, boxes of "Jane Ray" were begging to be bought; today, some collectors are buying lowly saucers for a $1.00 that couldn't be sold for 25¢ each then!

A 1947 chain store catalog of glassware by Anchor Hocking lists this as "Jade-ite Heat Proof Tableware," which is the only true "name" known. That record also lists the vegetable bowl as 8⅛" instead of 8¼", as indexed in later catalogs. I have never seen this smaller version, but there may be some. Most likely it's a typo or a wrong measurement.

Would you believe collectors now pay more than $50 for a piece of "Jane Ray" Jade-ite? Two pieces have reached that level already, the 9" flat, rimmed soup and the 6¼" bread and butter plate! (The demitasse set is technically two pieces.)

"Jane Ray" means Jade-ite to most collectors. I had it listed exclusively in Jade-ite in my first book. Notice that there are other colors!

There are demitasse cups and saucers in crystal, Peach Lustre, and amber. "Jane Ray" demitasse sets were the most difficult pieces to find until flat soups were unearthed.

Availability, as with blue "Bubble" and green Block, puts "Jane Ray" in front of many new collectors. If you like this pattern, start collecting now and buy the harder-to-find pieces when you discover them! You will not be sorry!

	Ivory	Jade-ite	Vitrock		Ivory	Jade-ite	Vitrock
Bowl, 4⅞", dessert	30.00	10.00	10.00	Plate, 6¼"		95.00	
Bowl, 5⅞", oatmeal		24.00	20.00	Plate, 7¾", salad		12.00	
Bowl, 7⅝", soup plate		25.00		Plate, 9⅛", dinner	45.00	11.00	20.00
Bowl, 8¼", vegetable		24.00	30.00	Platter, 9" x 12"		25.00	
Bowl, 9", flat soup		200.00		Saucer	10.00	2.00	2.00
Cup	30.00	7.00	8.00	**Saucer, demitasse		45.00	20.00
*Cup, demitasse		40.00	20.00	Sugar		9.00	
Creamer		9.00		Sugar cover		20.00	

*Peach Lustre $10.00

**Peach Lustre $15.00

FIRE-KING MEADOW GREEN ANCHOR HOCKING GLASS CORPORATION, 1967 – 1977

Meadow Green was a line of glassware and ovenware introduced at the time that avocado green colored appliances were all the rage. Today's collectors are beginning to warm to it, and since I keep reading that green and gold decor is about to return, maybe that will jump start the collecting of this line. As with Blue Mosaic, cups, creamers, and sugars are solid colors (two different shades of green) on the exteriors without the floral decal. The lid for the sugar is white without a decal.

In any case, this pattern is still inexpensive and can be used in ovens and microwaves. Be sure to test for hot spots before leaving it in the microwave for very long. Casseroles came with (non-decaled) white lids as well as crystal. Crystal seems to be preferred by cooks since you can check on what's cooking without lifting the lid. However a premium of a couple of dollars is asked for white lids since they are more difficult to find. Add that to the price listed below since prices are for items with clear lids. If you want to collect a pattern without a lot of competition, then this might be the one. Start collecting fast; others also read!

	White w/decal		White w/decal
Bowl, 4⅝", dessert	2.50	Creamer	3.00
Bowl, 5", cereal	3.00	Cup	2.50
Bowl, 6⅝", soup	4.50	Custard, 6 oz.	1.50
Bowl, 8¼", vegetable	7.00	Loaf pan, 5" x 9"	6.50
Cake dish, 8", square	6.00	Mug, 9 oz.	4.00
Cake dish, 9" round	6.50	Plate, 7⅜", salad	2.50
Casserole, 12 oz., hndl.	3.50	Plate, 10", dinner	4.00
Casserole, 1 qt. w/cover	7.00	Platter, 12" x 9"	8.00
Casserole, 1½ qt. w/cover	8.00	Saucer	.50
Casserole, 1½ qt., oval w/cover	8.00	Sugar w/lid	5.00
Casserole, 2 qt., w/cover	9.00	Utility dish, 1½ qt.	6.00
Casserole, 3 qt., w/cover	12.00	Utility dish, 2 qt.	7.00

FIRE-KING PEACH LUSTRE, "LAUREL"

ANCHOR HOCKING GLASS CORPORATION, 1952 – 1963

"The New Sensation" is how Peach Lustre color/pattern was described in a 1952 catalog. This laurel leaf design was also made in other colors such as Gray Laurel. The laurel design was incorporated in the name of that pattern, but Peach Lustre was the only name ever used for this pattern. Twelve years of production made a rather large collecting base for today. The name Peach Luster was also used to refer to the color of other patterns, so don't get that confused. For example, "Jane Ray" demitasse sets can be found in Peach Lustre, i.e., Jane Ray **pattern**, but Peach Lustre color.

Unfortunately, this color was not enduring. Prices listed below are for pieces with good color and **no deterioration.** The major detraction to collecting Peach Lustre is color wear. Dishwashers and harsh detergents are lethal to the glaze. Wear creates white streaks on the surface. **Recognize that worn or rubbed pieces will be hard to sell for even half the listed price.** Because there is so much still around, collectors can afford to be picky about what they buy in Peach Lustre. The 11" serving plate was discontinued as of 8-25-60. It is the most difficult piece to find, especially with good color. It's a great serving dish!

Crystal stemware like that shown under "Bubble" was also engraved with a "Laurel" cutting to go with all laurel patterns.

	Peach Lustre			Peach Lustre
Bowl, 4⅞", dessert	4.00		Plate, 7⅜", salad	9.00
Bowl, 7⅝", soup plate	10.00		Plate, 9⅛", dinner	5.00
Bowl, 8¼", vegetable	10.00		Plate, 11", serving	15.00
Creamer, ftd.	4.00		Saucer, 5¾"	1.00
Cup, 8 oz.	3.50		Sugar, ftd.	4.00

FIRE-KING PRIMROSE

ANCHOR HOCKING GLASS CORPORATION, 1960 – 1962

Primrose was a pattern that Anchor Hocking utilized to bridge the gap between dinnerware and ovenware usage. Primrose was created with pieces designed for either duty. Many of Anchor Hocking's patterns were produced as dinnerware, even though they were openly marked "ovenware" to allow customers to know that they were "heat-proof" and could be "pre-warmed" in the oven. No ovenware was intended for use on the stove top, but most can be used in the microwave with prudence.

Primrose was only listed in the 1960 – 1961 and 1961 – 1962 catalogs. From its lack of availability today, it might even be very limited — or, as with the Sapphire Blue ovenware, many cooks are still using it instead of parting with it to buy newer wares. Primrose may not have been as acceptable to the public as Anchor Hocking hoped.

All tumblers, along with most of the lidded ovenware items, are the most difficult pieces to find in this pattern. The 11 oz. white tumblers are the only Fire-King ones known besides those of the "Game Bird." Crystal Primrose tumblers were packed in boxed sets and came in at least two sizes. The crystal tumblers have become harder to find than the white ones! Many Primrose sets have been accumulated without finding tumblers of any kind!

All Primrose casserole covers are clear crystal Fire-King. All pieces of ovenware were guaranteed against oven breakage for two years. Dealers would exchange a new item for the broken pieces. The one quart casserole, baking pan, and oval casserole were all sold with a brass finished candle warmer and candle. I have received numerous letters saying that those brass holders are still working as they were intended!

The deep loaf pan was sold as a baking pan by adding a crystal glass cover. All the crystal glass lids are harder to find than their respective pans. Lids have a tendency to be dropped or broken.

	White w/decal		White w/decal		White w/decal
Bowl, 4⅝", dessert	3.50	Casserole, 2 qt., knob cover	16.00	Plate, 9⅛", dinner	5.00
Bowl, 6⅝", soup plate	8.00	Creamer	5.00	Platter, 9" x 12"	15.00
Bowl, 8¼", vegetable	14.00	Cup, 5 oz., snack	3.00	Saucer, 5¾"	1.00
Cake pan, 8", round	12.00	Cup, 8 oz.	3.00	Sugar	5.00
Cake pan, 8", square	12.00	Custard, 6 oz., low or dessert	3.50	Sugar cover	5.00
Casserole, pt., knob cover	9.00	Pan, 5" x 9", baking, w/cover	18.00	Tray, 11" x 6", rectangular, snack	5.00
Casserole, ½ qt., oval,		Pan, 5" x 9", deep loaf	14.00	Tumbler, 5 oz., juice (crystal)	25.00
au gratin cover	15.00	Pan, 6½" x 10½", utility baking	12.00	Tumbler, 5 oz., (white)	32.00
Casserole, 1 qt., knob cover	12.00	Pan, 8" x 12½", utility baking	18.00	Tumbler, 10 oz., water (crystal)	25.00
Casserole, 1½ qt., knob cover	12.00	Plate, 7⅜", salad	4.50	Tumbler, 11 oz., (white)	28.00

FIRE-KING RESTAURANT WARE

ANCHOR HOCKING GLASS CORPORATION, 1948 – 1967

Colors: Jade-ite, Milk White

Anchor Hocking's Restaurant Ware line is adaptable to microwave use. As far as I know, any of these pieces can be used this way. Remember to put the dish in the microwave for just a little time to see if it gets hot as you would test any other dish.

You can see a catalog sheet at the bottom of this page which will show you the differences in the three sizes of Restaurant Ware cups and the mug. For more detailed information and to view some remarkably rare items in Jade-ite, pick up a copy of my *Anchor Hocking's Fire-King & More*.

White Restaurant Ware is being found in small quantities and is beginning to generate some collector interest!

	Jade-ite		Jade-ite
Bowl, 4¾", fruit G294	12.00	Plate, 5½", bread/butter G315	12.00
Bowl, 9¼", flat soup	120.00	Plate, 6¾", pie or salad G297	12.00
Bowl, 8 oz., flanged rim, cereal G305	25.00	Plate, 8⅞", oval partitioned G211	75.00
Bowl, 10 oz., deep G309	30.00	Plate, 8", luncheon G316	65.00
Bowl, 15 oz., deep G300	32.00	Plate, 9⅝", 3-compartment G292, 2 styles	28.00
Cup, demitasse	35.00	Plate, 9⅝", 5-compartment G311	38.00
Cup, 6 oz., straight G215	9.00	Plate, 9", dinner G306	24.00
Cup, 7 oz., extra heavy G299	10.00	Platter, 9½", oval G307	55.00
Cup, 7 oz., narrow rim G319	10.00	Platter, 11½", oval G308	45.00
Mug, coffee, 7 oz. G212	10.00	Saucer, 6" G295	4.00
Pitcher, ball jug, 3 styles	550.00	Saucer, demitasse	40.00

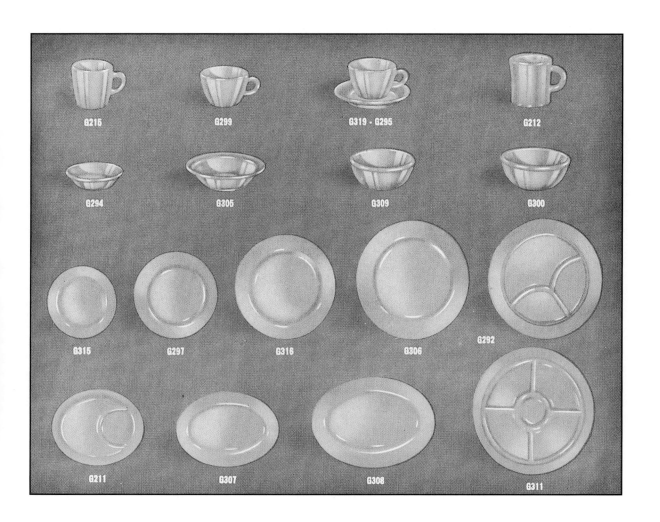

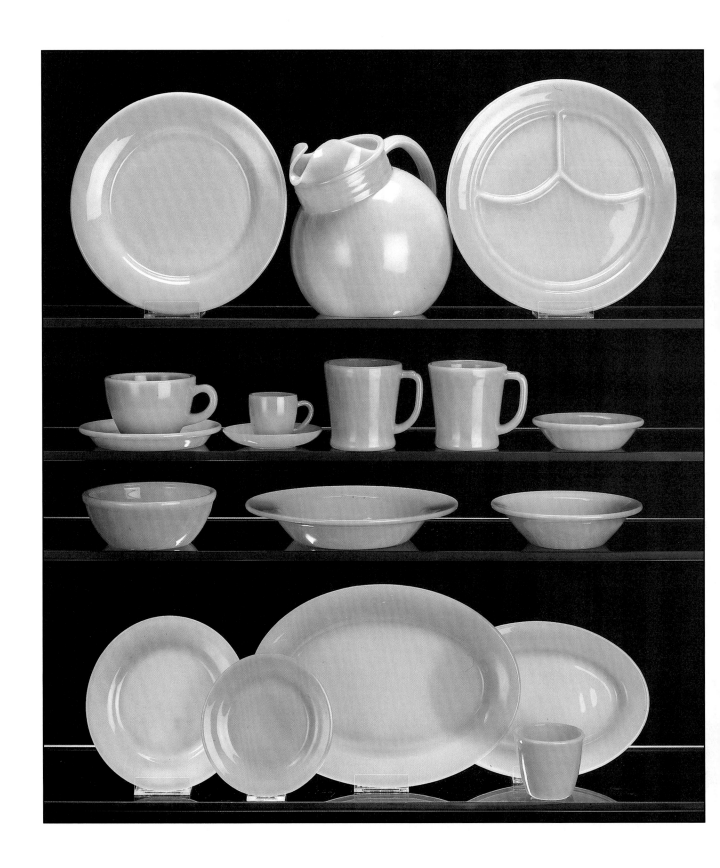

FIRE-KING SAPPHIRE BLUE OVEN GLASS,

ANCHOR HOCKING GLASS CORPORATION, 1942 – 1950s

Colors: Sapphire blue, crystal; some Ivory and Jade-ite

It used to be that when Fire-King was mentioned, Sapphire blue oven glass was what immediately came to mind; today, the word Fire-King is nearly synonymous with Jade-ite. Times do change. Everyone remembers grandma or mom making their favorite dessert in Fire-King Sapphire blue. My mom used half of the large roaster to make wonderful bread pudding! She'd only make it with her "from scratch biscuits"; so, I did see it many times over the years. Sapphire was the ovenware that was recognized for its durability. Fire-King had a two year guarantee. All you had to do was take the broken pieces to your local dealer and your piece was replaced at no charge.

This blue is great for standard ovens, but it tends to develop heat cracks from sudden temperature changes if used in the microwave. We learned that the hard way — experience! Cathy had to quit using the deep cereals for oatmeal when they kept splitting after coming out of the microwave!

Collectors favor the casseroles with pie plate covers above those with knobbed covers. Cooks prefer the knobbed lids because they are easier to lift when hot than the pie plate style — but there are fewer bottoms for these! Those knobbed lids survived better than their counterparts.

That 8 ounce nurser (bottle) is not as available as the 4 ounce. In the late 1970s, cases of the smaller nurser were found in a warehouse in New York. That supply has kept the market saturated over the years. The skillet on page 83 is shown compliments of Anchor Hocking's morgue. The skillets are found occasionally, but they were never released as a part of this line because the handles tended to break off where it joins the body! Sporadically, nipple covers have surfaced. These blue covers are embossed "BINKY'S NIP CAP U.S.A." (and not Fire-King). I just bought one. The dealer had two and wanted only $20.00 less for a chipped one. She still owns it and probably will for a while. Damaged glass will bring half or less than mint glass unless the damage is very slight or the piece is very rare.

The dry cup measure looks like a mug with eight ounce measurements up the side and no spout for pouring. Without these measurements on the side, it is the normally found mug! Regular mugs come in two styles — thick and thin. The thin is uncommon.

The reason the juice saver pie plate is priced so highly comes from the fact that most were heavily utilized. Many are deeply scarred. To obtain the price below, this pie plate has to be mint! Jade-ite ones are very rarely seen, as the price indicates.

The prices with asterisks under the Ivory listing are for Jade-ite items with the Fire-King embossing. Those items with asterisks (Jade-ite) are not found in Ivory. All Ivory is plain without embossed design. You will find plain Ivory and Jade-ite mugs, but they hold eight ounces, not seven. The Jade-ite mug with the embossed Fire-King pattern is rare!

	Ivory	Sapphire		Ivory	Sapphire
Baker, 1 pt., 4½" x 5"		8.00	Loaf pan, 9⅛" x 5⅛", deep	15.00	22.00
Baker, 1 pt., round	4.00	8.00	Mug, coffee, 7 oz., 2 styles	*90.00	28.00
Baker, 1 qt., round	6.00	12.00	Nipple cover		250.00
Baker, 1½ qt., round	6.00	16.00	Nurser, 4 oz.		20.00
Baker, 2 qt., round	8.50	16.00	Nurser, 8 oz.		30.00
Baker, 6 oz., individual	5.00	5.00	Percolator top, 2⅛"		5.00
Bowl, 4⅜", individual pie plate		20.00	Pie plate, 8⅜", 1½" deep		9.00
Bowl, 5⅜", cereal or deep dish pie plate	6.50	22.00	Pie plate, 9⅝", 1½" deep		10.00
Bowl, measuring, 16 oz.		25.00	Pie plate, 9", 1½" deep	9.00	10.00
Cake pan (deep), 8¾" (½ roaster)		30.00	Pie plate, 10⅜", juice saver	*350.00	150.00
Cake pan, 9"	15.00		Refrigerator jar & cover, 4½" x 5"	**35.00	15.00
Casserole, 1 pt., knob handle cover	30.00	14.00	Refrigerator jar & cover, 5⅛" x 9⅛"	**75.00	32.50
Casserole, 1 qt., knob handle cover	25.00	18.00	Roaster, 8¾"		55.00
Casserole, 1 qt., pie plate cover		18.00	Roaster, 10⅜"		80.00
Casserole, 1½ qt., knob handle cover	20.00	22.00	Table server, tab handles (hot plate)	18.00	22.00
Casserole, 1½ qt., pie plate cover		20.00	Utility bowl, 6⅞", 1 qt.		18.00
Casserole, 2 qt., knob handle cover	25.00	22.00	Utility bowl, 8⅜", 1½ qt.		23.00
Casserole, 2 qt., pie plate cover		25.00	Utility bowl, 10⅛"		25.00
Casserole, individual, 10 oz.		13.00	Utility pan, 8⅛" x 12½", 2 qt.		90.00
Cup, 8 oz. measuring, 1 spout		22.00	Utility pan, 10½" x 2" deep	15.00	25.00
Cup, 8 oz., dry measure, no spout		850.00			
Cup, 8 oz., measuring, 3 spout		30.00	*Jade-ite w/embossed design (Not Ivory)		
Custard cup or baker, 5 oz.	5.00	5.00	**Jade-ite (Not Ivory)		
Custard cup or baker, 6 oz.	6.00	5.00			

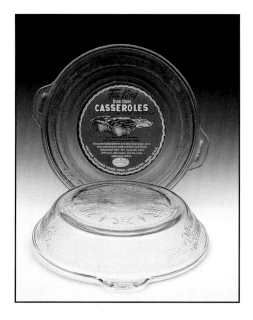

FIRE-KING "SHELL," ANCHOR HOCKING GLASS CORPORATION, 1965 – 1976

Colors: white, white trimmed in gold, Jade-ite, and Lustre Shell

The "Shell" pattern name evolved from the Golden Shell pattern which was milk white with a 22K gold trim and Lustre Shell which was a re-introduction of the old Peach Lustre. Jade-ite Shell was never actually named and is shown in several catalog listings as being in the "English Regency" styling causing some collectors to refer to it as "Regency Shell." This Jade-ite Shell" has attracted quite a following lately.

One of the problems facing collectors is knowing the difference between Fire-King Shells and Fire-King Swirls. Note the Shells have scalloped edges whereas the Swirl patterns (shown on page 88 through page 90) do not. Creamers and sugars in Shell are footed and Swirl creamer and sugar sets are flat. There are other differences; notice the shapes of cups, etc.

In 1966, Lustre Shell was introduced and was in catalogs until 1976. This Lustre Shell was the same color used for Peach Lustre, introduced in 1952. Peach Lustre was dropped in 1963. This Lustre finish also deteriorates easily, so look for pieces that were used sparingly. Some Lustre Shell color is only found on the outside of the pieces.

The soup bowl in Lustre Shell was enlarged from 6⅜" to 7⅝". Lustre was Anchor Hocking's name for the color and shell was the design. Now why didn't they add "shell" to the Jade-ite and solve our pattern name problems today? "Jade-ite Shell" should have been the name!

A demitasse cup and saucer were introduced to the Lustre Shell line in 1972. As with other Fire-King patterns, demitasse saucers are harder to find than cups.

You may find pieces of Golden Shell decorated. One of the more popular decorations is of the 1964 New York World's Fair.

	Golden Shell	Jade-ite "Shell"	Lustre Shell
Bowl, 4¾", dessert	3.50	14.00	4.00
Bowl, 6⅜", cereal	11.00	30.00	10.00
Bowl, 7⅝", soup plate	12.00	40.00	10.00
Bowl, 8½", vegetable	9.00	28.00	12.00
Creamer, ftd.	3.50	25.00	8.00
Cup, 8 oz.	3.25	10.00	4.00
Cup, 3¼ oz., demitasse	7.50		10.00
Saucer, 4¾", demitasse	10.00		10.00
Plate, 7¼", salad	4.00	25.00	3.50
Plate, 10", dinner	6.00	28.00	7.00
Platter, 9½" x 13"	9.00	85.00	
Saucer, 5¾"	1.00	4.00	2.00
Sugar, ftd.	4.00	25.00	10.00
Sugar cover	4.00	75.00	6.00

FIRE-KING "SWIRL," ANCHOR HOCKING GLASS CORPORATION, 1950s

Colors: Azur-ite, Ivory, Ivory trimmed in gold or red, white or white trimmed in gold, and Pink

The first "Swirl," introduced in 1950, was Azur-ite which is the light blue shown on top of page 88; that was followed by Sunrise (red trimmed, shown on bottom of page 88). Pictured on the bottom of 89 are Ivory and White "Swirls." Ivory "Swirl" was introduced in 1953; later in the 1950s, Anchorwhite took over for the Ivory. Golden Anniversary was introduced in 1955 by adding 22K gold trim to Ivory "Swirl." In the latter 1950s, a gold border was added to Anchorwhite, but labels on this say "22K." The Ivory is a beige tint as opposed to the flatter white of Anchorwhite. They are sometimes confused when shopping by flash-light at early morning flea markets. Both patterns were heavily marketed and are available! Watch for worn gold edges, since most collectors avoid those pieces for collections. If you are buying these to use, pieces with worn gold edges may be a bargain!

Pink "Swirl" top page 88) was introduced in 1956 as **Pink.** Note the pink footed sugar and creamer. These do not have the typical white bottoms normally found on Pink. They are from a pattern called **Rose-ite.** Basically, Pink was first introduced as a solid, opaque pink named Rose-ite. Production difficulties with color consistency caused Anchor Hocking to change the color to a pink color which was sprayed-on over white. There is a wide variance in Pink tints, but none of the Pink approaches the intensity of the Rose-ite pink! The picture illustrates it as well or better than I can describe it to you! A pitcher and tumblers only were made to go with the Pink "Swirl" as far as I can determine. The tumbler pictured is from an original boxed set. Actually, the catalog lists this pitcher as "Wrought Iron."

On page 90 is a photograph of "Swirl" with hand-painted scenes. I finally heard from a friend of the J. Kinney who painted this ware. The J. stands for Jesse. She painted scenes on white glassware and most of it was Fire-King "Swirl." I have more information on Jesse in my computer in Kentucky, but I am writing in Florida! It was great to finally make contact with some-one who knew J. (Jesse) Kinney! There is some collector demand for her pieces now!

	Anchorwhite Ivory	Azur-ite	Golden Anniversary	Jade-ite	Pink	Sunrise
Bowl, 4⅞", fruit or dessert	7.00	8.00	4.00		8.00	8.00
Bowl, 5⅞", cereal	25.00	25.00				35.00
Bowl, 7¼", vegetable					40.00	
Bowl, 7⅝", soup plate	2.75	20.00	10.00		20.00	25.00
Bowl, 8¼", vegetable	20.00	35.00	20.00		30.00	30.00
Bowl, 9¼", flanged soup	75.00	150.00				
Creamer, flat	10.00	10.00			9.00	9.00
Creamer, ftd.	2.75		3.25			
Cup, 8 oz.	8.00	6.00	3.00	40.00	7.00	7.50
Plate, 7⅜", salad	8.00	9.00	2.50		10.00	10.00
Plate, 9⅛", dinner	10.00	10.00	4.00	80.00	10.00	12.00
Plate, 11", serving					30.00	
Platter, 12" x 9"	20.00	20.00	6.50		20.00	22.00
Saucer, 5¾"	2.00	2.00	1.00	20.00	2.00	3.00
Sugar lid, for flat sugar	5.00	10.00			10.00	15.00
Sugar, flat, tab handles	10.00	10.00			8.00	12.00
Sugar, ftd., open handles	3.00		3.50			
Tumbler, 5 oz., juice					12.00	
Tumbler, 9 oz., water					15.00	
Tumbler, 12 oz., iced tea					20.00	

FIRE-KING "SWIRL"

FIRE-KING TURQUOISE BLUE, ANCHOR HOCKING GLASS CORPORATION, 1957 – 1958

Color: Turquoise Blue

Turquoise Blue was cataloged by Anchor Hocking as dinnerware, but all pieces are signed ovenware except the egg plate which is not marked at all. Most dinnerware patterns made by Anchor Hocking are stamped ovenware. This allowed the consumer to know that the item could be pre-warmed in the oven before using. Turquoise Blue has become very collectible.

We used Turquoise Blue as our dinnerware for five years. From that experience I can tell you that 10" serving plates are rarely found and the 6⅛" plate may even be harder to find. Several collectors have told me they have never found either one! The traditional 9" dinner with its upturned edges does not make an adequate sized plate to feed teenage boys!

The batter bowl was never shown in catalogs. Few of these have been found and big prices are being asked. I do not believe Anchor Hocking only made eight of these as I understand one dealer told his customer. I've seen half that many myself! I'd be interested in knowing the source of this belief. I have a photograph from an Illinois couple who pictured six of these batter bowls. Illinois may have been a promotional area for these Turquoise batters.

There are two different mixing bowl sets that go with this pattern. Both sets are pictured on the bottom row. The three-piece set on the left was called Splash Proof and the four-piece set on the right was called Swedish Modern by Hocking. Collectors commonly call them "tear drop" bowls, today. The 1 quart round mixing bowl and the 3 quart tear-shaped mixing bowls are the most difficult sizes to find in these bowl sets. However, the 1 quart tear-shaped bowl is always the first to sell at shows. Many people want these to use as small serving dishes. I can vouch for their being great for egg scrambling.

The 5¾" ash tray was discontinued before the 1957 – 1958 catalog was out of print. It should be rarer than the others. Especially promoted were the three-part relish, egg plate, and the snack sets with 22K gold decorations. Do not put these gold-edged pieces in the microwave because the gold creates sparks. All other pieces worked well in our microwave.

Cups, saucers, 9" dinner plates, creamers, and sugars are readily found. Mugs and small berry bowls are the next easiest pieces to gather. Although the 9" plate with cup indent is not as plentiful as the dinner plate, it does not demand the price of the dinner since many collectors do not buy snack sets…yet! Of course, that leaves more for the snack set collectors.

	Blue
Ash tray, 3½"	9.00
Ash tray, 4⅝"	12.00
Ash tray, 5¾"	17.00
Batter bowl, w/spout	300.00
Bowl, 4½", berry	8.00
Bowl, 5", cereal	15.00
Bowl, 6⅝", soup/salad	25.00
Bowl, 8", vegetable	20.00
Bowl, "tear drop," mixing, 1 pt.	25.00
Bowl, "tear drop," mixing, 1 qt.	30.00
Bowl, "tear drop," mixing, 2 qt.	40.00
Bowl, "tear drop," mixing, 3 qt.	60.00
Bowl, round, mixing, 1 qt.	20.00
Bowl, round, mixing, 2 qt.	24.00
Bowl, round, mixing, 3 qt.	25.00
Creamer	6.00
Cup	5.00
Egg plate, 9¾"	18.00
Mug, 8 oz.	10.00

	Blue
Plate, 6⅛"	22.00
Plate, 7¼"	13.00
Plate, 9"	10.00
Plate, 9", w/cup indent	6.00
Plate, 10"	33.00
Relish, 3-part, 11⅛"	12.00
Saucer	1.50
Sugar	6.00

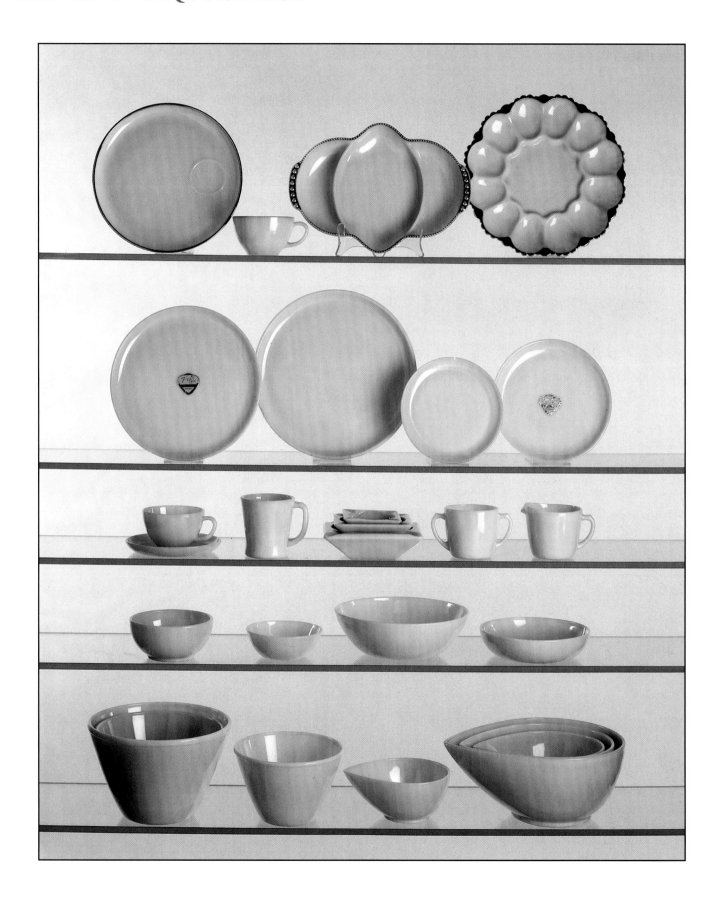

FIRE-KING WHEAT, ANCHOR HOCKING GLASS CORPORATION, 1962 – LATE 1960s

Production of Wheat began in 1962, and it was one of Anchor Hocking's most prolific lines. Like Sapphire blue Fire-King of the 1940s, everyone has seen the Wheat pattern of the 1960s! Wheat patterns were produced by several glass and pottery companies. It was a popular motif of the time. You will find crystal glasses with wheat cuttings that were made to go with all the wheat patterns being used. Not everyone is fond of Wheat, but there are enough who remember it to keep the collecting spark alive. Wheat will not break your checking account; so, you might stock some for future dispersal!

Ovenware lids create quandaries today because casserole sizes of yesteryear do not accept most modern day lids! Replacement lids for the older casseroles will cost up to half the price of the entire dish. Those lids are valuable commodities, so treat them gently. Both the oval and round 1½ quart casseroles and the 10½" baking pan were used with candle warmers. These candle warmers were brass finished with walnut handles plus the candle. Many were never used! They are being found with the original candles intact! Replacement candles can be found at most kitchenware stores should you need one. Several readers say that they still use these today for keeping food warm. Food never lasted that long with my boys. It never had a chance to get cold!

	Wheat			Wheat
Bowl, 4⅝", dessert	3.50		Cup, 8 oz.	4.00
Bowl, 5", chili	15.00		Custard, 6 oz., low or dessert	3.00
Bowl, 6⅝", soup plate	8.00		Mug	20.00
Bowl, 8¼", vegetable	12.00		Pan, 5" x 9", baking, w/cover	16.00
Cake pan, 8", round	11.00		Pan, 5" x 9", deep loaf	12.00
Cake pan, 8", square	10.00		Pan, 6½" x 10½" x 1½",	
Casserole, 1 pt., knob cover	8.00		utility baking	12.00
Casserole, 1 qt., knob cover	10.00		Pan, 8" x 12½" x 2",	
Casserole, 1½ qt., knob cover	11.00		utility baking	15.00
Casserole, 1½ qt., oval,			Plate, 7⅜", salad	6.00
au gratin cover	14.00		Plate, 10", dinner	5.00
Casserole, 2 qt., knob cover	15.00		Platter, 9" x 12"	12.50
Casserole, 2 qt., round,			Saucer, 5¾"	1.00
au gratin cover	15.00		Sugar	4.50
Creamer	5.00		Sugar cover	4.00
Cup, 5 oz., snack	3.00		Tray, 11" x 6", rectangular, snack	4.00

FLORAGOLD, "LOUISA," JEANNETTE GLASS COMPANY, 1950s

Colors: Iridescent, some Shell Pink, ice blue, and crystal

Floragold was formerly in *The Collector's Encyclopedia of Depression Glass*. However, Floragold was made long after the Depression era and rightly belongs here. Floragold is often mistaken for an older "carnival glass" pattern called "Louisa." Antique dealers, who do not sell much glassware, will price this early 1950s glassware quite high believing it to be original "carnival glass" made in the early 1900s. Collectors of "carnival glass" often accept some iridescent glassware made in the 1920s and even, occasionally, a piece or two from the 1930s; but I have not met one yet who considers any piece made in the 1950s collectible! The rose bowl in the carnival pattern "Louisa" is regularly offered for sale as Floragold which turns the quandary around the other way. I recently encountered a note from a collector wanting "Louise" (sic) wallpaper to go with her Floragold.

The vase and the 15 ounce tumblers need a strong iridized color before you spend much of your money for them. Weakly sprayed color is the only problem with Floragold. This color was made by applying an iridized spray over crystal and reheating. Overheating burned out the color! That rarely found vase was made by taking a 15 ounce tumbler and fluting the top. These tumblers are found in crystal and sell in the $15.00 to 20.00 range; add the iridized spray and you have to add another zero to that price. Apparently, many of these tumblers were never sprayed or perhaps, someone just ordered a batch of crystal ones.

Finally, some of the larger ruffled bowls have begun to sell. They remain reasonable; now might be the time to latch on to some of these. Mint condition shaker tops are hard to find. They were made of white or brown plastic, and many were cracked by twisting them too tightly. Tops are worth $15.00 to $18.00 each, which makes the tops more valuable than the shakers!

Cups abound because they were sold in sets of twelve without saucers as part of "egg nog" sets. The pitcher or the large bowl accompanied the cups for serving egg nog at Christmas! That 5¼" saucer (no cup ring) is the same as the sherbet plate.

Ice blue, crystal, red-yellow, Shell Pink, and iridized large comports were made in the late 1950s and into the early 1970s. An iridescent one is pictured in the middle of row 4 on the next page. All colored comports are selling in the $12.00 to $15.00 range except the iridized one which will fetch $25.00 on a good day.

For those who have never seen the 5½" square butter dish, it is pictured in the *Very Rare Glassware of the Depression Years*, fourth edition. There are two different 5¼" comports in Floragold. Both of these are pictured in the first edition of *Very Rare Glassware of the Depression Years*. You can see the ruffled style below. A couple of these have sold recently for the prices listed. There are a couple of more plain top ones being offered for sale.

	Iridescent
Ash tray/coaster, 4"	5.50
Bowl, 4½", square	5.50
Bowl, 5½", round cereal	40.00
Bowl, 5½", ruffled fruit	8.00
Bowl, 8½", square	14.00
Bowl, 9½", deep salad	45.00
Bowl, 9½", ruffled	8.00
Bowl, 12", ruffled large fruit	7.00
Butter dish and cover, ¼ lb. oblong	25.00
Butter dish and cover, round, 6¼" sq. base	45.00
Butter dish bottom	14.00
Butter dish top	28.50
Butter dish and cover, round, 5½" sq. base	850.00
Candlesticks, double branch, pr.	55.00
Candy dish, 1 handle	12.00
Candy or Cheese dish and cover, 6¾"	55.00
*Candy, 5¼" long, 4 feet	7.50
Comport, 5¼", plain top	950.00
Comport, 5¼", ruffled top	1,000.00
Creamer	9.00
Cup	6.00
Pitcher, 64 oz.	37.50
Plate or tray, 13½"	22.00
Plate or tray, 13½", with indent	75.00
Plate, 5¼", sherbet	12.00
Plate, 8½", dinner	40.00
Platter, 11¼"	25.00
*Salt and pepper, plastic tops	55.00
Saucer, 5¼" (no ring)	12.00
Sherbet, low, footed	16.00
Sugar	6.50
Sugar lid	12.00

	Iridescent
Tidbit, wooden post	40.00
Tumbler, 10 oz., footed	20.00
Tumbler, 11 oz., footed	20.00
Tumbler, 15 oz., footed	115.00
Vase or celery	400.00

* Shell pink $20.00

FOREST GREEN, ANCHOR HOCKING GLASS COMPANY CORPORATION, 1950 – 1967

Color: Forest Green

Forest Green was the color name of glassware made by Anchor Hocking. Even Hocking's "Bubble" was called Forest Green when it was first made. Forest Green was used for the square Charm blank (1950), but the glassware became better known by its color than its name. I have removed all the Charm pieces from the listing below and you will now find them listed only under Charm.

According to one Anchor Hocking catalog, "Bubble" stemware was originally called Early American line. The other stemware line sold along with "Bubble" has been called "Boopie" by another author; but documentation from Hocking shows the name to be Berwick. On page 97 the Early American line is pictured on the left in row two and Berwick is pictured on the right in that row.

After you remove Charm from the listing, Forest Green is reduced to being an accessory pattern, albeit a plentiful one. Forest Green can supply all sorts of beverage items, vases, and serving pieces. The Forest Green oval vegetable is scalloped along the edges and has a swirled effect on the sides. These were a premium item for a flour company in the South; look for them there.

You will spot many dark green pieces on the market that are mislabeled Forest Green. Unfortunately, Forest Green has become synonymous with any dark colored green. To be truly Forest Green, it must have been made by Anchor Hocking! That name was patented by them!

Decorated tumblers such as "A Bicycle for Two" will bring a dollar or two more than regular tumblers. However, undecorated tumblers sell faster to collectors.

Forest Green was widely distributed as premium items. Hocking must have provided their products at an extremely attractive price since so many tumblers and vases are found today. In the Kentucky area, tumblers were used as containers for Sealtest brand dairy products. A reader reported finding an unopened box of twenty-four 7 ounce tumblers marked, "Clover Honey Delight, Packed by National Honey Packers Mt. Sterling Illinois." Tea bags were another commodity often found in Anchor Hocking tumblers.

Massive quantities of 4" ball-shaped ivy vases testify to successful sales of Citronella candles packaged in those. I have previously pictured a boxed set of "Moskeeto-Lites." Those candles originally sold for $1.19. After using the candles, you had two free vases. I considered using these two on my dock in Florida!

	Green		Green		Green
Ash tray, 3½", square	5.00	Stem, 6 oz., sherbet	9.00	Tumbler, 10 oz., ftd., 4½"	6.50
Ash tray, 4⅝", square	6.00	*Stem, 6 oz., sherbet	8.00	Tumbler, 11 oz.	7.00
Ash tray, 5¾", square	9.00	*Stem, 9 oz., goblet	12.00	Tumbler, 13 oz., iced tea	7.50
Ash tray, 5¾", hexagonal	8.00	Stem, 10¾ oz., goblet	14.00	Tumbler, 14 oz., 5"	7.50
Batter bowl w/spout	30.00	*Stem, 14 oz., iced tea	18.00	Tumbler, 15 oz., long boy	12.00
Bowl, 4¾", dessert	5.50	Tumbler, 5 oz., 3½"	4.00	Tumbler, 15 oz., tall iced tea	14.00
Bowl, 5¼" deep	12.00	Tumbler, 7 oz.	4.00	Tumbler, 32 oz, giant iced tea	18.00
Bowl, 6", mixing	9.00	Tumbler, 9 oz, table	5.00	Vase, 4" ivy ball	5.00
Bowl, 8½", oval vegetable	22.00	Tumbler, 9 oz., fancy	6.00	Vase, 6⅜"	6.00
Pitcher, 22 oz.	22.50	Tumbler, 9½ oz., tall	6.50	Vase, 9"	12.00
Pitcher, 36 oz.	25.00				
Pitcher, 86 oz., round	40.00				
Plate, 6¾", salad	8.00				
Punch bowl	25.00			*Berwick	
Punch bowl stand	25.00				
Punch cup (round)	2.25				
Saucer, 5⅜"	1.50				
Sherbet, flat	7.50				
*Stem, 3½ oz., cocktail	10.00				
*Stem, 4 oz., juice	10.00				
Stem, 4½ oz., cocktail	12.50				
Stem, 5½ oz., juice	12.50				

GOLDEN GLORY, FEDERAL GLASS COMPANY, 1959 – 1966; 1978 – 1979

Color: White with 22K gold decorations

Golden Glory is sprouting a modest following in collecting circles. Be cautious since the 22K gold decorations deteriorate easily and detergents will lighten them. You might run across some items that were rarely used or are still boxed. Discovery of mint condition pieces always makes collectors happy!

I have received a couple of letters from readers asking about crystal tumblers with Golden Glory decorations. I have not personally seen them and pictures for documentation have not been forthcoming. However, it's possible that they were made! See if you can spot them!

Originally, only a dozen pieces of Golden Glory were cataloged. It was reissued by Federal in 1978 and three additional pieces were added to the line. These included the larger 10" dinner plate, the smaller 6⅜" soup, and the 11¼" round platter. Incidentally, this later release did not include the oval platter, larger soup, sugar, creamer, and tumblers. This ought to make those items harder to find; but, according to an devoted collector, the hardest-to-find pieces are the 8½" vegetable bowl, tumblers, and the 7¾" salad plate. I have been unable to locate the round platter, so they could be uncommon. I did see one that you could barely make out an outline of the pattern on the plate! I decided to look further. Perhaps I made a mistake!

Bowl, 4⅞", dessert	4.50	Plate, 10", dinner	6.50
Bowl, 6⅜", soup	8.00	Platter, 11¼", round	15.00
Bowl, 8½", vegetable	12.00	Platter, 12", oval	11.00
Bowl, 8", rimmed soup	10.00	Saucer	.50
Creamer	4.00	Sugar	3.00
Cup	3.00	Sugar lid	4.00
Plate, 7¾", salad	3.00	Tumbler, 9 oz., ftd.	10.00
Plate, 9⅛", dinner	5.00	Tumbler, 10 oz., 5"	10.00

HARP, JEANNETTE GLASS COMPANY, 1954 – 1957

Colors: crystal, crystal with gold trim, and cake stands in Shell Pink, pink, iridescent white, red, and ice blue

A new collector admired some Harp pieces at a recent show. She recognized the cake stand as being one her mom once used. She was surprised that it was only $25 and bought it. She then proceeded to my booth to buy a book to learn about Harp. When she opened the book and began reading, she suddenly let out a gasp! She had just read the cup and saucer prices! Her first question to me was along the lines of how can those little pieces be worth more than this beautiful cake stand? It's all about supply and demand!

With so many new collectors starting on smaller sized patterns, the need for basic pieces has more than doubled the prices of hard to find items. There is genuinely not enough of this smaller pattern to provide everyone a set who wishes one. Harp has been used for bridge parties for years. With the cake stand, cups, saucers, and the 7" plates, it's an ideal pattern for entertaining small groups. Cake sets made up of the cake stand and eight 7" plates were a hit with consumers. Cake plates prevail today but the supply of 7" plates is dwindling; but if you run into the cup and saucers, do not hesitate — buy!

If gold trim bothers you, an art gum eraser and a little elbow grease will take care of that! Although that trim is 22K gold, it did not adhere well to most glass; it has a propensity to erode if ever used.

The normally found vase is 6", but there is a different style being found that has a little indentation at the foot. I haven't received any other information, but be on the lookout for it!

The Harp cake stand is reminiscent of late 1800s and early 1900s glassware. Most patterns after that time had cake plates instead of a stand. The following thirteen types of Harp stands have been documented. Shell Pink, red, and iridescent ones are the most coveted!

1., 2. Crystal with smooth or ruffled rim
3., 4. Either of above with gold trim
5. Iridescent with smooth rim
6., 7. White or Shell Pink (opaque) with beads on rim and foot
8., 9. Ice blue with beads on foot and smooth or ruffled rim

10. Pink transparent
11. Platinum decorated with smooth rim
12. Red
13. Fired-on red

Do write if you find any other variety so it can be documented.

	Crystal			Crystal
* Ash tray/coaster	5.00	Plate, 7"		15.00
Coaster	4.50	Saucer		12.50
Cup	32.50	*** Tray, 2-handled, rectangular		35.00
** Cake stand, 9"	25.00	Vase, 7½"		25.00

* Platinum, decoration $8.00
** Ice blue, white, pink or Shell Pink $45.00
*** Shell Pink $60.00

99

HEATHER Etching #343, Fostoria Glass Company, 1949 – 1976

Colors: crystal

Heather is a Fostoria pattern that was introduced in *Elegant Glassware of the Depression Era* due to appeals from readers. Although it certainly fits the elegant terminology, its dates of manufacture best fit this fifties era book. Heather is being seen more often at markets. Too, younger family members are now searching for it, trying to fill in partial sets that have been passed down.

All listings in Heather that do not have a line number below are etched on Century blank #2630. The pattern shown below is a #2470, 10" footed vase. I have tried to give as accurate a listing for this pattern as possible from old catalogs, but I am sure there are additional pieces. Any help from Heather admirers will be treasured and passed along.

Heather, like all patterns etched on #2630 blank, has problems with scratches and scuffs on the surfaces of any flat piece. All plates, and in particular dinner plates, have been, and still are, subject to that abuse. Protect them by what you serve on them and by how you store them between use! Many collectors use paper plates between plates to keep the sharp, ground bottom edges from scratching the plate below it! These dishes were meant to be used and most were! No one knew that someday they would become valuable!

Basket, 10¼" x 6½", wicker hndl.	85.00	Plate, 7½", salad	10.00	Tray, 9⅛", hndl., utility	45.00
Bowl, 4½", hndl.	15.00	Plate, 8½", luncheon	15.00	Tray, 11½", center hndl.	37.50
Bowl, 5", fruit	16.00	Plate, 8", party, w/indent for cup	30.00	Tumbler, #6037, 4⅞", 5 oz., ftd.,	
Bowl, 6", cereal	25.00	Plate, 9½", small dinner	35.00	juice	20.00
Bowl, 6¼", snack, ftd.	20.00	Plate, 10", hndl., cake	30.00	Tumbler, #6037, 6⅛", 12 oz.,	
Bowl, 7⅛", 3 ftd., triangular	20.00	Plate, 10½", dinner,		ftd., tea	25.00
Bowl, 7¼", bonbon, 3 ftd.	25.00	large center	45.00	Vase, 5", #4121	50.00
Bowl, 8", flared	32.50	Plate, 10½", snack tray,		Vase, 6", bud	30.00
Bowl, 9", lily pond	37.50	small center	30.00	Vase, 6", ftd. bud, #6021	55.00
Bowl, 9½", hndl., serving bowl	42.50	Plate, 14", torte	50.00	Vase, 6", ftd., #4143	55.00
Bowl, 9½", oval, serving bowl	45.00	Plate, 16", torte	80.00	Vase, 7½", hndl.	75.00
Bowl, 10", oval, hndl.	45.00	Platter, 12"	85.00	Vase, 8", flip, #2660	95.00
Bowl, 10½", salad	47.50	Preserve, w/cover, 6"	70.00	Vase, 8", ftd., bud, #5092	85.00
Bowl, 10¾", ftd., flared	50.00	Relish, 7⅜", 2-part	20.00	Vase, 8½", oval	85.00
Bowl, 11, ftd., rolled edge	55.00	Relish, 11⅛", 3-part	32.50	Vase, 10", ftd., #2470	115.00
Bowl, 11¼", lily pond	45.00	Salt and pepper, 3⅛", pr.	47.50		
Bowl, 12", flared	55.00	Salver, 12¼", ftd. (like cake stand)	65.00		
Butter, w/cover, ¼ lb.	75.00	Saucer	4.50		
Candlestick, 4½"	22.00	Stem, #6037, 4", 1 oz., cordial	42.00		
Candlestick, 7", double	37.50	Stem, #6037, 4", 4½ oz., oyster			
Candlestick, 7¾", triple	50.00	cocktail	18.00		
Candy, w/cover, 7"	55.00	Stem, #6037, 4¾", 7 oz.,			
Comport, 2¾", cheese	20.00	low sherbet	14.00		
Comport, 4⅜"	30.00	Stem, #6037, 5", 4 oz., cocktail	20.00		
Cracker plate, 10¾"	30.00	Stem, #6037, 6⅛", 6 oz., parfait	25.00		
Creamer, 4¼"	20.00	Stem, #6037, 6⅜", 9 oz.,			
Creamer, individual	15.00	low goblet	30.00		
Cup, 6 oz., ftd.	17.00	Stem, #6037, 6", 4 oz.,			
Ice bucket	75.00	claret-wine	32.50		
Mayonnaise, 3 pc.	37.50	Stem, #6037, 6", 7 oz., saucer			
Mayonnaise, 4 pc., div. w/2 ladles	42.50	champagne	18.00		
Mustard, w/spoon, cover	35.00	Stem, #6037, 7⅞", 9 oz., goblet	26.00		
Oil, w/stopper, 5 oz.	50.00	Sugar, 4", ftd.	20.00		
Pickle, 8¾"	25.00	Sugar, individual	15.00		
Pitcher, 6⅛", 16 oz.	80.00	Tidbit, 8⅛", 3-ftd., upturned edge	30.00		
Pitcher, 7⅛", 48 oz.	165.00	Tidbit, 10¼", 2-tier, metal hndl.	45.00		
Plate, 6", bread/butter	7.00	Tray, 7⅛", for ind. sug/cr.	17.50		
Plate, 7½", crescent salad	45.00	Tray, 9½", hndl., muffin	33.00		

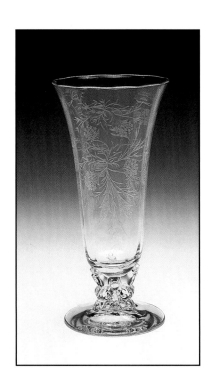

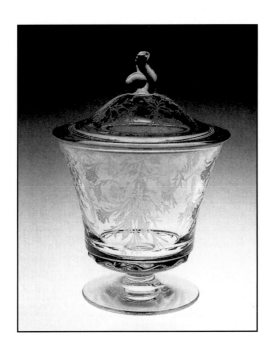

HERITAGE FEDERAL GLASS COMPANY, 1940 – 1955

Colors: crystal, some pink, blue, green, and cobalt

Heritage is another smaller pattern that captures the eyes of discerning collectors. For the moment, prices for crystal creamers, sugars, and 8½" berry bowls have slowed their upward surge. These are the most pesky pieces to find. For some reason, the sugar turns up with more regularity than the creamer. As a matter of fact, most creamers of this time are harder to find than their counterparts.

The reproduction berry bowls from several years ago are so crudely made that they are causing little trouble for collectors. Reproductions of Heritage bowls were marketed by McCrory's and similar stores in the late 1980s. These were made in amber, crystal, and green. Many are marked "MC" in the center. I say "many" because not all reports from readers have mentioned this mark. In any case, the smaller berry bowls sold three for $1.00 and the larger for $1.59 each. The pattern on these pieces is not very good and should not fool even beginning collectors. Compare the fully designed hobs in the photograph to the sparsely designed hobs on the reproductions. The green reproduction is much darker and closer to the 1970s avocado green. Notice the Depression green of the original bowl in the photo. Federal never made Heritage in amber.

Authentic pink, blue, and green berry bowls remain scarce. These are unquestionably rare! It is a shame that only berry bowl sets were made in these colors. (I have never shown the cobalt blue bowl before, so enjoy it, compliments of a couple of Oklahoma collectors! Now, if I could just get my hands on a pink one!)

Heritage was advertised as late as 1954 in women's magazines.

Crystal Heritage sets can be assembled more easily than sets of many other patterns since there are so few pieces. There are only 10 separate objects to find. The limitation you have is whether to search for four, six, eight, or twelve place settings. Thankfully, you only have to find one creamer and one 8½" berry bowl no matter how many place settings you collect. Some collectors are buying several of the larger fruit bowls, ignoring the harder to find berry bowl.

Refer to Daisy (page 47) for an explanation of Indiana's green Heritage pattern.

	Crystal	Pink	Blue Green
Bowl, 5", berry	8.00	50.00	75.00
Bowl, 8½", large berry	40.00	150.00	225.00
Bowl, 10½", fruit	15.00		
Cup	7.00		
Creamer, footed	30.00		
Plate, 8", luncheon	9.00		
Plate, 9¼", dinner	12.00		
Plate, 12", sandwich	15.00		
Saucer	4.00		
Sugar, open, footed	25.00		

HOBNAIL, FENTON ART GLASS COMPANY

Color: white

We were able to capture so much of Fenton's Hobnail for your viewing pleasure in this book because this large collection was graciously made available to us. This kind of generosity is almost as startling as it is appreciated! Since I am using the same photos, you need to know that I had one letter stating that there were three pieces shown last time that were not Fenton. Sorry.

Measurements were done as we photographed and not all these agree with catalog listings. I have used actual measurements when we had the piece in our photograph. I hope you enjoy this wonderful collection! Listings from catalogs were furnished by Carrie Domitz who willingly shared her access to said information. Catalog numbers are listed for each piece. Watch for this! Milk glass is gathering new devotees all the time!

White		White		White	
Apothecary jar, 11", w/cover #3689	125.00	Basket, 5¾", 1¾" base #3336	22.00	Bonbon, 5" x 2" #3630	15.00
Ash tray, 3¼" x 4½", rectangular #3693	10.00	Basket, 6½" x 4½", oval, two-hndl. #838	25.00	Bonbon, 5" x 2¾", star #3921	12.00
Ash tray, 3½", round #3972	6.00	Basket, 6½" x 7½", double crimped #3736	27.50	Bonbon, 6" x 1⅝", double crimped #3926	10.00
Ash tray, 4", ball #3648	35.00	Basket, 7" x 7", deep #3637	60.00	Bonbon, 7" x 2½", two-hndl. #3937	15.00
Ash tray, 4", octagon #3876	10.00	Basket, 7½" x 7", #3837	27.50	Bonbon, 8" x 2¼" #3716	18.00
Ash tray, 5", round #3973	10.00	Basket, 8" x 7¾", 3" base #3032	30.00	Bonbon, 8" x 5½" #3706	20.00
Ash tray, 5", square #3679	17.50	Basket, 8", 2¼" diameter base #3335	30.00	Boot, 4" #3992	14.00
Ash tray, 5¼", octagon #3877	10.00	Basket, 8½", double crimped #3638	30.00	Bottle, vanity, 5⅜" w/stopper #3865	45.00
Ash tray, 6½", octagon #3878	12.00	Basket, 10" #3830	50.00	Bowl, 4", berry, square #3928	15.00
Ash tray, 6½", pipe w/center flower #3773	50.00	Basket, 10½" x 11½", deep #3734	55.00	Bowl, 4", candle orifice #3873	22.50
Ash tray, 6½", round #3776	10.00	Basket, 13" x 7", oval #3839	65.00	Bowl, 5", cereal, 2" high #3719	75.00
Basket, 4" x 6", 4-ftd., oval #3634	25.00	Bell, 5½" #3645	15.00	Bowl, 5½" x 6¾", candy, ribbon top #3730	85.00
Basket, 4½" #3834	17.50	Bell, 6" #3667	25.00	Bowl, 5½", rose #3022	15.00
Basket, 5½" x 5½", double crimped #3735	15.50	Bell, 6¾" #3067	18.00	Bowl, 6" x 6", octagonal, peanut #3627	18.50
		Bonbon, 5" x 2½", two-hndl. #3935	20.00	Bowl, 6½", candle orifice #3872	17.50

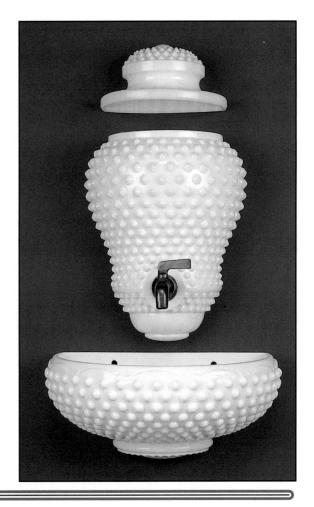

HOBNAIL

	White		White		White
Bowl, 7", double crimped #3927	12.50	Candy dish, 6½" x 4¾" #3668	42.50	Jam & jelly set, 2 4¾" jars, lid, ladle/ double crimped chrome hndl. tray #3915	45.00
Bowl, 7½", candle, ftd., 5" high #3971	50.00	Candy dish, 6½" x 6½" #3668	42.50	Jam set, 4 pc., 4¾" jar, lid, label, and 6" crimped saucer #3903	50.00
Bowl, 8", 3-toed #3635	22.00	Candy dish, 6½", heart #3033	22.50	Jar, 5", jam w/spoon and lid #3601	35.00
Bowl, 8", candle, double crimped #3771	27.50	Candy jar, 5¼", w/cover #3883	32.00	Jar, 7¼", honey, round, ftd., w/cover #3886	65.00
Bowl, 8", double crimped #3639	30.00	Candy jar, 6½", w/cover, 4½" wide #3688	45.00	Jardiniere, 4½", scalloped #3994	12.00
Bowl, 8", oval #3625	25.00	Candy jar, 7½", w/cover #3688	45.00	Jardiniere, 5½", scalloped #3898	35.00
Bowl, 8½", console, rippled top #3724	65.00	Candy jar, 8½", ftd., w/pointed knob cover #3885	38.50	Jardiniere, 6", scalloped, 6" diameter #3898	25.00
Bowl, 9", cupped #3735	135.00	Candy jar, 8½", ftd., w/rounded knob cover #3887	35.00	Jelly, 5½" x 4½" #3725	30.00
Bowl, 9", double crimped, 5" high #3924	22.50	Celery, 12" #3739	100.00	Kettle, 2½", 3-toed, 3" diameter #3990	14.00
Bowl, 9", oval, ftd. #3621	55.00	Chip n' dip, 12¼" x 3¼" bowl w/division #3922	250.00	Lamp, 8", hurricane, hndl. base scalloped top #3998	65.00
Bowl, 9", scalloped/flared #3626	55.00	Comport #3703	45.00	Lamp, 9", courting, electric, crimped top #3713	135.00
Bowl, 9", square #3929	65.00	Cigarette box, 4¼", sq. #3685	35.00	Lamp, 9", courting, oil, crimped top #3713	135.00
Bowl, 9½", chip n' dip candle #3924	25.00	Cigarette lighter 2¼", cube #3692	18.00	Lamp, 11", hurricane, crimped top #3713	115.00
Bowl, 10", ftd., double crimped #3731	38.50	Comport, 3¾", double crimped #3727	17.50	Lamp, 19", student, crimped top #3707	250.00
Bowl, 10¼", shallow #3622	55.00	Comport, 5½", double crimped #3920	86.00	Lamp, 21", student, double crimped top #3807	225.00
Bowl, 10½" #3623	85.00	Comport, 5¼", double crimped #3728	16.00	Lamp, 22", Gone with the Wind #3808	210.00
Bowl, 10½", double crimped #3624	30.00	Comport, 6" x 5½", octagonal stem #3628	18.00	Lamp, 22½", student, w/prisms #1174	235.00
Bowl, 10½", ftd., crimped #3723	35.00	Cookie jar, 11", w/lid #3680	110.00	Lamp, 26", double crimped, pillar #3907	210.00
Bowl, 11", 3 holes for hanging, #3705	135.00	Creamer, 2⅛", plain hndl. and edge #3900	9.00	Lavabo, 3-pc. (urn w/lid and basin) #3867	115.00
Bowl, 12" x 5", banana #3620	40.00	Creamer, 3½", plain hndl. #3901	10.00	Margarine tub, 5¼" #3802	22.00
Bowl, 12" x 7", banana #3720	45.00	Creamer, 3½", scalloped edge #3708	17.50	Mayonnaise set, 3-pc., bowl, 6" ruffled saucer, ladle #3803	30.00
Bowl, 12", double crimped #3938	25.00	Creamer, 3", beaded hndl. and edge #3665	20.00	Mustard jar, 3½", w/spoon and lid #3605	35.00
Butter and cheese, 4¼", w/8" plate, cover #3677	150.00	Creamer, 3", beaded hndl. and ruffled edge #3702	20.00	Mustard jar, 3½", w/spoon and lid #3889	18.00
Butter, ¼ lb., oval, 7¾" x 3¾", #3777	35.00	Creamer, 3", star shaped edge #3906	12.50	Mustard, 3⅝", kettle #3979	18.00
Butter, ¼ lb., rectangular, 7½" x 2⅛" #3977	20.00	Creamer, 4" #3606	10.00	Napkin ring, 2" diameter #3904	35.00
Cake plate, 12⅞" x 5", pie crust crimped edge #3913	50.00	Creamer, 4¾", scalloped edge #3902	22.50	Nut dish, 2½" x 4¾" $3650	58.00
Candleholder, 2" x5", pr. #3670	28.00	Cruet, 7¾" #3863	50.00	Nut dish, 2½" x 5" $3729	45.00
Candleholder, 2¾" x4¼", ftd., pr. #3673	40.00	Cup, child's #489	60.00	Nut dish, 2¾" x 4", ftd. #3631	35.00
Candleholder, 3", flat, ruffled edge, pr. #3974	30.00	Decanter, 12", hndl., w/stopper #3761	225.00	Nut dish, 5" x 3¼", oval, #3732	20.00
Candleholder, 3½", cornucopia, pr. #3971	70.00	Egg cup, 4" #3647	65.00	Nut dish, 5" x 5½", ftd. #3629	17.00
Candleholder, 3½", hndl., pr. #3870	50.00	Epergne candle, 2" high x 5" wide, petite #3671	40.00	Nut dish, 7" x 3½", oval #3633	14.00
Candleholder, 3½", rounded, flared top, pr. #3974	30.00	Epergne candle, 6" wide, for 7" candleholder #3746	70.00	Oil, 4¾", w/stopper #3869	15.00
Candleholder, 3½", single, ruffled edge, pr. #3770	90.00	Epergne set, 6½", 2-pc. 7" horn #3704	75.00	Oil, 8", w/stopper #3767	55.00
Candleholder, 5½", 2-light, pr. #3672	125.00	Epergne set, 6½", 4-pc., 6" tri-horns #3801	50.00	Pickle, 8" x 4", oval #3640	15.00
Candleholder, 6½", cornucopia, pr. #3874	57.50	Epergne set, 9½", 4-pc. 8" tri-horns #3701	50.00	Pitcher, 5¼", squat, 4" diameter top #3965	37.50
Candleholder, 6", pr. #3674	28.00	Epergne set, 9", 5-pc. (#3920 comport, frog, 5" tri-horns) #3800	200.00	Pitcher, 7" #3365	32.00
Candleholder, 7" #3745	35.00	Fairy light, 4½", 2-pc. #3608	14.00	Pitcher, 7¾", 80 oz., no ice lip (fat neck) #3967	125.00
Candleholder, 8", crescent, pr. #3678	150.00	Fairy light, 8½", 3-pc. #3804	85.00	Pitcher, 8", 54 oz., no ice lip (fat neck) #3764	65.00
Candleholder, 10", pr. #3774	65.00	Goblet, 3⅞", 3 oz., wine #3843	15.00		
Candy box, 5¼", shoe w/cover #3700	35.00	Goblet, 4½", 4 oz., wine #3843	14.00		
Candy box, 6", w/cover #3600	32.00	Goblet, 5⅝", 8 oz., water #3845	12.50		
Candy box, 6", w/cover, 6" diameter #3984	50.00	Hat, 2⅝", burred #3991	15.00		
Candy box, 6¾", w/cover #3886	35.00	Hat, 2⅝", plain #3991	25.00		
Candy box, 8⅛", w/cover, ftd. #3784	42.50				

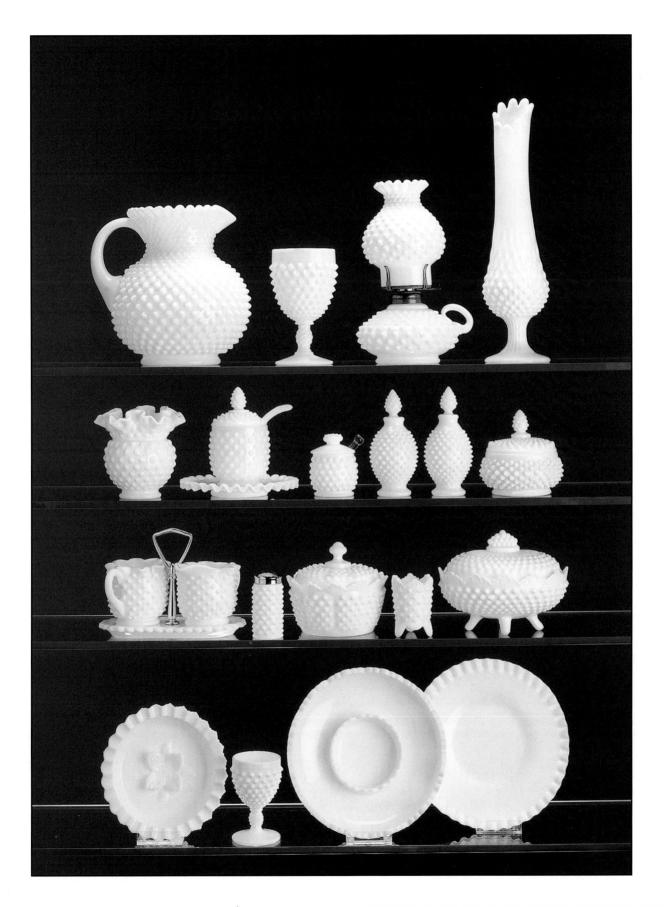

HOBNAIL

White

	White
Pitcher, 9½", w/ice lip, 70 oz. #3664	55.00
Pitcher, 11" #3360	60.00
Planter, 4½", square, scalloped top #3699	14.00
Planter, 8½" long, scalloped top #3690	20.00
Planter, 8", crescent, 4-ftd., #3798	30.00
Planter, 9½" long, scalloped top #3690	27.50
Planter, 9" wall, #3836	57.50
Planter, 10" long, rectangular box #3799	27.50
Planter, 10", crescent, 4-ftd., #3698	47.50
Plate, 8½", round, pie crust crimped edge #3912	25.00
Plate, 8¼", round, pie crust crimped edge #3816	25.00
Plate, 13½", crimped edge #3714	50.00
Plate, 16", torte #3817	65.00
Powder box, 6½", round w/lid #3880	50.00
Puff box, 4½", round #3885	75.00
Punch base, 3¾" x 8½" #3778	100.00
Punch bowl, 10½"" x 5¼", plain edge #3827	260.00
Punch bowl, 11¼"" x 6½", octagon #3820	465.00
Punch bowl, 15" x 7½", crimped edge #3722	325.00
Punch cup, 2½" x 3", octagonal #3840	20.00
Punch cup, 2¼" x 2¾" #3847	15.00
Punch ladle #9520	55.00
Punch ladle (crystal) #9527	30.00
Relish, 5¼" x 7½", 3-part #3607	35.00
Relish, 7½", 3-sections #3822	16.00
Relish, 7½", non divided #3822	50.00
Relish, 7½", scalloped, 3-sections #3822	16.00
Relish, 8½", heart-shaped #3733	25.00
Relish, 12⅜", 3-sections #3740	35.00
Salt & pepper, 3", flat, pr. #3806	20.00
Salt & pepper, 3¾" pr. #3609	24.00
Salt & pepper, 4¼" pr. #3602	40.00
Salt dip, 2⅜" x 2¼" x ⅜", shell shape #9496	45.00
Server, 10", two-tier, 12" bowl & 3-section top #3709	50.00
Shaker, 4¾", cinnamon sugar #3797	135.00
Sherbet, 4" #3825	15.00

	White
Slipper, 5", kitten head and paws #3995	10.00
Spoon holder, 7¼" long #3612	115.00
Stein, 6¾", 14 oz., #3646	110.00
Sugar, 2⅛", plain handle and edge #3900	9.00
Sugar, 3", beaded handle and edge #3665	20.00
Sugar, 3", beaded handle and ruffled edge #3702	20.00
Sugar, 3", star-shaped edge #3906	12.50
Sugar, 3½", plain handle #3901	10.00
Sugar, 3½", scalloped edge #3708	17.50
Sugar, 4¾", scalloped edge #3902	22.50
Sugar, 5¾" w/lid #3606	12.50
Syrup pitcher, 5¼", 12 oz. #3660	32.50
Syrup pitcher, 5¾", 12 oz. #3762	27.50
Tidbit, two-tier, 13½" and 8½" #3794	55.00
Toothpick, 2¾" #3895	40.00
Toothpick, 3" #3795	12.00
Tray, 7½" x 3¾", oil/mustard #3715	12.50
Tray, 7¾", chrome handle #3879	25.00
Tray, 12½" x 7", vanity #3775	100.00
Tray, 13½" sandwich w/metal handle #3791	55.00
Tumbler, 3½", 5 oz., flat #3945	10.00
Tumbler, 4¾", 9 oz. flat #3949	15.00
Tumbler, 5", 12 oz., iced tea #3942	18.50
Tumbler, 5", 12 oz., iced tea, barrel shape #3947	37.50
Tumbler, 5¾", iced tea, ftd. #3842	38.50
Tumbler, 6", 16 oz., flat #3946	50.00
Urn, 11", covered #3986	185.00
Vanity bottle, 7⅛", 3-pc. #3986	235.00
Vase, 2¼", violet, ribbon crimped #3754	35.00
Vase, 3", crimped #3855	12.50
Vase, 3¾", double crimped #3850	10.00
Vase, 4", 3¾" diameter #3952	10.00
Vase, 4", 4¾" diameter #3775	50.00
Vase, 4", fan, pie crust edge #3953	12.50
Vase, 4½", double crimped #3854	15.00
Vase, 5", 3-toed #3654	12.50
Vase, 5", double crimped #3850	17.50
Vase, 5", scalloped #3655	17.50
Vase, 5½", double crimped #3656	30.00
Vase, 5½", ivy ball, ruffled, ped. ft. #3726	20.00
Vase, 5¾", ivy, ribbed, ped. ft. #3757	20.00

	White
Vase, 6", double crimped #3856	20.00
Vase, 6", double crimped #3954	25.00
Vase, 6", ftd., swung, handkerchief #3651	40.00
Vase, 6", hand #3355	30.00
Vase, 6¼", 3" diameter base, fan #3957	22.00
Vase, 6¼", 5" diameter, double crimped #3954	25.00
Vase, 6½", ftd., swung, handkerchief #3651	50.00
Vase, 6½", swung, handkerchief #3750	22.50
Vase, 7½", handkerchief #3657	22.50
Vase, 8", 4" diameter base, fan #3959	40.00
Vase, 8", bud, ftd., swung #3756	18.00
Vase, 8", double crimped, 3½" diameter #3859	55.00
Vase, 8", double crimped, 6½" diameter #3958	28.00
Vase, 8", double crimped, 6¼" diameter #3858	50.00
Vase, 8½" fan #3852	150.00
Vase, 8½", Jack in the Pulpit #3356	28.00
Vase, 9" #3659	55.00
Vase, 9", swung #3755	50.00
Vase, 10", swung, ftd., bud #3950	15.00
Vase, 10", swung, handkerchief #3855	40.00
Vase, 11", double crimped #3752	40.00
Vase, 12", 3-toed #3658	175.00
Vase, 12", swung, ftd., 2½" diameter #3758	25.00
Vase, 12", swung, ftd., 3¼" diameter #3753	27.50
*Vase, 14", swung, handkerchief #3755	50.00
*Vase, 14", swung, pitcher, 3¼" diameter #3750	45.00
Vase, 18", ftd., 3¼" diameter #3753	47.50
Vase, 24", swung #3652	37.50

* size varies upward

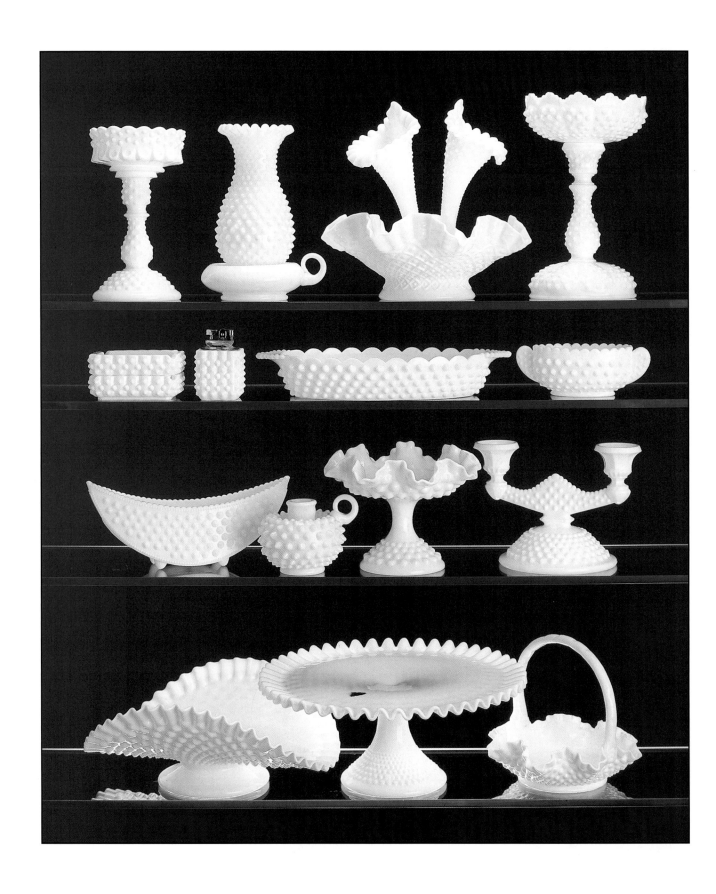

HOLLY CUTTING #815, FOSTORIA GLASS COMPANY, 1942 – 1980

Color: crystal

I have had repeated requests to add Holly to my book. Numerous brides chose this Fostoria pattern over Navarre and Meadow Rose; that choice has today's collectors searching to fill out family sets or simply buying it because they like the pattern. Holly cuttings are found on many of Fostoria's blanks as you can see from the listing. Its cut band is distinctive and easily recognized.

If you are trying for a full set, you will have two sizes of tumblers and eight different stems to contend with, and those are the easiest pieces to find. Serving pieces and basic dinnerware items are not as easily accumulated.

As with many elegant patterns of all companies of this time, stemware and tumblers were often bought to go with china sets. Glass serving dishes and dinnerware items were never even considered to be necessary. "Food just looks better on solid, colored dishes than it does on crystal," said an older, elegantly dressed lady recently when I asked if she had any pieces other than stemware in her Fostoria pattern. She informed me that she never wanted any glass dishes to go with her Bavarian china. That reasoning may well be why only stemware is so abundant in most elegant patterns today.

The double candlestick was referred to as a duo by Fostoria. You can see the #2364 ash tray and cigarette holder pictured in Buttercup. These little items are rarely found.

	Crystal		Crystal
Ash tray, #2364, 2⅝", individual	20.00	Plate, #2337, 8½", luncheon	12.50
Bowl, #1769, finger	35.00	Plate, #2337, 9½", dinner	35.00
Bowl, #2364, 5", fruit	12.00	Plate, #2364, 11", sandwich	30.00
Bowl, #2364, 8", rimmed soup	25.00	Plate, #2364, 14", torte	40.00
Bowl, #2364, 9", salad	30.00	Plate, #2364, 16", torte	50.00
Bowl, #2364, baked apple	15.00	Plate, #2364, cracker	25.00
Bowl, #6023, 9", ftd.	50.00	Relish, #2364, 8¼", two-part	22.00
Bowl, #2364, 12", flared	35.00	Relish, #2364, 10", three-part	25.00
Bowl, #2364, 12", lily pond	35.00	Saucer, #2350	3.00
Bowl, #2364, 13", fruit	40.00	Shaker, #2364, 2⅝", individual pr.	40.00
Candlestick, #2324, 4"	20.00	Shaker, #2364, 3¼", pr.	40.00
Candlestick, #6023, 5½", duo	30.00	Stem, #6030, 3⅞", 1 oz., cordial	30.00
Celery, #2364, 11"	25.00	Stem, #6030, 3¾", 4 oz., oyster cocktail	15.00
Cheese comport, #2364, ftd.	18.00	Stem, #6030, 4⅜", 6 oz., low sherbet	11.00
Cigarette holder, #2364, 2" high	30.00	Stem, #6030, 5¼", 3½ oz., cocktail	12.00
Comport, #6030, 5"	25.00	Stem, #6030, 5⅝", 6 oz., high sherbet	12.00
Comport, #2364, 8"	32.00	Stem, #6030, 6", 3½ oz., claret/wine	30.00
Cream, #2350½, 3¼"	15.00	Stem, #6030, 6⅜", 10 oz., low goblet	18.00
Cream, #2666, ind.	20.00	Stem, #6030, 7⅞", 10 oz., water goblet	20.00
Cup, #2350½	10.00	Sugar, #21350½, 3⅛"	15.00
Ladle, mayonnaise	10.00	Sugar, 2666, ind.	20.00
Mayonnaise, #2364, 5"	30.00	Tray, #2364, 11¼", center hndl.	35.00
Pickle, #2364, 8", oval	22.00	Tray, #2666, individual sug/cr (no cutting)	15.00
Pitcher, #2666, 32 oz.	75.00	Tumbler, #6030, 4⅝", 5 oz., juice, ftd.	15.00
Pitcher, #6011, 53 oz., 8⅞", ftd. jug	195.00	Tumbler, #6030, 6", 12 oz., iced tea, ftd.	20.00
Plate, #2337, 6", dessert	5.00	Vase, #2619½, 6"	65.00
Plate, #2364, 6¾", mayonnaise	10.00	Vase, #2619½, 7½"	75.00
Plate, #2337, 7½", salad	10.00	Vase, #2619½, 9½"	95.00

HOLIDAY, "BUTTONS AND BOWS," JEANNETTE GLASS COMPANY, 1947 – MID 1950s

Colors: Pink, iridescent; some Shell Pink and crystal

There are distinct variations of Holiday pieces which cause problems for collectors. I have used an extra page in the pas describing these discrepancies. Unfortunately, that space is needed to introduce new patterns.

Quickly, there are three styles of cup and saucer sets. One style cup and saucer have plain centers. These are easy to match Two other cup styles have a rayed center. You cannot mix these since one cup's base size of 2" will only fit a 2⅛" cup ring and the 2⅜" cup base will fit a 2⅛" saucer ring. Two styles of 10 ounce tumblers occur. One is flat bottomed and the other has a smal raised foot and is narrower at the bottom. These are from different moulds, but inexperienced collectors sometimes get upse with differences on similar items purchased. Two styles of sherbets are known. One has a rayed foot while the other is plain. Two distinct sherbet plates have 2¾" centers, but one has a "beads" effect in the center, while the other has a center ring with a "diamond" effect in the center. Mould variations occur in nearly all patterns, but Holiday's variations are especially unsettling. It is okay to mix styles!

I remember when $10.00 seemed like a high price for the Holiday 6" footed tumblers and now $175.00 is the asking price They were not easily found when they were $10.00!

Holiday cake plates, candlesticks, and console bowls remain difficult pieces to find. If you are thunderstruck by how such . recently manufactured (relatively speaking) glassware could have so many hard-to-find pieces, welcome to the club. We know the iced teas went to the Philippines. Apparently, there were few requests for serving pieces or they were unpopular premiun items. So far, no facts have surfaced on this mystery.

Iridescent pieces of Holiday are bought by some collectors to enhance their sets. Only four different pieces were made and only the sandwich tray is not pictured.

Holiday was a well liked pattern and well used, judging by the wealth of shopworn pieces I have examined in various sets over the years. Be sure to examine the underside of the edges. Pointed edges are prone to chips, nicks, and "chigger bites," an auction term that varies from place to place. Some areas of the country have bigger chiggers than others! Remember, damaged glass **cannot be** "almost mint." Prices listed here are for mint condition glassware!

	Pink	Crystal	Iridescent
Bowl, 5⅛", berry	12.50		
Bowl, 7¾", soup	55.00		
Bowl, 8½", large berry	30.00		
Bowl, 9½", oval vegetable	27.50		
*Bowl, 10¾", console	135.00		
Butter dish and cover	40.00		
Butter dish bottom	10.00		
Butter dish top	30.00		
Cake plate, 10½", 3-legged	110.00		
Candlesticks, 3" pr.	110.00		
Creamer, footed	8.00		
Cup, three sizes	8.00		
Pitcher, 4¾", 16 oz. milk	65.00	15.00	22.50
Pitcher, 6¾", 52 oz.	38.00		
Plate, 6", sherbet	6.00		

	Pink	Crystal	Iridescent
Plate, 9", dinner	17.00		
Plate, 13¾", chop	110.00		
Platter, 11⅜", oval	20.00		12.50
Sandwich tray, 10½"	17.50		15.00
Saucer, 3 styles	4.00		
Sherbet, 2 styles	6.00		
Sugar	10.00		
Sugar cover	15.00		
Tumbler, 4", 10 oz., flat	22.50		
Tumbler, 4", footed, 5 oz.	45.00		12.00
Tumbler, 4¼", footed, 5¼ oz.		8.00	
Tumbler, 6", footed	160.00		

* Shell Pink $40.00

HORIZON #2650 LINE, FOSTORIA GLASS COMPANY, 1951 – 1958

Color: crystal, Cinnamon, Spruce Green

Horizon is an intriguing Fostoria pattern that few collectors have taken much note of in recent years. It was not a huge line for Fostoria and was only made for eight years. It is very 50s-looking, sleek and svelte; and right now, 50s are **in** as people try to remake their childhood memories. Many couples are decorating in the styles they remember growing up with. Have you noticed all the 50s diners springing up?

The brown and green colors were called Cinnamon and Spruce Green by Fostoria. I'll admit, Cinnamon, isn't my cup of tea; but my taste runs to blue. Cathy assures me it would make a dynamite table setting. When I recently called a dealer about some pieces of Horizon she had listed on her web page, she said, "You want to buy WHAT?" I had noticed that we were missing four or five items from our photograph that she had for sale. They won't be missing the next time. Once it appears in my book, the pieces tend to cost me more than when they were not listed; so, I buy when I can.

Both colors can be found now and seem to be very durable and modernistic looking. If this is your forte, you'd better jump in and collect it before the supply runs out.

	Cinnamon Crystal Spruce		Cinnamon Crystal Spruce
Bowl, #5650, 2⅝" high, dessert/finger	10.00	Plate, 7", salad	8.00
Bowl, 4½", fruit	7.00	Plate, 10", dinner	15.00
Bowl, 5", cereal	12.00	Plate, 11", sandwich	15.00
Bowl, 8½", salad	18.00	Plate, 14", torte	14.00
Bowl, 10½", salad	20.00	Platter, 12", oval	22.00
Bowl, 11½", four-part, server	20.00	Relish, 12", three-part	20.00
Bowl, 12", two-handled, server	25.00	Saucer	2.00
Candy, 5" w/cover	25.00	Sugar, 3⅛"	12.00
Coaster	10.00	Tumbler, #5650, 3⅜", juice/cocktail	6.00
Cream, 3½"	12.00	Tumbler, #5650, 3⅜", sherbet/old fashioned	8.00
Cup, 8½ oz.	10.00	Tumbler, #5650, 5", water/scotch & soda	9.00
Mayonnaise, 3-pc. set	25.00	Tumbler, #5650, 6", iced tea/highball	12.00

Colors: crystal, iridescent; some pink; recently bi-colored red/yellow and blue/green combinations, and white

Iridescent Iris belongs entirely within the blueprint of this 50s book; and although crystal production goes back to 1928 for its start, some crystal was made as late as the 1940s and 1950s. Additionally, candy bottoms and vases were manufactured as late as the 1970s. Those had sprayed-on colors over crystal. Accordingly, I have decided to include crystal Iris prices in this book. Besides, it is hard to price only one color Iris without incurring collectors' wrath!

Realize that those iridescent candy bottoms are a product of the 1970s when Jeannette made crystal and iridized or flashed bottoms with two-tone colors such as red/yellow or blue/green. These candy bases were sold as vases. Some of these colors have since washed off or peeled over time, again making them crystal candy bottoms. Some have been purposely stripped of their color to fool unaware collectors. These newly made pieces have a **non-rayed foot**; no tops were ever made. Similarly, the regular 9" vases were made in white and sprayed green, red, and blue on the outside. Many of these vases have lost the colors on the outside and are now only white. White vases sell in the $12.00 – 15.00 range. White vases were never made before the early 1970s regardless of what story you hear of it belonging to a ninety-eight-year-old who only used it for her prize roses!

Iris prices have finally settled down, but almost all scarce pieces have at least doubled in price in the last few years. That is noteworthy! It even beats the stock market, but not Fire-King Jade-ite which has done the same in a little over a year. What will be next? I wish I knew!

The 8 ounce water goblet, 5¾", 4 ounce goblet, 4" sherbet, and the demitasse cup and saucer are the most difficult pieces to find in iridescent. The 5¾", 4 ounce goblet is displayed in *Very Rare Glassware of the Depression Era, 4th Series* and you can see the demitasse cup and saucer on the right as well as three other rarely seen colors of amethyst, blue, and red! The iridescent tall sherbet and water goblet are finally shown here as well as a nut dish. All of these are elusive, but nut dishes should be the easiest to find in this group!

I have not found any supplementary information on the decorated red and gold "Corsage" Iris that is found on crystal. We know it was styled by Century in 1946 because of a card attached to a "Corsage" wedding gift that a reader shared with me. A few more sprayed-on red pieces are surfacing; but, so far, there is no documentation for these!

Published reports on "new" Iris iced teas and berry bowls were premature and erroneous. These tea tumblers turned out to be a years-old stash of originally issued Iris packaged in original Jeannette boxes and not scare-touted reproductions.

	Crystal	Iridescent	Green/Pink
*** Bowl, 4½", berry, beaded edge	45.00	10.00	
Bowl, 5", ruffled, sauce	9.00	28.00	
Bowl, 5", cereal	125.00		
Bowl, 7½", soup	165.00	60.00	
Bowl, 8", berry, beaded edge	85.00	25.00	
Bowl, 9½", ruffled, salad	12.50	13.00	150.00
Bowl, 11½", ruffled, fruit	15.00	14.00	
Bowl, 11", fruit, straight edge	65.00		
Butter dish and cover	47.50	45.00	
Butter dish bottom	12.50	12.50	
Butter dish top	35.00	32.50	
Candlesticks, pr.	45.00	48.00	
Candy jar and cover	175.00		
Coaster	110.00		
Creamer, footed	12.00	12.00	150.00
Cup	15.00	14.00	
*Demitasse cup	35.00	150.00	
*Demitasse saucer	145.00	250.00	
Fruit or nut set	110.00	150.00	
Goblet, 4", wine		30.00	

	Crystal	Iridescent	Green/Pink
Goblet, 4¼", 4 oz., cocktail	27.50		
Goblet, 4¼", 3 oz., wine	17.00		
Goblet, 5¾", 4 oz.	28.00	225.00	
Goblet, 5¾", 8 oz.	26.00	225.00	
** Lamp shade, 11½"	95.00		
Pitcher, 9½", footed	40.00	42.50	
Plate, 5½", sherbet	15.00	14.00	
Plate, 8", luncheon	110.00		
Plate, 9", dinner	55.00	48.00	
Plate, 11¾", sandwich	33.00	33.00	
Saucer	12.00	11.00	
Sherbet, 2½", footed	28.00	15.00	
Sherbet, 4", footed	28.00	225.00	
Sugar	11.00	11.00	150.00
Sugar cover	12.00	12.00	
Tumbler, 4", flat	150.00		
Tumbler, 6", footed	18.00	16.00	
***Tumbler, 6½", footed	35.00		
Vase, 9"	27.50	25.00	195.00

*Ruby, Blue, Amethyst priced as Iridescent
**Colors: $65.00
***Has **not** been reproduced

JAMESTOWN, FOSTORIA GLASS COMPANY, 1958 – 1982

Colors: Amber, amethyst, blue, brown, crystal, green, pink, and red

Jamestown is one of the many Fostoria patterns whose pieces (other than stems) seem to be invisible! Amber or brown Jamestown is not sought by many collectors, but I rarely see serving pieces in those colors either. Service items were not manufactured by Fostoria for the same production span as the stemware line; that leaves both collectors and dealers scrounging for serving pieces! Not every piece was made in each color. I have grouped colors into three pricing groups based upon sales reports. You may find prices even less than those listed for amber and brown. If you are looking for either of those colors, ask for them. You should be able to find some bargains!

In the middle pricing group, crystal is most in demand, but green is beginning to close the gap. You might find some bargains in amethyst Jamestown since it sometimes is mistaken for Moroccan Amethyst.

Ruby Jamestown has always sold well, but there is not a complete line of Ruby. Pink and blue Jamestown are selling better than Ruby at the present time. A distasteful note for collectors is that Ruby stemware has once again been made and sold in the Fostoria outlet stores. Those newer stems were selling for $16.00 each which has caused prices to adjust on older Ruby Jamestown stemware. Unhappily, there is little distinction between the old and newly made items. Both older stems and newer ones have three mould lines which I overheard someone touting as a point of distinction. Now that Viking has gone out of business, this problem may be solved since Viking was making this Ruby for Lancaster Colony who bought the Fostoria moulds. Where is the marketing imagination to come up with **new** colors to captivate the public?

My listings below came from two different Fostoria catalogs. The line numbers on each stem in those catalogs have two different dimensions and capacities listed. That is one of the many things that muddles writing a book. Which figure do you use? I have recorded both stem listings for the purists. Either someone measured incorrectly one year or the sizes were actually changed. I don't believe those half ounces and eighth inches are going to matter much in the overall scheme of things! I have referred to this problem before in the measurements section of the *Collector's Encyclopedia of Depression Glass*. Accordingly, your measurements could differ from those I have listed!

	Amber/Brown	Amethyst/Crystal/Green	Blue/Pink/Ruby
Bowl, 4½", dessert #2719/421	8.50	13.50	16.00
Bowl, 10", salad #2719//211	21.00	40.00	50.00
Bowl, 10", two hndl. serving #2719/648	21.00	45.00	60.00
Butter w/cover, ¼ pound #2719/300	24.00	45.00	55.00
Cake plate, 9½", hndl. #2719/306	16.00	35.00	40.00
Celery, 9¼" #2719/360	18.00	32.50	37.50
Cream, 3½", ftd. #2719/681	11.00	17.50	25.00
Jelly w/cover, 6⅛" #2719/447	32.50	57.50	80.00
Pickle, 8⅜" #2719/540	21.00	40.00	45.00
Pitcher, 7⁵⁄₁₆", 48 oz., ice jug #2719/456	45.00	95.00	135.00
Plate, 8" #2719/550	8.50	16.00	23.00
Plate, 14", torte #2719/567	26.00	42.50	60.00
Relish, 9⅛", 2-part #2719/620	16.00	32.00	37.50
Salad set, 4-pc. (10" bowl, 14" plate w/wood fork & spoon) #2719/286	55.00	85.00	100.00
Salver, 7" high, 10" diameter #2719/630	60.00	**120.00	120.00
Sauce dish w/cover, 4½" #2719/635	18.00	35.00	40.00
Shaker, 3½", w/chrome top. pr. #2719/653	26.00	40.00	50.00
Stem, 4⁵⁄₁₆", 4 oz., wine #2719/26	10.00	20.00	24.00
*Stem, 4¼", 6½ oz., sherbet #2719/7	6.50	12.50	16.00
*Stem, 4⅛", 7 oz., sherbet #2719/7	6.50	12.50	16.00
*Stem, 5¾", 9½ oz., goblet #2719/2	10.00	16.00	16.00
*Stem, 5⅞", 10 oz., goblet #2719/2	10.00	16.00	16.00
Sugar, 3½", ftd. #2719/679	11.00	17.50	25.00
Tray, 9⅜", hndl. muffin #2719/726	26.00	42.50	55.00
Tumbler, 4¼", 9 oz. #2719/73	9.00	21.00	25.00
Tumbler, 4¾", 5 oz., juice #2719/88	9.50	21.00	26.00
Tumbler, 5⅛", 12 oz. #2719/64	9.00	21.00	26.00
Tumbler, 6", 11 oz., ftd. tea #2719/63	10.00	21.00	24.00
Tumbler, 6", 12 oz., ftd. tea #2719/63	10.00	21.00	24.00

*Made in recent years
**Green $195.00

KING'S CROWN, THUMBPRINT LINE No. 4016, U.S. GLASS (TIFFIN) COMPANY

LATE 1800s – 1960s; INDIANA GLASS COMPANY, 1970s

Colors: Crystal, crystal with ruby or cranberry flash, crystal with gold or platinum

King's Crown is one of the fastest selling patterns that I stock as long as I stay away from the multitude of stems that are available. Unfortunately, stems are what I keep running into and I have had to learn to control buying them no matter how reasonable they are. Buy any of the serving pieces and customers will attack your booth as soon as the doors are open at a show!

King's Crown was made for so long and by over twenty different companies that I doubt a truly **complete** listing will ever be accomplished! There is a calculable number of pieces; but like counting stars, you'll probably never be finished. This pattern causes chaos among both old and new collectors. Originally issued as Thumbprint Line No. 4016 by U. S. Glass in the late 1800s, this glassware was also made by Tiffin into the early 1960s. The Tiffin catalog reprint shown is from 1955. Confounding the issue, Indiana bought the Tiffin moulds and changed the design somewhat. Also, there were numerous other glassware companies who made similar patterns. If some pattern sold well for one company, another soon had similar wares!

For this book I am including both Indiana pieces as well as those made by Tiffin after 1940. You will find additional items, but please realize that many of those could be from an earlier time and a different company. The Tiffin plates seem to have starred designs in the center while the Indiana ones appear to be plain. I have discovered no hard, fast rules in researching this confounding pattern! One of the exhilarating things about King's Crown is that you never know what piece is available around the next corner. Collectors seem to like it all!

Most collectors prefer the deeper red shade of flashing to the lighter shade called "cranberry." Cranberry can be seen on the bottom of page 121 with a variety of other colors of King's Crown items that I have found. The pitcher and other purple pieces are Tiffin's Mulberry. There are pieces flashed with gold, platinum, blue, green, yellow, cranberry, or ruby. The prices for other flashed colors are being more firmly established. Most flashed colors are selling for less than ruby, although gold items are not far behind ruby. Demand makes ruby the desired color. For crystal without flashed-on colors, subtract fifty percent of the prices listed. Gold and platinum decorated products were also made at Indiana.

Bear in mind, that amber, cobalt blue, avocado green, and iridized carnival colors are all Indiana's production of the **late 1970s and 1980s**. In 1976, they also made a Smoky Blue for the Bicentennial. A duplicate blue was used in the Tiara Sandwich line that year!

The price on the punch bowl set has doubled in the last few years. Demand for these is almost inconceivable. Everyone collecting or wanting to collect King's Crown has to have the punch set! The 24" plate listed on the party server measures 22½" to 23" on the ones I have measured.

Elongated thumbprint designs are from the original Tiffin moulds. Some elongated thumbprint style may have been made at Indiana before they changed the moulds; but if the pieces you have show **circular** thumbprints, you definitely have King's Crown made by Indiana. Most Tiffin made tumblers are flared at the top while Indiana's are straight. Expect to pay less than the prices below for the more recently issued Indiana tumblers. You alone can decide what you are willing to buy and the price you are willing to pay!

	Ruby Flashed		Ruby Flashed
Ash tray, 5¼", square	25.00	Plate, 5", bread/butter	8.00
Bowl, 4", finger	17.50	Plate, 7⅜", mayonnaise liner	12.50
Bowl, 5", mayonnaise	45.00	Plate, 7⅜", salad	12.00
Bowl, 5", divided mayonnaise	65.00	Plate, 9¾", snack w/indent	15.00
Bowl 5¾"	20.00	Plate, 10", dinner	40.00
Bowl, 6", diameter, ftd., wedding or candy	55.00	Plate, 14½", torte	85.00
Bowl, 8¾", 2-hndl., crimped bon bon	85.00	Plate, 24", party	185.00
Bowl, 9¼", salad	90.00	Plate, 24", party server (w/punch ft.)	295.00
Bowl, 10½", ftd., wedding or candy, w/cover	165.00	Punch bowl foot	150.00
Bowl, 11½", 4½" high, crimped	125.00	Punch bowl, 2 styles	450.00
Bowl, 11¼" cone	85.00	Punch cup	15.00
Bowl, 12½", center edge, 3" high	95.00	Punch set, 15-pc. w/foot	850.00
Bowl, 12½", flower floater	85.00	Punch set, 15-pc. w/plate	800.00
Bowl, crimped, ftd.	100.00	Relish, 14", 5-part	110.00
Bowl, flared, ftd.	85.00	Saucer	8.00
Bowl, straight edge	80.00	Stem, 2 oz., wine	7.50
Cake salver, 12½", ftd.	75.00	Stem, 2¼ oz., cocktail	12.50
Candleholder, sherbet type	30.00	Stem, 4 oz., claret	13.00
Candleholder, 2-lite, 5½"	95.00	Stem, 4 oz., oyster cocktail	14.00
Candy box, 6", flat, w/cover	60.00	Stem, 5½ oz., sundae or sherbet	10.00
Cheese stand	25.00	Stem, 9 oz., water goblet	12.00
Compote, 7¼", 9¾" diameter	50.00	Sugar	25.00
Compote, 7½", 12" diameter, ftd., crimped	95.00	Tumbler, 4 oz., juice, ftd.	12.00
Compote, small, flat	25.00	Tumbler, 4½ oz., juice	14.00
Creamer	25.00	Tumbler, 8½ oz., water	13.00
Cup	8.00	Tumbler, 11 oz., iced tea	16.00
Lazy Susan, 24", 8½" high, w/ball bearing spinner	295.00	Tumbler, 12 oz., iced tea, ftd.	20.00
Mayonnaise, 3-pc. set	65.00	Vase, 9", bud	75.00
Pitcher	185.00	Vase, 12¼", bud	90.00

United States Glass Company
TIFFIN, OHIO
KINGS CROWN
Also known as No. 4016 Thumbprint

Sugar

Cream

5" Bread and Butter Plate

Cup and Saucer

10" Dinner Plate

AVAILABLE PLAIN CRYSTAL, DECORATED CRANBERRY OR RUBY

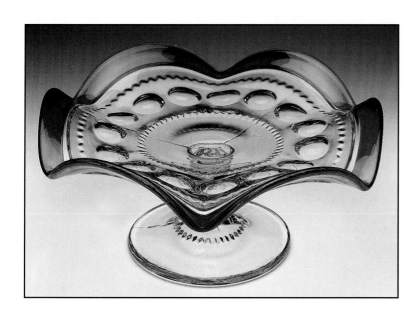

KINGS CROWN

Center Edge Bowl 12½″ Diameter 3″ High

2-Lite Candle Holder 5½″ High

Footed Fruit Compote 9¾″ Diameter 7¼″ High

Crimped Bowl 11½″ Diameter 4½″ High

Cone Bowl 11¼″ Diameter 4¾″ High

Page 2   AVAILABLE PLAIN CRYSTAL, DECORATED CRANBERRY OR RUBY

KINGS CROWN

Goblet 9 oz.

Wine 2 oz.

Juice 4 oz.

Claret 4 oz.

Cocktail 2¼ oz.

Oyster Cocktail 4 oz.

Sundae 5½ oz.

Water Tumbler 8½ oz.

Juice Tumbler 4½ oz.

Footed Ice Tea 12 oz.

Ice Tea Tumbler 11 oz.

Finger Bowl 4″ Diameter

7⅜″ Salad Plate

KINGS CROWN

Wedding Bowl and Cover
6" Diameter 10½" High

Flower Floater 12½" Diameter

Torte Plate 14" Diameter

Ash Tray 5¼" Square

Footed Cake Salver
12½" Diameter 4¾" High

Color: Crystal, Azure

Picture fireworks exploding overhead and you'll be able to remember this pattern. Fostoria made Lido in Azure blue, but it is rarely seen in anything other than crystal. You can see an Azure tumbler as the pattern shot on page 129! Unless you are supremely lucky in your pursuits of glass, that picture might be all you ever see in Azure. That piece was sold right after the photography session, but I have had several collectors ask to buy it! (By the time you see a picture in the book, it has been a **least** nine months since that **picture** was taken. Pictures are just the first step in the book process. It's kind of like having a baby time-wise!) Azure was discontinued during World War II. Blue fetches up to double the prices for crystal on hard-to-find items; but basic pieces sell for only a little more than crystal since there are fewer collectors searching for it. It's not that it's unwanted, there is just so little to be found that most people shy away from it.

I'll admit that I looked at that Lido pitcher (top page 129) at a glass show for several years before I pried the money loose to buy it. This pitcher is not commonly found; but the price for a photograph seemed discouraging. All in all, this is a reasonably priced Fostoria pattern, and there are precious few of those patterns left!

All items without a line number listed below are found on Baroque blank #2496. You may find other Lido items than those listed here. Let me know what you see!

Bowl, 4", one hndl., square	14.00		Plate, 10", hndl. cake	35.00
Bowl, 4⅜", one hndl.	14.00		Plate, 10¼", dinner	45.00
Bowl, 4⅝", one hndl., 3 cornered	14.00		Plate, 11", cracker	22.50
Bowl, 5", one hndl., flared	13.00		Plate, 14", torte	40.00
Bowl, 6¼", 3 ftd., cupped	20.00		Relish, 6", square, 2-part	17.50
Bowl, 7⅜" 3 ftd., bon bon	17.00		Relish, 10", 3-part	30.00
Bowl, 8½", 2 hndl.	40.00		Saucer	4.00
Bowl, 10½", 2 hndl.	45.00		Shaker, 2¾"	25.00
Bowl, 12", flared	50.00		Stem, #6017, 3⅝", 4 oz., oyster cocktail	20.00
Bowl, 12½", oval, #2545 "Flame"	50.00		Stem, #6017, 3⅞", ¾ oz. cordial	42.50
Bowl, finger, #766	22.00		Stem, #6017, 4½", 6 oz., low sherbet	14.00
Candlestick, 4½", duo	35.00		Stem, #6017, 4⅞", 3½ oz., cocktail	18.00
Candlestick, 4"	20.00		Stem, #6017, 5½", 3 oz., wine	27.50
Candlestick, 5½"	22.00		Stem, #6017, 5½", 6 oz., high sherbet	17.50
Candlestick, 6¾", duo, #2545 "Flame"	45.00		Stem, #6017, 5⅞", 4 oz., claret	30.00
Candy w/cover, 6¼", 3-part	85.00		Stem, #6017, 7⅜", 9 oz., water	22.50
Celery, 11"	22.50		Sugar	9.00
Comport, 3¼", ftd. cheese	17.50		Sugar, individual	10.00
Comport, 4¾"	17.50		Sweetmeat, 6", square, 2 hndl.	17.50
Comport, 5½"	25.00		Tidbit, 8¼", 3-ftd., flat	20.00
Comport, 5¾"	27.50		Tray, 6½" ind. sug/cr., #2496½	12.00
Creamer	10.00		Tumbler, #4132, 2⅛", 1½ oz., whiskey	25.00
Creamer, individual	11.00		Tumbler, #4132, 3½", 4 oz., sham	10.00
Cup, ftd.	15.00		Tumbler, #4132, 3⅛", 7½ oz., old fashioned	15.00
Ice bucket	75.00		Tumbler, #4132, 3¾", 5 oz., sham	10.00
Jelly w/cover, 7½"	55.00		Tumbler, #4132, 3¾", 9 oz., sham	13.00
Mayonnaise, 3-pc. set, 2496½	37.50		Tumbler, #4132, 4⅛", 7 oz., sham	12.00
Oil bottle w/stopper, 3½ oz.	85.00		Tumbler, #4132, 4⅞", 12 oz., sham	15.00
Pickle, 8"	17.50		Tumbler, #4132, 5⅜", 14 oz., sham	17.50
Pitcher, #6011, 8⅞", 53 oz., ftd.	175.00		Tumbler, #6017, 4¾", 5 oz., ftd. juice	14.00
Plate, 6"	6.00		Tumbler, #6017, 5½", 9 oz., ftd. water	18.00
Plate, 7", #2337	9.00		Tumbler, #6017, 6", 12 oz., ftd. iced tea	22.00
Plate, 7½"	9.00		Tumbler, #6017, 6½", 14 oz., ftd.	27.50
Plate, 8½"	12.50		Vase, 5"	75.00
Plate, 9½"	32.50			

LODESTAR, Pattern #1632, A.H. Heisey & Co.

Color: Dawn

This Heisey pattern in only the Dawn color is named Lodestar. Crystal pieces in the same design are called Satellite and th[e] prices decline sensationally! Each piece has the star-like shape for its base. Dawn is not inexpensive as you can see by the price[s] listed below. These are realistic selling prices, not hoped for or asking prices!

	Dawn
Ash tray	95.00
Bowl, 4½", sauce dish, #1626	40.00
Bowl, 5", mayonnaise	85.00
Bowl, 6¾", #1565	60.00
Bowl, 8"	70.00
Bowl, 11", crimped	100.00
Bowl, 12", deep floral	90.00
Bowl, 14", shallow	130.00
Candleblock, 2¾" tall, 1-lite star, #1543, pr. (Satellite)	275.00
Candlestick, 2" tall, 1-lite centerpiece, pr.	140.00
Candlestick, 5¾" tall, 2-lite, pr.	600.00
Candy jar, w/cover, 5"	135.00
Celery, 10"	60.00
Creamer	50.00
Creamer, w/handle	90.00
Jar, w/cover, 8", #1626	160.00
Pitcher, 1 qt., #1626	170.00
Plate, 8½"	65.00
Plate, 14"	90.00
Relish, 7½", 3-pt.	70.00
Sugar	50.00
Sugar, w/handles	90.00
Tumbler, 6 oz., juice	50.00
Vase, 8", #1626	160.00
Vase, 8", crimped, #1626	180.00

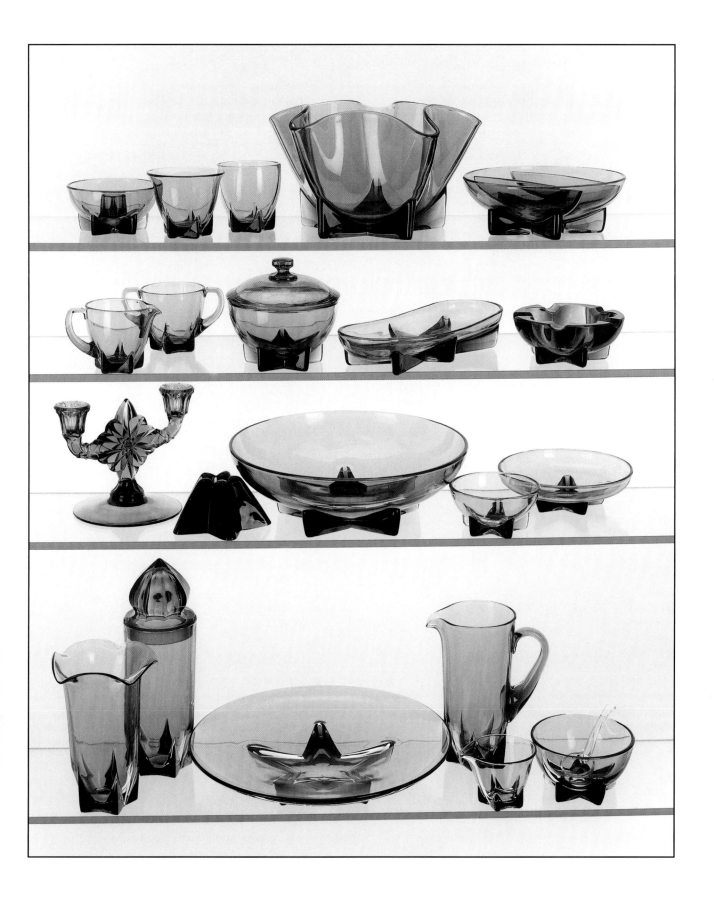

Color: crystal

Fostoria's **Mayflower** has a **cornucopia of flowers** as its predominate design. This pattern is occasionally confused with another Fostoria pattern, Corsage. Look at page 43 to observe the **cone-shaped** bouquet of flowers that makes up the **Corsage** design.

Fostoria's #2560 blank known as Coronet is used for most Mayflower etchings. Notice that there are **three undulating lines around the top of Coronet blanks.** You can spot these on the relish, comport, two-handled bowl, creamer, and sugar on page 133. The handles on the sugar and creamer are an unerring indication of blank #2560. I had a number of positive comments on the blue backgrounds for crystal patterns in the last book. One collector at the Houston show thought any color would be great, even black. Well, we tried that and it made the book look as if it were black and white instead of color.

The cordial in the top row represents line #6020 which is the only stemware line that you will find in Mayflower.

On the lower row is a #4140 jug which collectors refer to as a pitcher. This style is rarely found. The large vase on the end of that row stands 8" tall, but looks even larger due to its spacious aperture. This is the #2430 vase in the listing. The vase in the middle is the #5100 blank. Vases are rarely found in Fostoria crystal patterns, contrary to what you see pictured! It took thousands of miles of travel to round up these.

Fostoria's "Flame" #2545 blank is depicted by the oval bowl in the second row and a single candlestick on the left in the next row. Only a few pieces of Mayflower will be found on this blank. Speaking of candlesticks, there are a growing number of collectors of these throughout the country. Be sure to check out my newest book, *Glass Candlesticks of the Depression Era*, where a large number of them are to be found, all in one volume!

Any other unlisted pieces you find, feel free to drop me a postcard so we can get them documented.

Bowl, finger, #869	25.00	Plate, 6¼", hndl., lemon, #2560	6.00
Bowl, 5", hndl., whip cream, #2560	22.50	Plate, 7½", #2560	10.00
Bowl, 5½", hndl., sweetmeat, #2560	17.50	Plate, 8½", #2560	15.00
Bowl, 5¾" x 6¼", hndl., bon bon, #2560	20.00	Plate, 9½", #2560	37.50
Bowl, 7¼", 3-ftd., bon bon, #2560	22.50	Plate, 10½", hndl. cake, #2560	32.50
Bowl, 8½", hndl., #2560	45.00	Plate, 14", torte #2560	50.00
Bowl, 10", salad, #2560	45.00	Relish, 6½", hndl., 2-part, #2560	20.00
Bowl, 10½", hndl., #2496	45.00	Relish, 10" x 7¾", 3-part, #2560	32.50
Bowl, 11", hndl., #2560	55.00	Salt & pepper, pr.	65.00
Bowl, 11½", crimped, #2560	65.00	Saucer, #2560	5.00
Bowl, 12", flared, #2560	50.00	Stem, #6020, 3¾", 1 oz., cordial	40.00
Bowl, 12½", oval, #2545 "Flame"	50.00	Stem, #6020, 3¾", 4 oz., oyster cocktail	20.00
Bowl, 13", fruit, #2560	55.00	Stem, #6020, 4⅝", 6 oz., low sherbet	15.00
Candlestick, 4", #2560½	27.50	Stem, #6020, 4⅞", 3½ oz., cocktail	18.00
Candlestick, 4½", #2545 "Flame"	30.00	Stem, #6020, 5⅜", 3½ oz., wine	30.00
Candlestick, 4½", #2560	25.00	Stem, #6020, 5½", 6 oz., saucer champagne	18.00
Candlestick, 5", duo, #2496	35.00	Stem, #6020, 5¾", 4½ oz., claret	35.00
Candlestick, 5⅛", duo, #2560	40.00	Stem, #6020, 6⅛", 5½ oz., claret	35.00
Candlestick, 6¾", duo, #2545 "Flame"	45.00	Stem, #6020, 7¼", 9 oz., water	25.00
Celery, 11", #2560	35.00	Sugar, #2560	11.00
Comport, 5½"	30.00	Sugar, individual, #2560	12.00
Creamer, #2560	12.00	Tray, 7½", individual cr./sug #2560	15.00
Creamer, individual, #2560	12.50	Tray, 10" x 8¼", hndl., muffin, #2560	32.50
Cup, ftd., #2560	17.00	Tumbler, #6020, 4⅞", 5 oz., ftd. juice	17.50
Mayonnaise set, 3-pc., #2560	37.50	Tumbler, #6020, 5¾", 9 oz., ftd. water	20.00
Olive, 6¾", #2560	17.00	Tumbler, #6020, 6⅜", 12 oz., ftd. ice tea	25.00
Pickle, 8¾", #2560	20.00	Vase, 3¾", #2430	55.00
Pitcher, 7½", 60 oz., flat, #4140	265.00	Vase, 8", #2430	110.00
Pitcher, 9¾", 48 oz., ftd. #5000	265.00	Vase, 10", ftd., #2545, "Flame"	125.00
Plate, 6", #2560	6.00	Vase, 10", ftd., #5100	110.00

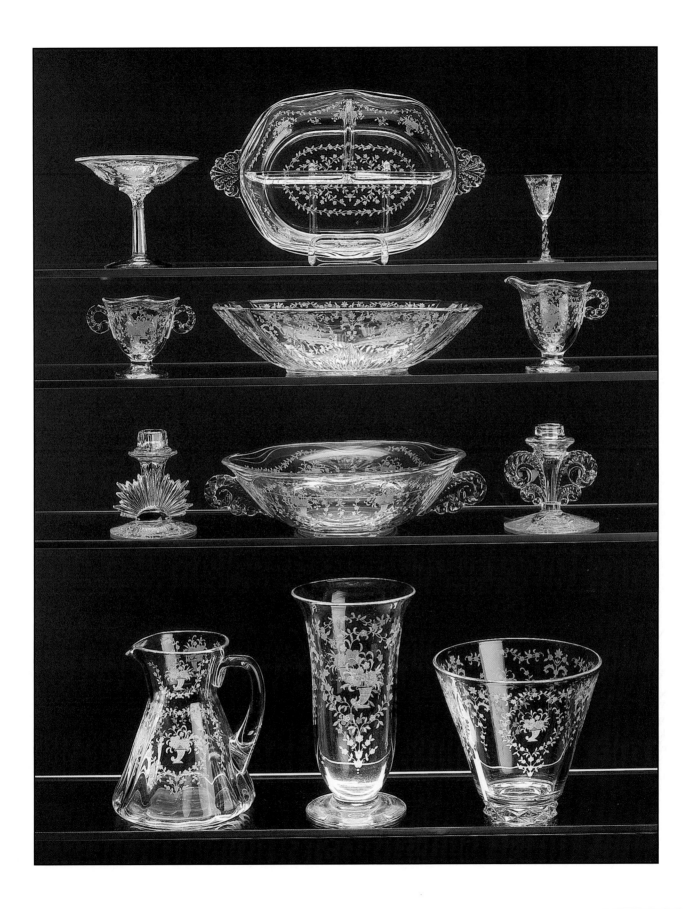

MEADOW ROSE Plate Etching #328, FOSTORIA GLASS COMPANY, 1936 – 1982

Colors: Crystal and Azure

Since the addition of Meadow Rose to this book four years ago, there has been less confusion between Fostoria's Navarre and Meadow Rose. Some of the antique mall and part-time dealers had often mislabeled these two patterns. Since Navarre is more expensive, guess which pattern was most often identified incorrectly? I have also observed that a larger number of collectors have been seeking Meadow Rose recently. Please notice the **opening** in the middle of the Meadow Rose medallion that is filled in Navarre. See the catalog reprint of Navarre on page 159. Buying a mislabeled piece in a mall usually means you are stuck with it. It is your responsibility to know what you are buying!

Meadow Rose was sold alongside its sister pattern, Navarre, for over 40 years. Matching stemware service was available until Fostoria's closing. Prices for Meadow Rose are edging toward Navarre's, but many items continue to sell for less. Meadow Rose collectors are presently still outnumbered by those pursuing Navarre; but, that might change!

I have only been able to round up five pieces of Azure. That color was discontinued during World War II in all Fostoria patterns. Pieces found in Azure will fetch an additional 50% – 75% more than crystal. Thanks for all those who have sent lists of what they have in Azure. By the next edition, I should be able to have a price listing for pieces in this color. If you are reading this for the first time, I need a list of any pieces you may have in Azure.

All pieces without a mould blank number in the listing below are #2496 or Baroque blank. Look for the raised fleur-de-lis motif on this line. All other mould blanks are listed with the item.

Bowl, 4", square, hndl.	11.00	Plate, 9½", dinner	45.00
Bowl, 4½", #869, finger	40.00	Plate, 10", hndl., cake	47.50
Bowl, 4⅝", tri-cornered	15.00	Plate, 11", cracker	30.00
Bowl, 5", hndl., flared	24.00	Plate, 14", torte	60.00
Bowl, 6", square, sweetmeat	17.50	Plate, 16", torte, #2364	90.00
Bowl, 7⅜", 3-ftd., bonbon	27.50	Relish, 6", 2-part, square	32.50
Bowl, 8½", hndl.	40.00	Relish, 10" x 7½", 3-part	45.00
Bowl, 10", oval, floating garden	50.00	Relish, 13¼", 5-part, #2419	85.00
Bowl, 10½", hndl.	55.00	Salad dressing bottle, #2083, 6½"	250.00
Bowl, 12", flared	62.50	Salt & pepper, #2375, 3½", ftd., pr.	95.00
Bowl, 12", hndl., ftd.	62.50	Sauce dish liner, 8", oval	30.00
Bowl, #2545, 12½", oval, "Flame"	55.00	Sauce dish, 6½" x 5¼"	125.00
Candlestick, 4"	25.00	Sauce dish, div. mayo., 6½"	45.00
Candlestick, 4½", double	35.00	Saucer	6.00
Candlestick, 5½"	32.00	Stem, #6016, ¾ oz., cordial, 3⅞"	47.50
Candlestick, 6", triple	55.00	Stem, #6016, 3¼ oz., wine, 5½"	40.00
Candlestick, #2545, 6¾", double, "Flame"	50.00	Stem, #6016, 3½ oz., cocktail, 5¼"	25.00
Candy, w/cover, 3-part	110.00	Stem, #6016, 4 oz., oyster cocktail, 3⅝"	27.50
Celery, 11"	37.50	Stem, #6016, 4½ oz., claret, 6"	40.00
Comport, 3¼", cheese	27.50	Stem, #6016, 6 oz., low sherbet, 4⅜"	24.00
Comport, 4¾"	30.00	Stem, #6016, 6 oz., saucer champagne, 5⅝"	24.00
Creamer, 4¾", ftd.	20.00	Stem, #6016, 10 oz., water, 7⅝"	30.00
Creamer, individual	17.50	Sugar, 3½", ftd.	18.00
Cup	20.00	Sugar, individual	16.00
Ice bucket, 4⅜" high	100.00	Tidbit, 8¼", 3 ftd., turned-up edge	22.00
Jelly w/ cover, 7½"	65.00	Tray, #2375, 11", center hndl.	35.00
Mayonnaise, #2375, 3-piece	55.00	Tray, 6½", 2496½, for ind. sugar/creamer	22.00
Mayonnaise, 2496½, 3-piece	55.00	Tumbler, #6016, 5 oz., ftd., juice, 4⅝"	25.00
Pickle, 8"	30.00	Tumbler, #6016, 10 oz., ftd., water, 5⅜"	25.00
Pitcher, #2666, 32 oz.	225.00	Tumbler, #6016, 13 oz., ftd., tea, 5⅞"	30.00
Pitcher, #5000, 48 oz., ftd.	350.00	Vase, #4108, 5"	75.00
Plate, 6", bread/butter	11.00	Vase, #4121, 5"	75.00
Plate, 7½", salad	15.00	Vase, #4128, 5"	75.00
Plate, 8½", luncheon	20.00	Vase, #2470, 10", ftd.	165.00

MODERNTONE PLATONITE, HAZEL ATLAS GLASS COMPANY, 1940 – EARLY 1950s

Colors: Platonite pastel, white, and white decorated

Platonite Moderntone is one of the more reasonably priced patterns of this era. You can still find pieces at garage and yard sales for a dollar or less. Not everyone is fond of this fired color ware; but if you are one of those who are, buy it every chance you can. No one thought the supply of Jade-ite Fire-King would ever cease to exist, but there are many dealers now kicking themselves for not buying more when it was readily available.

Blue and red decorated Platonite Moderntone is catching the eye of many new collectors. Unfortunately, there is little of either of these decorations being found. Exhibit a piece of Blue (or Red) Willow or Deco-trimmed Moderntone (shown on page 137 – 138) and you will see collectors' eyes sparkle! I have bought every piece of Willow decorated Moderntone I have found. Actually, I have only seen the Deco decorated blue items offered for sale once. I bought them and would like to find more for customers! All reports of this decoration have been from northern Ohio. The red Deco is found more frequently.

At present, demand is negligible for plain white Platonite. If you would like to find a set of white, go for it! The first item in row 4 on page 137 is a cone-shaped tumbler found only in white. The lid states that this tumbler was given free with the purchase of "Lovely" cherry gelatin, a competitor of Jello®. It cost 10¢. Many pieces of glass from this era were obtained by buying some product. Popular product items of yesteryear are often commonly found today; but those not-so-popular products packed in glassware may be treasures now.

Pastel colors are the lighter shades of blue, green, pink, and yellow. Pastel green is shown on the left atop page 139; pastel pink is at the bottom left of page 139; pastel yellow tops page 140; and pastel blue is on the right of page 142.

At the bottom of page 139 you may notice that there are two distinct shades of pink. I have been assured by Moderntone collectors that this difference in shade is of no significance to them. It disturbs me to the point that I placed the lighter shades on the far right of the photograph to illustrate the diversity of shades.

The four tumblers shown atop page 141 are fired-on Moderntone tumblers in color shades I had never seen before and were unusual enough that I had to buy them. They are fired over crystal and not white Platonite. If you have any other pieces of Moderntone fired over crystal, let me know. The dealer I bought them from had them labeled Swanky Swigs. The light blue one does not fit the known Swanky Swigs color scheme.

In pastel colors to date, there is no significant price difference between pieces with white interiors as opposed to those with colored interiors. I, personally, have found more demand for colored interiors than the white. It's a matter of preference. Buy what you like.

All Platonite bowls come with or without rims. Bowls without rims are more difficult to find, but those rimmed bowls tend to have more inner rim roughness which is a deterrent for collectors. Pastel pink 8" bowls with or without rims and yellow 12" platters are easier to find than other pastel colors. I suspect they were a premium item at one time which would account for their abundance. All other colored platters are rarely found. Children's dishes in this pattern have a section all their own, shown on pages 143 – 145.

	Pastel Colors	White or w/stripes	Deco/Red or Blue Willow
Bowl, 4¾", cream soup	6.50	4.00	20.00
Bowl, 5", berry, w/rim	5.00	3.00	12.50
Bowl, 5", berry, wo/rim	6.00		
Bowl, 5", deep cereal, w/white	7.50	4.00	
Bowl, 5", deep cereal, wo/white	9.00		
Bowl, 8", w/rim	*14.00	6.00	35.00
Bowl, 8", wo/rim	*20.00		
Bowl, 8¾", large berry		7.00	35.00
Creamer	5.00	4.00	20.00
Cup	3.50	2.50	20.00

	Pastel Colors	White or w/stripes	Deco/Red or Blue Willow
Mug, 4", 8 oz.		8.00	
Plate, 6¾", sherbet	4.50	2.50	9.00
Plate, 8⅞", dinner	6.50	3.50	25.00
Plate, 10½", sandwich	16.00	8.00	
Platter, 11", oval		12.50	35.00
Platter, 12", oval	**15.00	9.00	45.00
Salt and pepper, pr.	16.00	13.00	
Saucer	1.00	1.50	5.00
Sherbet	4.50	2.50	15.00
Sugar	5.00	4.00	20.00
Tumbler, 9 oz.	9.00		
Tumbler, cone, ftd.		6.00	

*Pink $9.00
* *Yellow $9.00

MODERNTONE PLATONITE, HAZEL ATLAS GLASS COMPANY, 1940 – EARLY 1950s (CONT.)

Colors: Dark Platonite fired-on colors

Unlike collecting pastel Moderntone, obtaining the darker, later colors will redefine perseverance! When compared to the quantities of pastel, there are minute amounts of darker colors available. Buy it whenever you find it.

The price listing below separates colors into two price groups based upon demand and availability. The first group consists of cobalt blue (page 142 left), turquoise green (top center page 139), lemon yellow (top left page 140), and orange (bottom page 140). All these colors can be eventually collected in sets with some effort. This group can be found with white or colored interiors. White interiors are more plentiful. Most collectors will take anything they can find. It only matters if you do not wish to mix the different color treatments made by Hazel Atlas. You can see both styles in each of these colors on the pages previously noted.

Gathering a set of any of the other colors, Chartreuse, Burgundy, Green, Gray, "rust," or "gold" is another mission. Should you undertake it, you will find that none of the previous colors are found with white interiors. These colors are shown at the top of page 143 except for Chartreuse that can only be seen on the right on page 139. Colors shown on the top of page 143 are as follows from left to right: Burgundy, Green, Gray, "rust," and "gold." Collectors have mistakenly called the Green "forest green" and the Burgundy "maroon." I have also heard the "gold" referred to as "butterscotch." As with pink, some collectors consider "gold" merely a variation of "lemon" yellow and not a separate color.

Several pieces listed under pastel are not to be found in the darker colors. So far, cream soups, bowls with rims, sandwich plates, and shakers have not been found in any of these darker colors! Green (dark) tumblers are the only color I have seen in the later colors. If you see others, please let me know!

With the advent of "rainbow" color collecting, many collectors are mixing the colors available with great success. I've seen pictures of some truly wonderful table arrangements.

	Cobalt Turquoise Lemon Orange	Burgundy Chartreuse Green/Gray Rust/Gold			Cobalt Turquoise Lemon Orange	Burgundy Chartreuse Green/Gray Rust/Gold
Bowl, 4¾", cream soup	10.00			Plate, 10½" sandwich	22.00	
Bowl, 5", berry, w/rim	11.00			Platter, 12" oval	22.00	32.00
Bowl, 5", berry, wo/rim	8.00	12.00		Salt and pepper, pr.	22.50	
Bowl, 5", deep cereal, w/white	12.00			Saucer	4.00	5.00
Bowl, 5", deep cereal, wo/white		15.00		Sherbet	7.00	9.00
Bowl, 8", w/rim	32.00			Sugar	8.00	11.00
Bowl, 8", wo/rim	32.00	37.50		Tumbler, 9 oz.	12.50	*25.00
Creamer	8.00	11.00				
Cup	7.00	8.00		*Green $17.50		
Plate, 6¾", sherbet	6.00	8.00				
Plate, 8⅞" dinner	12.00	13.00				

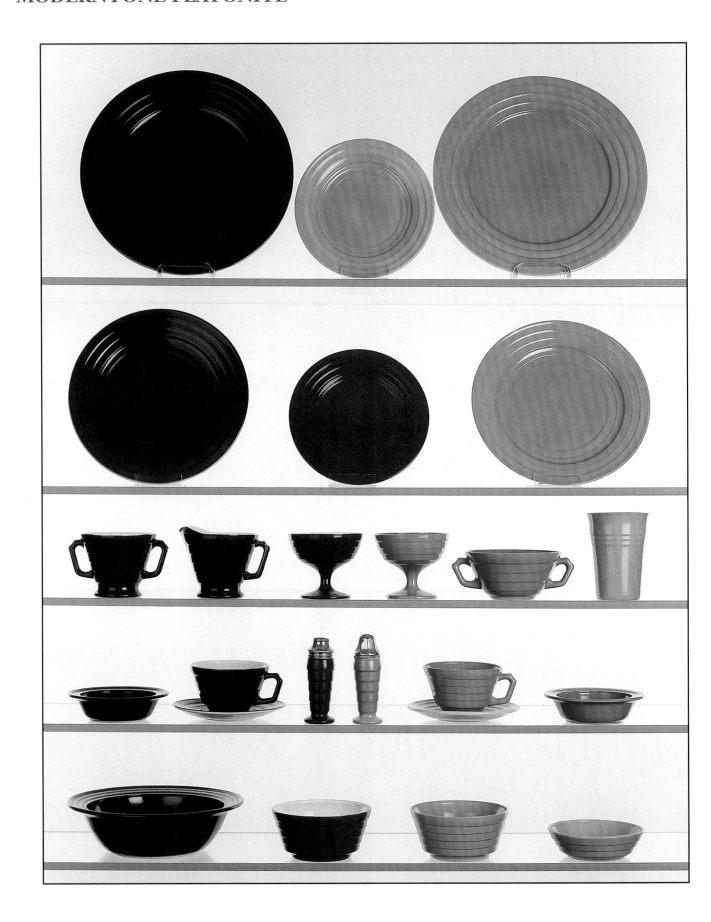

MODERNTONE "LITTLE HOSTESS PARTY DISHES"

HAZEL ATLAS GLASS COMPANY, EARLY 1950s

Moderntone "Little Hostess" sets cause a stir in collecting circles other than our Depression Glass world. Doll collectors and dealers also amass sets of children's dishes. Prices increase due to demand; and when there is **demand** from several collecting circles, prices tend to spiral accordingly.

The set pictured at the top of page 145 was a premium from Big Top Peanut Butter. My wife was given one as a gift in the early 50s. Big Top, the forerunner of Jif®, was also sold in juice, tea, and parfait glasses which are collectible today and referred to as "Peanut Butter" glass.

There is a price upsurge in the harder to find Moderntone colors. An unusual, all white set has been found in an original box. It is pictured in *Very Rare Glassware of the Depression Years, Fourth Series*. Teapots are the most difficult pieces to find, with the lids being harder to find than the bottoms. Mint condition teapot bottoms are rarely found. Lids were broken and thrown away, while bottoms, which were only chipped, were kept. Both parts sell about equally today. When buying Burgundy teapot tops or bottoms individually, you should be aware that Burgundy shades vary. The hues of color may not match.

The picture at the top of page 144 contains two sets, mixed. There are pieces from a pink and black set and an all-white set. I was trying to show several type sets in one photo, lest you be confused by this.

LITTLE HOSTESS PARTY SET Pink/Black/White (top 144)	
Cup, ¾", bright pink, white	17.50
Saucer, 3⅞", black, white	12.00
Plate, 5¼", black, bright pink, white	15.00
Creamer, 1¾", bright pink	20.00
Sugar, 1¾", bright pink	20.00
Teapot, 3½", bright pink	85.00
Teapot lid, black	85.00
Set, 16-piece	380.00

LITTLE HOSTESS PARTY SET Lemon/Beige/Pink/Aqua (bottom 144)	
Cup, ¾", bright pink/aqua/lemon	17.50
Saucer, 3⅞", same	12.00
Plate, 5¼", same	15.00
Creamer, 1¾", pink	20.00
Sugar, 1¾", pink	20.00
Teapot, 3½", brown	85.00

Teapot lid, lemon	85.00
Set, 16-piece	390.00

LITTLE HOSTESS PARTY SET Gray/Rust/Gold Turquoise (top 145)	
Cup, ¾", gray, rust	13.00
Cup, ¾", gold, turquoise	13.00
Saucer, 3⅞", all four colors	8.00
Plate, 5¼", same	8.00
Creamer, 1¾", rust	15.00
Sugar, 1¾", rust	15.00
Teapot, 3½", turquoise	62.50
Teapot lid, turquoise	62.50
Set, 16-piece	290.00

LITTLE HOSTESS PARTY SET Green/Gray/Chartreuse/ Burgundy (bottom 145 left)	
Cup, ¾", green, gray, chartreuse	10.00
Cup, ¾", burgundy	13.00

Saucer, 3⅞", Green, Gray & Burgundy, Chartreuse	7.00
Plate, 5¼", Burgundy	10.00
Plate, 5¼", green, gray, chartreuse	8.00
Creamer, 1¾", Chartreuse	12.50
Sugar, 1¾", Chartreuse	12.50
Teapot, 3½", Burgundy	55.00
Teapot lid, Burgundy	60.00
Set, 16-piece	245.00

LITTLE HOSTESS PARTY SET Pastel pink/green/blue yellow (bottom 145 right)	
Cup, ¾", all four colors	9.00
Saucer, 3⅞", same	7.00
Plate, 5¼", same	10.00
Creamer, 1¾", pink	15.00
Sugar, 1¾", pink	15.00
Set, 14-piece	110.00

MOONSTONE, ANCHOR HOCKING GLASS CORPORATION, 1941 – 1946

Colors: crystal with opalescent hobnails and some green with opalescent hobnails; other experimental colors

Moonstone is truly 1940s glassware. This was predominately displayed in all the five-and-dime stores during the middle of the war. The photograph of a J. J. Newberry store window display on page 148 is one example of how well this glassware was promoted. I wish more records like this could be found!

There are quite a few experimental pieces showing up in Moonstone, including a 9¼" dinner plate. Had that plate been a production item, this set would attract more collectors. Collectors tend to avoid sets without dinner plates. You can see the dinner plate, a toothpick, and a 7¾" divided relish without a crimped edge in *Very Rare Glassware of the Depression Years, Fifth Series.* Yes, new items continue to surface! Most of the pieces pictured below (and at the top of page 147) are from Hocking's morgue. (Discontinued or experimental items were stored in some place appropriately called a morgue.) Some of these pieces may have found their way home with factory workers on the days they were produced. It happened!

The most troublesome normal production pieces to find today are 5½" berry bowls (bottom of page 147) listed as M277 in the Hocking brochure on page 148. There are none of those in the store display photo either! Admittedly, goblets and cups and saucers are also excluded in that store window display; and they are easily found today.

Ruffled 5½" bowls are more available than their straight-side counterparts; but even they are not as abundant as once believed. The sandwich plate measures 10¾" instead of 10" as erroneously listed. I have seen very few of these of late. Moonstone is a pattern that has gently slipped away into collections. Little is seen at shows and there are fewer quantities appearing in the market place.

Green Moonstone was issued under the name "Ocean Green" and was made in sets containing goblets, cups, saucers, plates, creamer, and sugar. Notice the two pieces shown are slightly different from the standard line in the catalog pages on 148.

Fenton Opalescent Hobnail pitchers and tumblers are good companion pieces to go with Anchor Hocking Moonstone sets since there are no pitchers, flat tumblers, or shakers found in Moonstone. Those found are Fenton. There is also no Moonstone cologne bottle about which I must receive a dozen letters a year. The Fenton pieces look fine with Moonstone; and, if you would like additional pieces that are similar to your pattern, buy them! The hobs on the Fenton are more pointed than on Moonstone, but the colors match very well. Glass companies often mimicked contemporary wares. That still occurs.

	Opalescent Hobnail			Opalescent Hobnail
Bowl, 5½", berry	17.00	Cup		8.00
Bowl, 5½", crimped, dessert	9.50	Goblet, 10 oz.		18.00
Bowl, 6½", crimped, handled	10.00	Heart bonbon, one handle		14.00
Bowl, 7¾", flat	12.00	Plate, 6¼", sherbet		6.00
Bowl, 7¾", divided relish	12.00	Plate, 8⅜", luncheon		15.00
Bowl, 9½", crimped	25.00	Plate, 10¾", sandwich		27.50
Bowl, cloverleaf	13.00	Puff box and cover, 4¾", round		25.00
Candle holder, pr.	18.00	Saucer (same as sherbet plate)		6.00
Candy jar and cover, 6"	28.00	Sherbet, footed		7.00
Cigarette jar and cover	23.00	Sugar, footed		9.00
Creamer	9.00	Vase, 5½", bud		13.00

LADIES & CHILDREN ANKLETS
LADIES & CHILDREN ANKLETS
FOUNDATION GARMENTS
STAR DUST Slips
BEAUTIFUL
MOONSTONE
WARE
J. J. NEWBERRY CO.

Opalescent "MOONSTONE" Glassware
"MOONSTONE" Glassware
DOZ. TO CTN.
WT. OF CTN.
Tableware
M2779— 3⅞" Cup 6 32#
M2729— 6¼" Saucer 6 32#
M2713— 6 oz. Sherbet 6 32#
M2729— 6¼" Sherbet Plate 6 32#
M2775— 5½" Dessert 6 32#
M2716—10 oz. Goblet 4 36#
M2740— 8⅜" Luncheon Plate 4 44#
Gift Ware
M2769— 7¾" Divided Relish 2 27#
M2766— 6½" Crimped Handled Bowl 2 19#
M2755— 6¾" Clover Leaf Dish 2 22#
M2772— 6½" Heart Bonbon 2 20#
M2767— 7¾" Flat Bowl 2 23#
M2753— 3¼" Sugar 2 13#
M2754— 3¼" Creamer 2 12½#
M2722— 4¾" Puff Box & Cover 2 22#
M2799— 5" Cigarette Jar & Cover 2 25#
M2782— 5½" Vase 2 16#
M2792— 6" Candy Jar & Cover 1 20#
M2760—10¾" Sandwich Plate 1 21#
M2768— 9½" Crimped Bowl 1 21#
M2765— 5½" Crimped Dessert 6 33#
M2781— 4¼" Candleholder 2 10#
Suggested Sets - Bulk Packed
M2700/1—7 Pce. Dessert Set 12 Sets 54#
(Bulk Packed in 2 Cartons)
M2700/2—4 Pce. Buffet Set 12 Sets 52#
(Bulk Packed in 3 Cartons)
M 2779
M 2729
M 2713
M 2729
M 2775
M2716
M2740
M2769
M2766
M2772
M2755
M2767
M2722
M2792
M2753
M2754
M2799
M2782
M2768
M2700/1 SET
M2760
M2781
M2765
M2700/2 SET
Now Available at Low Prices
105
105

MOROCCAN AMETHYST, HAZEL WARE, DIVISION OF CONTINENTAL CAN, 1960s

Color: Amethyst

Moroccan Amethyst is an agreeable purple color found on several different mould lines of Hazel Ware glass. As with Anchor Hocking's Forest Green and Royal Ruby, the color took preference over the patterns on which it was made, hence its "color moniker" with collectors.

Square or rectangular based pieces (top page 150) are being called Colony as they are in Capri. Bottom of page 150 shows the Moroccan Swirl, also found in Capri. On the top of page 151 you can see Octagonal, Pentagonal, and other assorted designs that are also seen in Capri.

One of the most interesting pieces pictured on page 151 is the apple-shaped salad bowl with an apple blossom in the bottom. You may find this apple-shaped bowl in fired-on Platonite, usually in Chartreuse or Green; however the apple blossom design is missing from the bottom of these bowls. There is also a floral design in the bottom of the 4½" square ash tray, but it is covered by an original Moroccan Amethyst sticker which I wouldn't let the photographer remove! The 4½" five-pointed star candlesticks are an additional find.

The top of page 151 reveals other colors being found with the swirled design. Crystal and white stemware are also being found that match the Moroccan designs. You will find swirled bowls in green, amber, and white! These bowls are usually reasonably priced. I imagine that they are a later production made to go with the 1970s Avocado and Harvest Gold colors.

Pieces that are beginning to disappear from markets include the ice bucket, eight ounce old fashioned tumbler, cocktail shaker, and the short, covered candy dish. You can find the tall candy without much difficulty. The lids to these candy jars are interchangeable. This was another case of economy in mould usage. There is a new collecting fraternity that is buying boxed sets; these are now fetching a premium especially if the box has pictures of the glassware contained inside.

An amethyst and white punch bowl set, called Alpine by the factory, can be seen on the bottom of page 151. The punch cups have open handles to hang onto the side of the punch bowl. I have seen some exceptional prices on that set. (They are actually selling for $150.00.) A "Seashell" snack set in the same two colors was also labeled "Alpine." The amethyst bowl pictured on the left of page 150 served not only as a bowl, but also as the punch bowl base. Many companies' punch bowl bases had additional functions that saved paying for another expensive mould.

"The Magic Hour" 4-piece cocktail set on page 153 features a clock showing six o'clock and says "yours" on one side and "mine" on the other. In this boxed set are two 4 ounce tumblers (2½" tall) and a spouted cocktail mixer with a metal stirring spoon. You will find two and three-tier tidbit trays made from assorted pieces (bowls, plates, ash trays).

Not much sprayed red over crystal is being found; although uncommon, there is little demand for it at present. Crystal, amber, and green pieces made from these moulds may someday be desirable.

	Amethyst		Amethyst
Ash tray, 3¼", triangular	5.50	Goblet, 4⅜", 5½ oz., juice	9.00
Ash tray, 3¼", round	5.50	Goblet, 5½", 9 oz., water	10.00
Ash tray, 6⅞", triangular	9.50	Ice bucket, 6"	37.50
Ash tray, 8", square	13.00	Plate, 5¾"	4.50
Bowl, 4¾", fruit, octagonal	7.50	Plate, 7¼", salad	7.00
Bowl, 5¾", deep, square	10.00	Plate, 8", square	12.00
Bowl, 6", round	11.00	Plate, 8", square, snack	10.00
Bowl, 7¾", oval	16.00	Plate, 9¾", dinner	9.00
Bowl. 7¾", rectangular	14.00	Plate, 10", fan shaped, snack w/cup rest	8.00
Bowl. 7¾", rectangular w/ metal handle	18.00	Plate, 12", round	15.00
Bowl, 10¾"	30.00	Plate, 12", sandwich, w/metal /handle	17.50
Candy w/lid short	35.00	Saucer	1.00
Candy w/lid tall	35.00	Tumbler, 4 oz., juice, 2½"	8.50
Chip and dip, 10¾" & 5¾" bowls in metal holder	40.00	Tumbler, 8 oz., old fashioned, 3¼"	14.00
Cocktail w/stirrer, 6¼", 16 oz., w/lip	32.00	Tumbler, 9 oz., water	10.00
Cocktail shaker w/lid	30.00	Tumbler, 11 oz., water, crinkled bottom, 4¼"	12.00
Cup	5.00	Tumbler, 11 oz., water, 4⅝"	12.00
Goblet, 4", 4½ oz., wine	10.00	Tumbler, 16 oz., iced tea, 6½"	16.00
Goblet, 4¼", 7½ oz., sherbet	7.50	Vase, 8½", ruffled	37.50

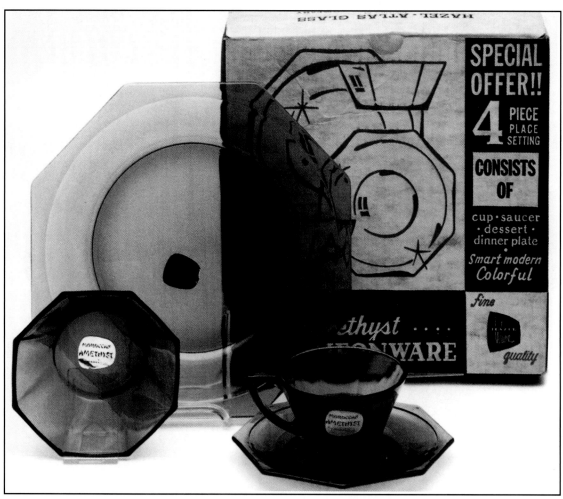

Colors: blue, crystal, pink, and Shell Pink

National is a Jeannette pattern recognized by collectors by sight, but rarely by name. Two pieces of National are more familiar to collectors of Shell Pink than anyone else. The candy bottom is seen frequently in Shell Pink, perhaps even more so than in crystal. You will find many crystal candy dishes are gold trimmed. The so called "heavy bottomed Shell Pink 9" vase" is actually a National vase. How that vase escaped being recognized as National for years is beyond me.

National is a heavy, bold pattern filled with serving pieces, but having only a basic luncheon set for the table. The log-like handles on the cup, creamer, and sugar are reminiscent of early pattern glass. The Lazy Susan and the punch set are reasonably priced and are sensible gifts for a beginning or non collector! They can be used. I am convinced there are additional pieces in the pattern. When adding new patterns to a book, I always try to find as many pieces and get as many items listed as possible, a formidable task. Complete listings (sometimes, even with company catalogs) is nearly impossible. I am always appreciative of your help in adding to the listings and recently, I have had several collectors tell me to express their thanks to all who write and make contributions to the body of knowledge.

Ash tray, small	3.00		Plate, 8", salad	5.00
Ash tray, large	4.00		Plate, 15", serving/punch liner	15.00
Bowl, 4½", berry	4.00		Punch bowl, 12"	25.00
Bowl, 8½", large berry	13.00		Punch bowl stand	15.00
Bowl, 12", flat	14.00		Punch cup	3.00
Candle, three ftd	15.00		Punch set, 15-pc.	90.00
Candy, ftd., w/cover	22.50		Relish, 13", 6-part	15.00
Cigarette box	12.50		Saucer	1.00
Creamer	5.00		Shakers, pr.	9.00
Cup	3.00		Sugar	5.00
Jar, relish	12.50		Tray, 8", hndl., sug/cr	5.00
Lazy Susan	35.00		Tray, 12½", hndl.	15.00
Pitcher, 20 oz., milk	17.50		Tumbler, 5⅛", ftd.	8.00
Pitcher, 64 oz.	27.50		Vase, 9"	18.00

NAVARRE, PLATE ETCHING #327, FOSTORIA GLASS COMPANY, 1937 – 1982

Colors: crystal, blue, pink, and rare in green

Most Navarre was sold after 1940, although it was first introduced in 1937. I have included it in this book as well as my *Elegar* book. This is the only overlapping pattern of Elegant glassware in this *Collectible Glassware of the 40s, 50s, 60s....* You will note there are a few patterns that were in the *Elegant* book that have now been moved to the time frame of this book.

Numerous (now hard to find) pieces were made near the end of Fostoria's reign (late 1970s and early 1980s). A majority of these pieces were signed "Fostoria" with acid etching on the base; a small number had only a sticker. Factory "seconds" that sold throug the outlet stores were rarely signed. Quality signed pieces were run through the outlets only when those stores ran short of second:

I had a knowledgeable Navarre collector approach me in Oregon last year and ask me to remove from the listing the #249 celery since it was never made; consider it done!

Shown on page 157 are a few of the later made pieces of Navarre. The price on many of these items has really skyrockete since the last book. They were already too exorbitantly priced for many Navarre collectors to own, but they are more so now You will find that assembling a crystal set of Navarre will be a time-consuming chore, but it can still be done with patience. Possibly only moneyed collectors can afford to build a set with all pieces.

The top row of page 157 shows water goblets, a magnum (center), and continental champagnes. The second row shows the large claret, regular claret, saucer champagnes, low sherbet, oyster cocktail, and bells. On the third row are footed teas, footed water, footed juice, double old fashioned, highball, and cordial. Some of the items pictured in the top three rows were made in blue and pink. Colored items are priced separately in the listings. The fourth row shows a 10½" footed #2470½ bowl, a three part candy, and a #2545 "Flame" oval bowl. The bottom shelf holds a #2482 triple candlestick, #2440 sugar and creamer, and the "Flame" double candlestick. Parts of several 1982 catalog sheets are reprinted on page 159. They display pieces made at the end of Fostoria's production.

	Crystal	Blue/Pink		Crystal	Blue/Pink
Bell, dinner	75.00	95.00	Plate, #2440, 10½" oval cake	55.00	
Bowl, #2496, 4", square, hndl.	12.00		Plate, #2496, 14", torte	65.00	
Bowl, #2496, 4⅜", hndl.	12.00		Plate, #2364, 16", torte	100.00	
Bowl, #869, 4½", finger	75.00		Relish, #2496, 6", 2-part, square	32.50	
Bowl, #2496, 4⅝", tri-cornered	25.00		Relish, #2496, 10" x 7½", 3-part	47.50	
Bowl, #2496, 5", hndl., ftd.	25.00		Relish, #2496, 10", 4-part	75.00	
Bowl, #2496, 6", square, sweetmeat	30.00		Relish, #2419, 13¼", 5-part	95.00	
Bowl, #2496, 6¼", 3 ftd., nut	22.00		Salt & pepper, #2364, 3¼", flat, pr.	70.00	
Bowl, #2496, 7⅜", ftd., bonbon	50.00		Salt & pepper, #2375, 3½", ftd., pr.	115.00	
Bowl, #2496, 10", oval, floating garden	80.00		Salad dressing bottle, #2083, 6½"	425.00	
Bowl, #2496, 10½", hndl., ftd.	75.00		Sauce dish, #2496, div. mayo., 6½"	50.00	
Bowl, #2470½, 10½", ftd.	75.00		Sauce dish, #2496, 6½" x 5¼"	75.00	
Bowl, #2496, 12", flared	62.50		Sauce dish liner, #2496, 8", oval	30.00	
Bowl, #2545, 12½", oval, "Flame"	85.00		Saucer, #2440	5.00	
Candlestick, #2496, 4"	25.00		Stem, #6106, ¾ oz., cordial, 3⅞"	50.00	
Candlestick, #2496, 4½", double	35.00		Stem, #6106, 3¼ oz., wine, 5½"	40.00	
Candlestick, #2472, 5", double	55.00		Stem, #6106, 3½ oz., cocktail, 6"	25.00	
Candlestick, #2496, 5½"	30.00		Stem, #6106, 4 oz., oyster cocktail, 3⅝"	30.00	
Candlestick, #2496, 6", triple	60.00		Stem, #6106, 4½ oz., claret, 6"	55.00	85.00
Candlestick, #2545, 6¾", double, "Flame"	75.00		Stem, #6106, 5 oz., continental		
Candlestick, #2482, 6¾", triple	85.00		champagne, 8⅛"	110.00	135.00
Candy, w/cover, #2496, 3-part	125.00		Stem, #6106, 6 oz., cocktail/sherry, 6³⁄₁₆"	75.00	
Celery, #2440, 11½"	50.00		Stem, #6106, 6 oz., low sherbet, 4⅜"	24.00	
Comport, #2496, 3¼", cheese	35.00		Stem, #6106, 6 oz., saucer champagne, 5⅝"	24.00	40.00
Comport, #2400, 4½"	35.00		Stem, #6106, 6½ oz., large claret, 6½"	50.00	70.00
Comport, #2496, 4¾"	30.00		Stem, #6106, 10 oz., water, 7⅝"	35.00	50.00
Cracker, #2496, 11" plate	42.50		Stem, #6106, 15 oz., brandy inhaler, 5½"	110.00	
Creamer, #2440, 4¼", ftd.	20.00		Stem, #6106, 16 oz., magnum, 7¼"	160.00	150.00
Creamer, #2496, individual	20.00		Sugar, #2440, 3⅝", ftd.	20.00	
Cup, #2440	20.00		Sugar, #2496, individual	20.00	
Ice bucket, #2496, 4⅜" high	120.00		Syrup, #2586, Sani-cut, 5½"	425.00	
Ice bucket, #2375, 6" high	150.00		Tidbit, #2496, 8¼", 3-ftd., turned up edge	30.00	
Mayonnaise, #2375, 3-piece	75.00		Tray, #2496½, for ind. sugar/creamer	35.00	
Mayonnaise, #2496½, 3-piece	75.00		Tumbler, #6106, 5 oz., ftd., juice, 4⅝"	25.00	
Pickle, #2496, 8"	30.00		Tumbler, #6106, 10 oz., ftd., water, 5⅜"	25.00	
Pickle, #2440, 6½"	37.50		Tumbler, #6106, 12 oz., flat, highball, 4⅞"	95.00	
Pitcher, #2666, 32 oz.	250.00		Tumbler, #6106, 13 oz., flat,		
Pitcher, #5000, 48 oz., ftd.	345.00		double old fashioned, 3⅝"	85.00	
Plate, #2440, 6", bread/butter	11.00		Tumbler, #6106, 13 oz., ftd., tea, 5⅞"	32.00	60.00
Plate, #2440, 7½", salad	15.00		Vase, #4108, 5"	90.00	
Plate, #2440, 8½", luncheon	22.50		Vase, #4121, 5"	90.00	
Plate, #2440, 9½", dinner	52.50		Vase, #4128, 5"	90.00	
Plate, #2496, 10", hndl., cake	50.00		Vase, #2470, 10", ftd.	225.00	

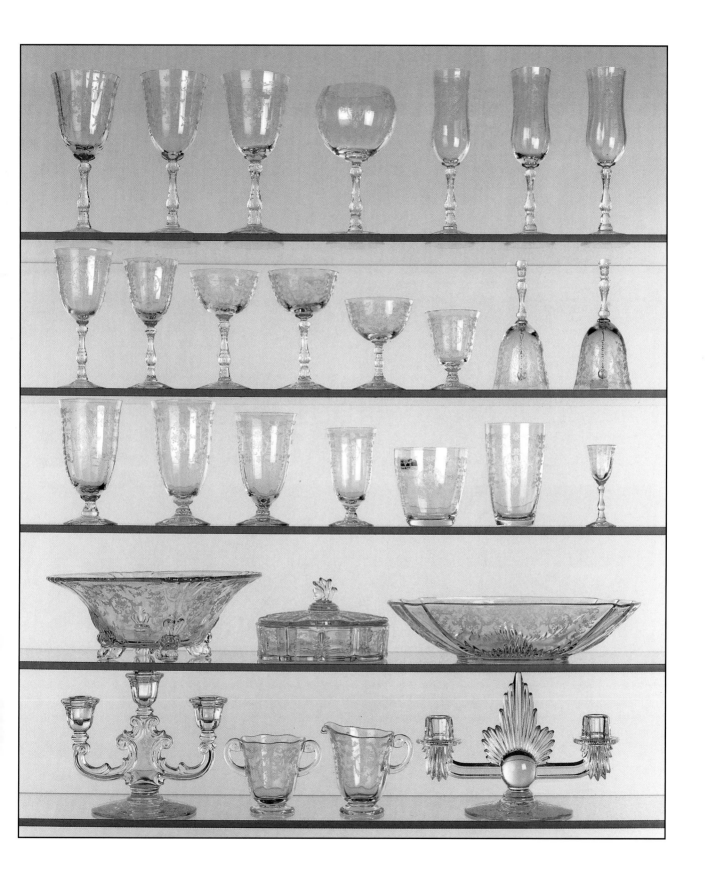

Yours ALL SPARKLE AND NICE

Every dinner is fun when table settings are all sparkle and nice. It's easy to have this glamour when you harmonize china for color, silver for gleam and crystal for glitter. So be sure to select with all three in mind. *Navarre*, for instance, is one of many handlaid "Master-Etchings". You'll love its bubble-thin bowl, its frosty, dainty decoration. You'll find *Navarre*, and many other Fostoria patterns, at better stores everywhere.

FOSTORIA

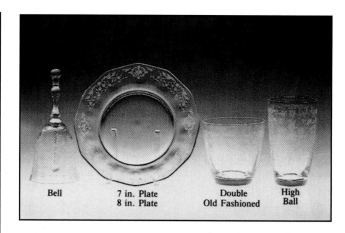

Bell · 7 in. Plate / 8 in. Plate · Double Old Fashioned · High Ball

Wilma Blue Goblet · Wilma Crystal Goblet · Navarre Crystal Goblet · Low Dessert/Champagne · High Dessert/Champagne

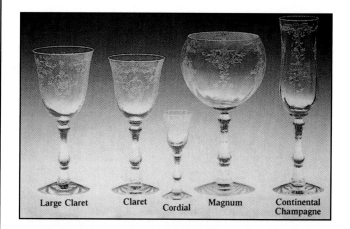

Large Claret · Claret · Cordial · Magnum · Continental Champagne

Luncheon Goblet/Ice Tea · Footed Juice · Brandy Inhaler · Cocktail/Sherry

NEW ERA #4044, A.H. Heisey Co., 1934 – 1941; 1944 – 1957 (stems, celery tray, and candlesticks)

Colors: crystal, frosted crystal, some cobalt with crystal stem and foot

Production of New Era was launched in the 1930s; but the abundant stemware seen these days fits the 50s setting of this book. New Era is often sought by Art Deco collectors. Stems always attract new collectors! Little do they realize how difficult any serving piece is to find. Fortunately, New Era stemware can be utilized with a diversity of patterns, old or new.

New Era stems **can** be found with cobalt bowls on crystal stems. Three are pictured. Any New Era piece with a cobalt bowl will fetch $125.00 to $150.00. Keep that in the memory bank on your excursions!

The double branched candelabra with the New Era bobeches is not terribly hard to find and is very appealing. Dinner plates without scratches in that plain, flat center and after-dinner cups and saucers will keep you shopping for a long time unless you are very lucky! Remember though, **searching** is part of the **fun** in collecting!

The decanter pictured below is rarely seen; watch for them. You will also find New Era pieces where the borders have been satinized (frosted). These tend to show off the pattern, but can go unrecognized as New Era. I confess, I once left six dinner plates in an antique mall in central Ohio for $10.00 each because I didn't recognize the pattern with the satinized look!

	Crystal		Crystal
Ash tray or indiv. nut	30.00	Stem, 1 oz. cordial	45.00
Bottle, rye w/stopper	120.00	Stem, 3 oz. wine	35.00
Bowl, 11" floral	35.00	Stem, 3½ oz., high, cocktail	12.00
Candelabra, 2 lite w/2 #4044 bobeche & prisms	70.00	Stem, 3½ oz. oyster cocktail	12.00
Creamer	37.50	Stem, 4 oz. claret	18.00
Cup	10.00	Stem, 6 oz. sherbet, low	12.50
Cup, after dinner	62.50	Stem, 6 oz. champagne	12.50
Pilsner, 8 oz.	27.50	Stem, 10 oz. goblet	16.00
Pilsner, 12 oz.	32.50	Sugar	37.50
Plate, 5½" x 4½" bread & butter	15.00	Tray, 13" celery	30.00
Plate, 9"x 7", luncheon	25.00	Tumbler, 5 oz. ftd. soda	8.00
Plate, 10" x 8", dinner	45.00	Tumbler, 8 oz. ftd. soda	11.00
Relish, 13" 3-part	25.00	Tumbler, 10 oz., low, ftd.	11.00
Saucer	5.00	Tumbler, 12 oz. ftd. soda	14.00
Saucer, after dinner	12.50	Tumbler, 14 oz. ftd. soda	17.50

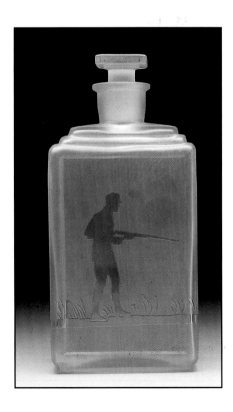 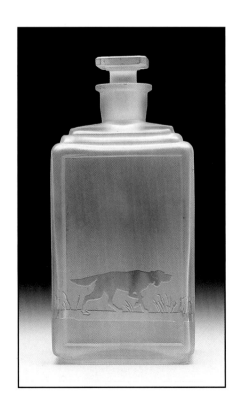

NEWPORT, "HAIRPIN," HAZEL ATLAS GLASS COMPANY, 1940 – EARLY 1950S

Colors: Platonite white and fired-on colors

Hazel Atlas made Newport in several transparent colors in the late 1930s; subsequently, they made it in Platonite until the early 1950s. Thus, Newport's listings are split between this 50s book and *The Collector's Encyclopedia of Depression Glass*. Cobalt blue, amethyst, and pink were made before 1940; and Platonite (opaque) white and white with fired-on colors was a popular line for Hazel Atlas beginning in the 1940s. Newport is another pattern that lends itself to "rainbow" collecting. The colors are numerous as you can see from the photographs. Actually, a mixture of colors seems to work well.

Notice the white edge on the fired-on pink plate in the rear. The edges and back of this plate are white. The pink (or other pastel color) decorates only the top. Evidently, the first colors manufactured all had white interiors. However, the turquoise blue bowl and dark green plate have colors fired both front and back. One collector mentioned that she bought the darker colors in both Newport and Moderntone. Since these were both made by Hazel Atlas, the colors do match.

There are nine tumblers illustrated on page 163. Have you any other color? I doubt that only nine colors were made. That is an odd number, if true.

White Platonite comes in two distinct hues. One is very opalescent white and the other is a flat white similar to milk glass. The Newport white shaker is often used by Petalware collectors for their pattern since there are no shakers in the MacBeth Evans set. It is not unprecedented for collectors to be fooled into thinking these shakers really are Petalware.

	White	Fired-on colors
Bowl, 4¾", berry	3.50	5.50
Bowl, 4¾", cream soup	5.50	9.00
Bowl, 8¼, large berry	9.50	15.00
Cup	3.50	6.00
Creamer	4.50	7.50
Plate, 6", sherbet	1.00	1.50
Plate, 8½", luncheon	3.00	5.00
Plate, 11½", sandwich	10.00	16.00
Platter, 11¾", oval	12.00	18.00
Salt and pepper, pr.	18.00	25.00
Saucer	.75	1.00
Sherbet	3.50	6.00
Sugar	4.50	7.50
Tumbler		22.00

ORCHID, ETCHING #1507 ON WAVERLY BLANK #1519 AND QUEEN ANN BLANK #1509,

A.H. HEISEY & CO., 1940 – 1957

Colors: crystal

Orchid is found etched on two Heisey mould blanks. Blank #1519, known as Waverly, is illustrated on page 165 as well as the plate on the left on page 166. Blank #1509, or Queen Ann, is pictured on page 167 along with the plate on the right on page 166.

Serving pieces and flatware items have risen slowly in price the past two years; but prices on a few pieces of stemware have been slowly dropping! Particularly, water goblets, high sherbets, and iced teas have softened due to an oversupply at present. Remember, I am noting what is going now and not attempting to foretell what will happen if suddenly everyone chooses to collect Orchid. If that happens, then the supply could diminish overnight!

	Crystal		Crystal
Ash tray, 3"	30.00	Bowl, 11", ftd., floral	115.00
Basket, 8½", LARIAT	1,200.00	Bowl, 12", crimped, floral, WAVERLY	95.00
Bell, dinner, #5022 or #5025	135.00	Bowl, 13", floral	115.00
Bottle, 8 oz., French dressings	195.00	Bowl, 13", crimped, floral, WAVERLY	95.00
Bowl, finger, #3309 or #5025	90.00	Bowl, 13", gardenia	70.00
Bowl, 4½", nappy, QUEEN ANN	37.50	Butter, w/cover, ¼ lb., CABOCHON	325.00
Bowl, 5½", ftd., mint, QUEEN ANN	37.50	Butter, w/cover, 6", WAVERLY	160.00
Bowl, 6", jelly, 2 hndl., QUEEN ANN.	37.50	Candleholder, 6", deep epernette, WAVERLY	1,000.00
Bowl, 6" oval, lemon, w/cover, QUEEN ANN	310.00	Candlestick, 1-lite, MERCURY	45.00
Bowl, 6", oval, lemon, w/cover, WAVERLY	895.00	Candlestick, 1-lite, QUEEN ANN, w/prisms	135.00
Bowl, 6½", ftd., honey, cheese, QUEEN ANN	42.50	Candlestick, 2-lite, FLAME	160.00
Bowl, 6½", ftd., jelly, WAVERLY	65.00	Candlestick, 5", 2-lite, TRIDENT	55.00
Bowl, 6½", 2 pt., oval, dressings, WAVERLY	50.00	Candlestick, 2-lite, WAVERLY	65.00
Bowl, 7", lily, QUEEN ANN	125.00	Candlestick, 3-lite, CASCADE	85.00
Bowl, 7", salad	60.00	Candlestick, 3-lite, WAVERLY	100.00
Bowl, 7", 3 pt., rnd., relish	55.00	Candy box, w/cover, 6", low ft.	175.00
Bowl, 7", ftd., honey, cheese, WAVERLY	55.00	Candy, w/cover, 5", high ft., WAVERLY	250.00
Bowl, 7", ftd., jelly	45.00	Candy, w/cover, 6", bow knot finial	175.00
Bowl, 7", ftd., oval, nut, WAVERLY	90.00	Cheese (comport) & cracker (11½") plate	135.00
Bowl, 8", mint, ftd., QUEEN ANN	65.00	Cheese & cracker, 14", plate	155.00
Bowl, 8", nappy, QUEEN ANN	70.00	Chocolate, w/cover, 5", WAVERLY	220.00
Bowl, 8", 2 pt., oval, dressings, ladle	55.00	Cigarette box, w/cover, 4", PURITAN	140.00
Bowl, 8", pt., rnd., relish	62.50	Cigarette holder, #4035	85.00
Bowl, 8½", flared, QUEEN ANN	67.50	Cigarette holder, w/cover	165.00
Bowl, 8½", floral, 2 hndl., ftd., QUEEN ANN	65.00	Cocktail icer, w/liner, UNIVERSAL, #3304	250.00
Bowl, 9", 4 pt., rnd., relish	75.00	Cocktail shaker, pt., #4225	275.00
Bowl, 9", ftd., fruit or salad	135.00	Cocktail shaker, qt., #4036 or #4225	225.00
Bowl, 9", gardenia, QUEEN ANN	65.00	Comport, 5½", blown	95.00
Bowl, 9", salad, WAVERLY	175.00	Comport, 6", low ft., WAVERLY	55.00
Bowl, 9½", crimped, floral, QUEEN ANN	75.00	Comport, 6½", low ft., WAVERLY	60.00
Bowl, 9½", epergne	525.00	Comport, 7", ftd., oval	145.00
Bowl, 10", crimped	72.50	Creamer, individual	35.00
Bowl, 10", deep salad	150.00	Creamer, ftd.	35.00
Bowl, 10", gardenia	75.00	Cup, WAVERLY or QUEEN ANN	42.50
Bowl, 10½", ftd., floral	115.00	Decanter, oval, sherry, pt.	250.00
Bowl, 11", shallow, rolled edge	70.00	Decanter, pt., ftd., #4036	325.00
Bowl, 11", 3-ftd., floral, seahorse ft.	150.00	Decanter, pt., #4036½	250.00
Bowl, 11", 3-pt., oblong, relish	70.00	Ice bucket, ftd., QUEEN ANN	250.00
Bowl, 11", 4-ftd., oval	125.00	Ice bucket, 2 hndl., WAVERLY	425.00
Bowl, 11", flared	135.00	Marmalade, w/cover	235.00
Bowl, 11", floral	70.00	Mayonnaise and liner, #1495, FERN	250.00

ORCHID

	Crystal
Mayonnaise, 5½", 1 hndl.	55.00
Mayonnaise, 5½", ftd.	55.00
Mayonnaise, 5½", 1 hndl., div.	50.00
Mayonnaise, 6½", 1 hndl.	65.00
Mayonnaise, 6½", 1 hndl., div.	65.00
Mustard, w/cover, QUEEN ANN	145.00
Oil, 3 oz., ftd.	185.00
Pitcher, 73 oz.	475.00
Pitcher, 64 oz., ice tankard	550.00
Plate, 6"	13.00
Plate, 7", mayonnaise	20.00
Plate, 7", salad	22.00
Plate, 8", salad, WAVERLY	24.00
Plate, 10½", dinner	150.00
Plate, 11", demi-torte	62.50
Plate, 11", sandwich	75.00
Plate, 12", ftd., salver, WAVERLY	250.00
Plate, 12", rnd sandwich, hndl.	70.00
Plate, 14", ftd., cake or salver	300.00
Plate, 14", torte, rolled edge	65.00
Plate, 14", torte, WAVERLY	90.00
Plate, 14", sandwich, WAVERLY	80.00
Plate, 15", sandwich, WAVERLY	75.00
Plate, 15½", QUEEN ANN	110.00
Salt & pepper, pr.	85.00
Salt & pepper, ftd., pr., WAVERLY	80.00
Saucer, WAVERLY or QUEEN ANN	12.50
Stem, #5022 or #5025, 1 oz., cordial	125.00

	Crystal
Stem, #5022 or #5025, 2 oz., sherry	125.00
Stem, #5022 or #5025, 3 oz., wine	80.00
Stem, #5022 or #5025, 4 oz., oyster cocktail	60.00
Stem, #5025, 4 oz., cocktail	40.00
Stem, #5022 or #5025, 4½ oz., claret	145.00
Stem, #5022 or #5025, 6 oz., saucer champagne	30.00
Stem, #5022 or #5025, 6 oz., sherbet	25.00
Stem, #5022 or #5025, 10 oz., low water goblet	37.50
Stem, #5022 or #5025, 10 oz., water goblet	42.50
Sugar, individual	35.00
Sugar, ftd.	35.00
Tray, indiv., creamer/sugar, QUEEN ANN	90.00
Tray, 12", celery	55.00
Tray, 13", celery	60.00
Tumbler, #5022 or #5025, 5 oz., fruit	55.00
Tumbler, #5022 or #5025, 12 oz., iced tea	65.00
Vase, 4", ftd., violet, WAVERLY	125.00
Vase, 6", crimped top	125.00
Vase, 7", ftd., fan, lariat	110.00
Vase, 7", ftd.	140.00
Vase, 7", crimped top, LARIAT	120.00
Vase, 8", ftd., bud	215.00
Vase, 8", sq., ftd., bud	225.00
Vase, 10", sq., ftd., bud	295.00
Vase, 12"	375.00
Vase, 14"	695.00

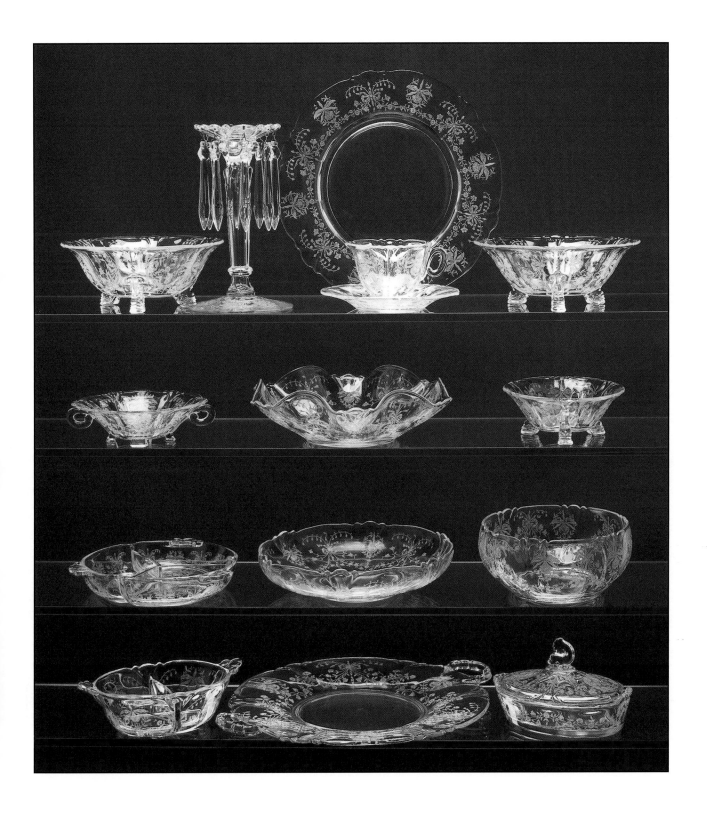

OVIDE, INCORRECTLY DUBBED "NEW CENTURY," HAZEL ATLAS GLASS COMPANY, 1930 – 1950s

Colors: green, black, white Platonite, and white with trimmed or fired-on colors in 1950s

As with Newport, Hazel Atlas's Ovide began production in the Depression era mostly in transparent colors; yet, it continued well into the 1950s with opaque Platonite. Pattern names have surfaced for some of the pastel-banded Platonite that was used in restaurants. It competed with Anchor Hocking's Jade-ite Restaurant Ware line. Very few of the combination colors pictured here are found today. Evidently, they were not as widely distributed or accepted as Hocking's Jade-ite. If many collectors should start searching for these patterns, the full extent of the shortage would be revealed.

A full-page ad is shown on page 170 introducing Sierra Sunrise. The charcoal and pink combination shown below was named Informal as can be seen in the 1955 ad on page 171. That ad exuberantly asserts that pink and charcoal were popular color combinations in 1955. (My wife remembers having a charcoal gray skirt with an appliquéd pink poodle near the hem. That combination of colors wasn't limited to dishes, obviously.) I have been unable to find a name for the chartreuse and darker green color. Have you any ads or boxed sets with names for this or any other color blends?

Collectors are buying this inexpensively priced glassware to use as everyday dishes; according to them, it works well in both the microwave and the dishwasher. There is only a hint of collector interest in Platonite with pastel edges at the present time; but a few years ago, that could have been said of Jade-ite!

Colors shown at the bottom of page 169 have been hard to uncover. I have never found a platter in any color other than the one shown which I refer to as "Butterscotch." Platters in all Hazel Atlas' Platonite patterns seem to prevail in that one color. All basic pieces should be found in all colors; but serving pieces may only be "Butterscotch." Let me know if you find something different.

One of the difficulties in ordering glass through the mail or via the Internet is miscommunication between buyer and seller. I once ordered an 18-piece set of dark "Moderntone" colors through the mail expecting to receive Moderntone pattern. I got Moderntone Ovide. Evidently, *Moderntone* at the factory referred to the colors and not the pattern. You will find Ovide pieces in the 50s Moderntone colors Burgundy, Chartreuse, Green, and Gray. That **Green** is the actual color designation by Hazel Atlas in spite of collectors calling it forest or dark green. This colored Ovide ware seemed to be Hazel Atlas Glass Company's answer to the popular 50s Fiesta dinnerware.

	White w/trims	Decorated White	Fired-on Colors	Art Deco
Ash tray, square			4.00	
Bowl, 4¾", berry	3.50	7.00	5.50	
Bowl, 5½", cereal, deep		15.00		
Bowl, 8", large berry			18.00	
Creamer	4.50	18.00	5.50	95.00
Cup	3.50	12.50	4.50	65.00
Plate, 6", sherbet	1.50	2.50		
Plate, 8", luncheon	2.50	13.00	4.00	50.00
Plate, 9", dinner	3.50			
Platter, 11"	7.50	25.00		
Refrigerator stacking set, 4-pc.		47.50		
Salt and pepper, pr.	13.00			
Saucer	1.00	2.50		20.00
Sherbet	5.50	2.00		60.00
Sugar, open	4.50	18.00	5.50	95.00
Tumbler		17.00		95.00

PANELED GRAPE, PATTERN #1881 WESTMORELAND GLASS COMPANY, 1950 – 1970s

Colors: white and white w/decorations, and some mint green in 1979

Westmoreland's Paneled Grape may be their most recognized pattern after English Hobnail. Production began in 1950 and continued for nearly thirty years. Pattern #1881 (Paneled Grape) was soon comprised of over a hundred pieces. Westmoreland listed this pattern with both designations as you can see from the catalog copies on the following pages. (Pieces shown on the catalog sheets as line #1884 are termed Beaded Grape and are not priced in the Paneled Grape listing below.) Paneled Grape is both cherished, and despised. Some people cannot stand white milk glass; others think it is the most exquisite glass on earth. Gratefully, there are enough different colors and patterns from this era to accommodate every collecting taste.

Rarely found pieces of Paneled Grape have continued to rise in price, albeit slowly. Prices for basic pieces remain steady. Produced for so long, #1881 has been well able to keep up with present collector demand. Punch sets are not quite as rare as once thought; but there is demand for them. We have sold five sets in the last few years and they do sell at the price listed!

Mint green Paneled Grape can be found, but there seem to be few overt buyers for it. It is uncommon. Many Westmoreland collectors are very close-mouthed about values on their glass and no one I asked wanted to share information on pricing green other than to say it was hard to sell. To answer a question recently posed about vases in this pattern, swung vases are actually swung while hot to extend their shape and therefore, their sizes vary.

Catalog pages from 1973 are depicted on pages 176 – 186. Company pictures and descriptions are always helpful.

	White w/decorations		White w/decorations
Appetizer or canapé set, 3 pc. (9" three-part relish/round fruit cocktail/ladle)	65.00	Candle holder, 4", octagonal, pr.	27.50
Basket, 5½", ruffled	55.00	Candle holder, 5", w/colonial hndl.	37.50
Basket, 6½", oval	25.00	Candle holder, 8", 2-lite (4 of these form a circular center piece)	27.50
Basket, 8"	77.50	Candy jar, 3-ftd., w/cover	32.50
Basket, 8", ruffled	65.00	Candy jar, 6¼", w/cover	25.00
Bon bon, 8", ruffled w/metal handle	50.00	Canister, 7"	150.00
Bottle, 5 oz., toilet	62.50	Canister, 9½"	175.00
Bottle, oil or vinegar, w/stopper, 2 oz.	22.00	Canister, 11"	225.00
Bowl, pedestal base, 5" (used w/12"/12½" lipped/10" rnd. bowls & epergne)	70.00	Celery or spooner, 6"	40.00
Bowl, 4", crimped	22.00	Cheese/old fashioned butter, 7", round w/cover	57.50
Bowl, 6", crimped, stemmed	30.00	Chocolate box, 6½", w/cover	55.00
Bowl, 6", ruffled edge, stemmed	30.00	Compote, 4½", crimped	30.00
Bowl, 6½" x 12½", 3⅛" high	115.00	Compote, 7" covered, ftd.	47.50
Bowl, 6½", oval	23.00	Compote, 9" ftd., crimped	80.00
Bowl, 8", cupped	38.00	Condiment set, 5-pc. (oil and vinegar, salt and pepper on 9" oval tray)	125.00
Bowl, 8½", shallow	55.00	Creamer, 6½ oz.	16.00
Bowl, 9", ftd., 6" high, skirted base	50.00	Creamer, individual	11.00
Bowl, 9", ftd., w/cover	70.00	Creamer, large (goes w/lacy edge sugar)	22.50
Bowl, 9", lipped	110.00	Creamer, small	10.00
Bowl, 9", lipped, ftd.	115.00	Cup, coffee, flared	13.00
Bowl, 9", square, w/cover	35.00	Cup, punch, cupped	12.00
Bowl, 9½", bell-shaped	45.00	Decanter, wine	150.00
Bowl, 9½", ftd., bell-shaped	110.00	Dresser set, 4-pc. (2)5 oz. toilet bottles, puff box and 13½" oval tray	250.00
Bowl, 10", oval	37.50	Egg plate, 12"	85.00
Bowl, 10½", round	77.50	Egg tray, 10", metal center handle	65.00
Bowl, 11", oval, lipped, ftd.	125.00	Epergne vase, 8½", bell	60.00
Bowl, 11½", oval, ruffled edge	80.00	Epergne vase, pattern at top	195.00
Bowl, 12", lipped	120.00	Epergne set, 2-pc. (9" lipped bowl/8½" epergne vase)	125.00
Bowl, 12" ftd., banana	160.00	Epergne set, 2-pc. (11½" epergne flared bowl/8½" epergne vase)	125.00
Bowl, 12½", bell-shaped	135.00	
Bowl, 13", punch, bell or flared	325.00	Epergne set, 2-pc. (12" epergne lipped bowl/8½" epergne vase)	225.00
Bowl, 14", shallow, round	150.00	
Bowl, ftd., ripple top	75.00	Epergne set, 2-pc. (14" flared bowl/8½" epergne vase)	235.00
Butter w/cover, ¼ pound	25.00	
Cake salver, 10½"	65.00	Epergne set, 3-pc. (12" epergne lipped bowl/5" bowl base/8½" epergne vase)	325.00
Cake salver, 11", round ftd., w/skirt	70.00	
Canapé or set, 3 pc. (12½" canapé tray/3½" cocktail/ladle)	120.00	Epergne set, 3-pc. (14" flared bowl/5" bowl base/8½" epergne vase)	350.00
Candelabra, 3-lite, ea.	295.00	

PANELED GRAPE

	White w/decorations		White w/decorations
Flower pot	47.50	Relish, 9", 3-part	40.00
Fruit cocktail, 3½" w/6" sauce plate, bell-shaped	22.50	Salt and pepper, 4¼", small, ftd., pr.	22.50
Fruit cocktail, 4½" w/6" sauce plate, round	25.00	*Salt and pepper, 4¼", small, ftd., pr.	27.50
Ivy ball	47.50	Salt and pepper, 4½", large, flat, pr.	52.50
Jardiniere, 5", cupped and ftd.	25.00	Sauce boat	30.00
Jardiniere, 5", straight sided	25.00	Sauce boat tray, 9"	30.00
Jardiniere, 6½", cupped and ftd.	35.00	Saucer	8.50
Jardiniere, 6½", straight sided	35.00	Sherbet, 3¾", low foot	16.00
Jelly, 4½", covered	27.50	Sherbet, 4¾", high foot	17.50
Ladle, small	10.00	Soap dish	100.00
Ladle, punch	47.50	Stem, 2 oz. cordial or wine goblet	22.50
Lighter in 2 oz. goblet	30.00	Stem, 3 oz.	30.00
Lighter in tooth pick	33.00	Stem, 5 oz., wine goblet	30.00
Marmalade, w/ladle	57.50	Stem, 8 oz. water goblet	18.00
Mayonnaise set, 3-pc. (round fruit cocktail/6" sauce plate/ladle)	35.00	Sugar w/cover, lacy edge on sugar to serve as spoon holder	35.00
Mayonnaise, 4", ftd.	27.50	Sugar, 6½"	14.00
Napkin ring	20.00	Sugar, small w/cover	14.00
Nappy, 4½", round	14.00	Tidbit or snack server, 2-tier (dinner and breakfast plates)	65.00
Nappy, 5", bell shape	22.00	Tidbit tray, metal handle on 8½" breakfast plate	27.50
Nappy, 5", round w/handle	30.00	Tidbit tray, metal handle on 10½" dinner plate	47.50
Nappy, 7", round	30.00	Toothpick	24.00
Nappy, 8½", round	30.00	Tray, 9", oval	50.00
Nappy, 9", round, 2" high	40.00	Tray, 13½", oval	80.00
Nappy, 10", bell	45.00	Tumbler, 5 oz. juice	24.00
Oil bottle	25.00	Tumbler, 6 oz. old fashioned cocktail	27.50
Parfait, 6"	25.00	Tumbler, 8 oz.	22.50
Pedestal, base to punch bowl, skirted	140.00	Tumbler, 12 oz. iced tea	25.00
Pickle, oval	21.00	Vase, 4", rose	20.00
Pitcher, 16 oz.	47.50	Vase, 4½, rose, ftd., cupped, stemmed	35.00
Pitcher, 32 oz.	37.50	Vase, 6", bell shape	20.00
Planter, 3" x 8½"	35.00	Vase, 6½" or celery	35.00
Planter, 4½", square	40.00	Vase, 8½", bell shape	25.00
Planter, 5" x 9"	38.00	Vase, 9", bell shape	25.00
Planter, 6", small, wall	85.00	Vase, 9", crimped top	35.00
Planter, 8", large, wall	135.00	Vase, 9½", straight	35.00
Plate, 6", bread	4.00	Vase, 10" bud (size may vary)	20.00
Plate, 7" salad, w/depressed center	25.00	Vase, 11", rose (similar to bud vase but bulbous at bottom)	35.00
Plate, 8½", breakfast	22.00	Vase, 11½", bell shape	47.50
Plate, 10½", dinner	45.00	Vase, 11½", straight	35.00
Plate, 14½"	120.00	Vase, 12", hand blown	175.00
Plate, 18"	175.00	Vase, 14", swung (size varies)	22.00
Puff box or jelly, w/cover	27.50	Vase, 15"	30.00
Punch set, 15-pc. (13" bowl, 12 punch cups, pedestal and ladle)	595.00	Vase, 16", swung (size varies)	22.00
Punch set, 15-pc. (same as above w/11" bowl w/o scalloped bottom)	525.00	Vase, 18", swung (size varies)	25.00

*All-over pattern

"*Panel Grape*"
GIFT SUGGESTIONS TO PLEASE THE DISCRIMINATING

1881
Bowl, Crimp.

1881 Bowl,
Lip. Ftd.

1881 Bowl,
Shallow

1881
Basket, Hld.

1881
Bowl, Lip.

1881
Bowl, Oval

1881/6½"
Basket

1881
Appetizer Set

1881
Bowl, Bell

1881
Bowl, Rose

1881
Butter

1881
Bon Bon

FAMOUS *"Panel Grape"* THE COLLECTORS FAVORITE

1881 Plates, 14½", 10½" & 8½"

1881
3 pc. Canister Set

1881
Jug, Qt.

1881
Egg Tray

1881
Salver, Skirted

1881
Salver, Ftd.

1881 Snack Server

1881
Ice Tea

1881
Goblet

1881
Sauce Boat/Tray

1881
Mayonnaise

1881
Condiment Set

1881
Salt/Pepper,
Lg.

1881
Oil

1881
Salt/Pepper
(Min. 3 Sets)

1881
Candy

1881
Dish, 3 Ftd.

1881
Puff Box/
Jelly

1881
Chocolate Box

1881
Candy, Crimp.

1881
Pickle

1881
Starter Set

1881
Candlestick

1881
Mayo
Set

1881
Cup/Saucer

1881
Dish, Oval

4

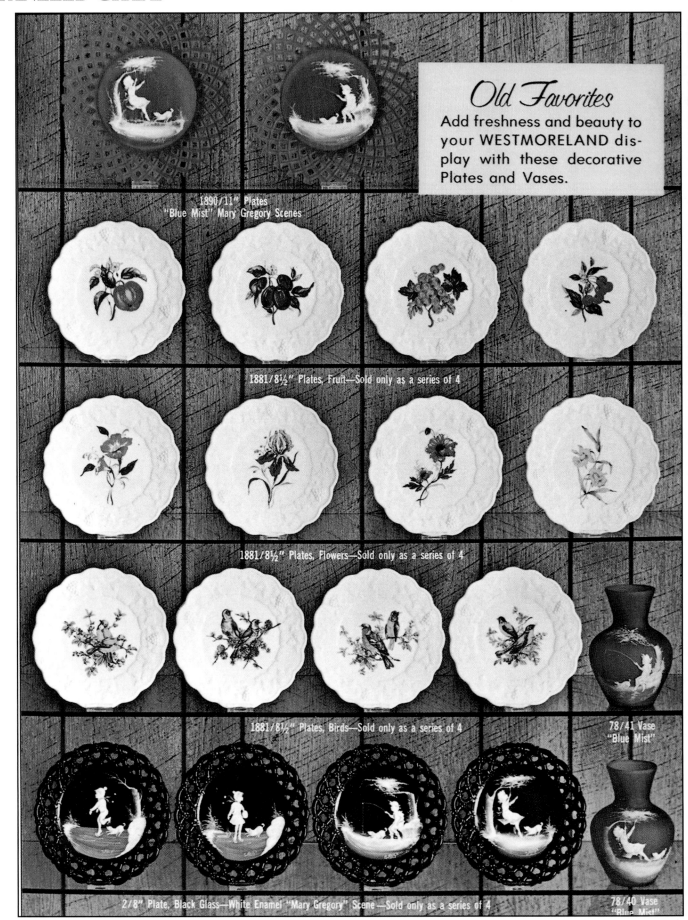

Old Favorites

Add freshness and beauty to your WESTMORELAND display with these decorative Plates and Vases.

1890/11" Plates "Blue Mist" Mary Gregory Scenes

1881/8½" Plates, Fruit—Sold only as a series of 4

1881/8½" Plates, Flowers—Sold only as a series of 4

1881/8½" Plates, Birds—Sold only as a series of 4

78/41 Vase "Blue Mist"

2/8" Plate, Black Glass—White Enamel "Mary Gregory" Scene—Sold only as a series of 4

78/40 Vase "Blue Mist"

MGT0731
Plate, 14½"

MGT0730
Plate, 10½"

MGT0729
Plate, 8½"

MGT0734
Sauce Boat

MGT0724
Cup & Saucer

MGT0733
Salt & Pepper
Small, Height, 4¼"

MGT0721
Appetizer Set

MGT0737
Sugar & Cream, Small

MGT0726
Jug, 1 Qt.

MGT0725
Goblet

MGT0736
Sugar & Cream,
Large

MGT0722
Butter

MGT0732
Salt & Pepper
Large, Height, 4½"

MGT0739
Wine

MGT0738
Tid Bit Tray

Milk Glass Tableware

1881
Sauce Boat/Tray

1881
Goblet
8 oz.

1881
Sugar/Cream, Lg.

1881
Jug, Qt.

1881 Salt/Pepper

small

large

small

1881 Oil, 2 oz.

1881 Sugar/Cream

1881
Appetizer
Set

1881
Marmalade
W/Ladle

1881
Tid Bit
Tray

1881
Snack
Server

1881 Plate, 14½"

1881 Plate, 10½"

1881 Plate, 8½"

1881
Cheese

1881 Butter

1881 Cup/Saucer

...Kitchen & Table Accessories

29

109
Cookie Jar

Collector's items from the vast "Paneled Grape" pattern

1881/9"
Bowl, Sq.

1881/9"
Compote, Crimped

1881
Compote, Crimped

1881/7"
Compote

1881
Candy Jar

1881
Decanter

1881
Celery/Vase

1881
Dish, 3 Ftd.

1881
Chocolate Box

1881
Candleholder

1881
Cocktail, Fruit

1881
Cheese

1881/9"
Bowl, Bell

1881/¼ #
Butter

1881
Cup/Saucer

1881
Candle

1881
Dish

1881/12"
Bowl, Lipped

1881
Bowl, Banana

1881
Bowl, Oval Lpd.

PANELED GRAPE

Excellent Gift Suggestions in a treasured pattern

1881/14½"
Plate

1881/10½"
Plate

1881/8½"
Plate

1881/6"
Plate

1881
Mayonnaise

1881/2 oz.
Oil

1881/4½"
Nappy

1881
Ice Tea

1881
Goblet

1881/1 Pt.
Jug

1881/1 Qt.
Jug

1881/6½"
Jardiniere

1881/5"
Jardiniere

1881
Pickle

1881
Mayo Set

1881
Puff Box/Jelly

1881
Flower Pot

1881
Planter, Oblong

1881
Planter, Window

1881
Planter, Sq.

1881
Ivy Ball

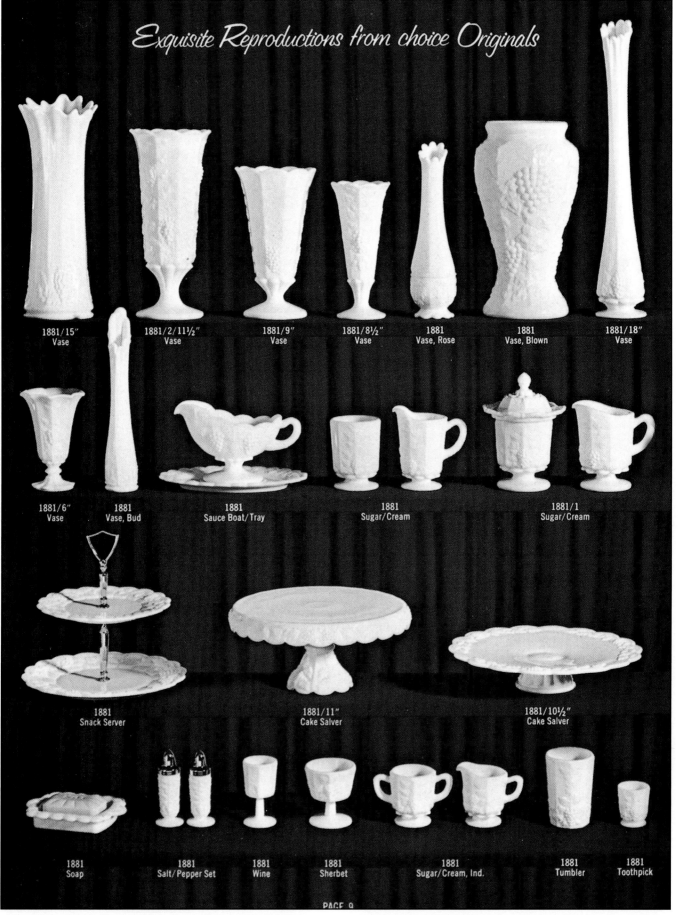

Exquisite Reproductions from choice Originals

1881/15"
Vase

1881/2/11½"
Vase

1881/9"
Vase

1881/8½"
Vase

1881
Vase, Rose

1881
Vase, Blown

1881/18"
Vase

1881/6"
Vase

1881
Vase, Bud

1881
Sauce Boat/Tray

1881
Sugar/Cream

1881/1
Sugar/Cream

1881
Snack Server

1881/11"
Cake Salver

1881/10½"
Cake Salver

1881
Soap

1881
Salt/Pepper Set

1881
Wine

1881
Sherbet

1881
Sugar/Cream, Ind.

1881
Tumbler

1881
Toothpick

PAGE 9

PANELED GRAPE

1881
Decanter

1881
Jug, Pt.

1881
Jug, Qt.

1881
Dish, 3 Ftd.

1881/9"
Compote, Crimp.

1881/4½"
Compote, Crimp.

1881
Goblet

1881
Ice Tea

1881
Compote

1881
Candy

1881
Celery/Vase

1881
Flower Pot

1881
Candlestick

1881
Condiment Set

1881
Candy, Crimp.

1881
Canape Server

1881
Cheese

1881
Choc. Box

1881 Dish, Oval

1881 Wine

1881 Cup/Saucer

1881 Cocktail, Fruit

13

1881
15 Pc. Punch Set
(Ind. Boxed)

1881
Pickle

1881
Snack Server

1881
Sauce Boat/Tray

1881
Oil

1881
Salt/Pepper, Lg.

1881
Cake Salver
(Ind. Boxed)

1881
Planter, Obl.

1881
Puff Box/Jelly

1881
Salt/Pepper
(Packed 3 Sets Per Box)

1881
Mayonnaise

1881
Mayo Set

1881/10½"
Plate
14½" Plate Also Available

1881/8½"
Plate

1881/6"
Plate

14

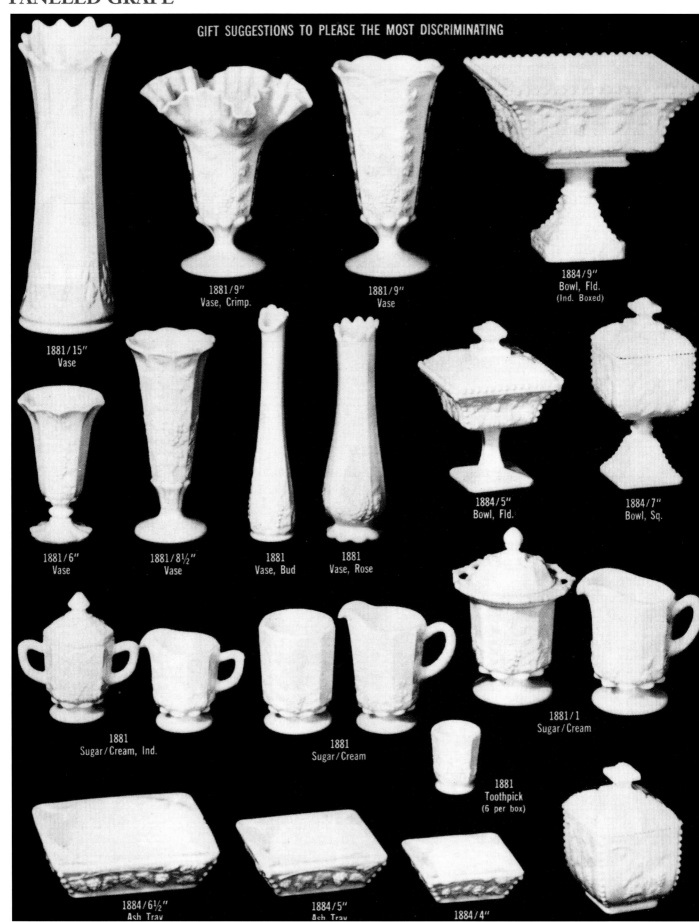

GIFT SUGGESTIONS TO PLEASE THE MOST DISCRIMINATING

1881/15"
Vase

1881/9"
Vase, Crimp.

1881/9"
Vase

1884/9"
Bowl, Fld.
(Ind. Boxed)

1881/6"
Vase

1881/8½"
Vase

1881
Vase, Bud

1881
Vase, Rose

1884/5"
Bowl, Fld.

1884/7"
Bowl, Sq.

1881
Sugar/Cream, Ind.

1881
Sugar/Cream

1881
Toothpick
(6 per box)

1881/1
Sugar/Cream

1884/6½"
Ash Tray

1884/5"
Ash Tray

1884/4"

PARK AVENUE, FEDERAL GLASS COMPANY, 1941 – EARLY 1970s

Colors: amber, crystal, and crystal w/gold trim

Park Avenue's amber is the color being sought by most collectors. I have found very little as you can see by my one tumbler in the photo below. I have separated the colors in the listing to better show the demand for amber. Gold-trimmed pieces are laborious to find with strong gold decorations. Gold wears off easily since it is a very soft 22K. If the gold is so worn that it looks awful, you can remove it with an art gum eraser or a light use of Soft Scrub®. Evidently, crystal Park Avenue was distributed in the central Florida area. I found the bowl with the wire hanging vases in this area. I doubt if it was factory made, but it does enhance the picture.

You will find the Federal Glass Company trademark (F within a shield) embossed on the bottom of most of the pieces. No Park Avenue pitchers, per se, were made as far as catalog records indicate. Star pitchers shown on page 228 were marketed with tumblers from this set.

The small whisky tumbler (as well as other sizes of tumblers) in Park Avenue may be found with jelly labels still affixed to them. Peach preserves were enclosed in one I found. Evidently, the small tumblers were used as samples or perhaps for jelly containers in gift sets. I recently had a letter from a collector who found some of these embossed "Delited," as is the paper labeled one in my picture.

All pieces listed were made into the early 1960s except the whisky glass that was in production until the early 1970s. Before I get letters, let me point out that Federal's catalog used the British spelling of whisky without the "e"; so, it seemed appropriate here that I follow their lead.

	Amber	Crystal
Ash tray, 3½", square		5.00
Ash tray, 4½", square		7.00
Bowl, 5", dessert	6.00	2.00
Bowl, 8½", vegetable	15.00	8.00
Candleholder, 5"		8.00
Tumbler, 2⅛", 1¼ oz., whisky		4.00
Tumbler, 3½", 4½ oz., juice	5.00	3.00
Tumbler, 3⅞", 9 oz.	6.00	4.00
Tumbler, 4¾", 10 oz.	7.00	5.00
Tumbler, 5⅛", 12 oz., iced tea	12.00	6.00

PRESSED TUMBLERS

Matching lines . . . such as the famed Park Avenue
on this page, or the Star Line on the next . . . new,
unusual shapes, and standard staples, are shown here in
Federal's selection of pressed tumblers. All are designed
and engineered for eye-appeal, serviceability, and
good value.

PARK AVENUE

TUMBLERS

1122 — 1¼ oz.
PARK AVENUE WHISKY
Ht. 2⅛"
Pkd. 12 doz. ctn. Wt. 16 lbs.

1122 — 4½ oz.
PARK AVENUE JUICE TUMBLER
Ht. 3½"
Pkd. 12 doz. ctn. Wt. 35 lbs.

1122 — 9 oz.
PARK AVENUE TUMBLER
Ht. 3⅞"
Pkd. 12 doz. ctn. Wt. 56 lbs.

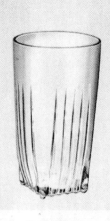

1142—10 oz.
PARK AVENUE TUMBLER*
Ht. 4¾"
Pkd. 6 doz. ctn. Wt. 37 lbs.

1122 — 12 oz.
PARK AVENUE ICED TEA
Ht. 5⅛"
Pkd. 6 doz. ctn. Wt. 43 lbs.

*CK 1142—10 oz. PARK AVENUE TUMBLER IN CARRY-KITS
are available factory-packed: 6 tumblers to each
Carry-Kit, 12 kits to ctn. Wt. 40 lbs.

19

PLANTATION, BLANK #1567, A.H. HEISEY & CO.

Colors: crystal; rare in amber

I cannot keep Plantation in stock! What few pieces I find sell at the first show! This pattern is hot with collectors right now, even pushing the desirable Rose and Orchid patterns aside as Heisey's most avidly sought pattern.

The plate in the second row, page 190, picturing a lady with a pineapple on her head, is a coupe plate that sells in the $400.00 range, if you should spot one.

You will have a major problem finding stems and tumblers in Plantation unlike many other Heisey patterns where stemware abounds! All flat tumblers are rare; do not let any escape!

	Crystal		Crystal
Ash tray, 3½"	45.00	Cup, punch	35.00
Bowl, 9 qt., Dr. Johnson, punch	600.00	Marmalade, w/cover	190.00
Bowl, 5", nappy	25.00	Mayonnaise, 4½", rolled ft.	65.00
Bowl, 5½", nappy	35.00	Mayonnaise, 5¼", w/liner	55.00
Bowl, 6½", 2 hndl., jelly	45.00	Oil bottle, 3 oz., w/#125 stopper	130.00
Bowl, 6½", flared, jelly	60.00	Pitcher, ½ gallon, ice lip, blown	400.00
Bowl, 6½", ftd., honey, cupped	75.00	Plate, coupe (rare)	400.00
Bowl, 8", 4-pt., rnd., relish	70.00	Plate, 7", salad	25.00
Bowl, 8½", 2-pt., dressing	70.00	Plate, 8", salad	35.00
Bowl, 9", salad	170.00	Plate, 10½", demi-torte	70.00
Bowl, 9½", crimped, fruit or flower	85.00	Plate, 13", ftd., cake salver	200.00
Bowl, 9½", gardenia	85.00	Plate, 14", sandwich	120.00
Bowl, 11", 3-part, relish	60.00	Plate, 18", buffet	110.00
Bowl, 11½", ftd., gardenia	140.00	Plate, 18", punch bowl liner	120.00
Bowl, 12", crimped, fruit or flower	100.00	Salt & pepper, pr.	70.00
Bowl, 13", celery	70.00	Saucer	10.00
Bowl, 13", 2-part, celery	60.00	Stem, 1 oz., cordial	125.00
Bowl, 13", 5-part, oval relish	90.00	Stem, 3 oz., wine, blown	75.00
Bowl, 13", gardenia	90.00	Stem, 3½ oz., cocktail, pressed	35.00
Butter, ¼ lb., oblong, w/cover	110.00	Stem, 4 oz., fruit/oyster cocktail	35.00
Butter, 5", rnd. (or cov. candy)	150.00	Stem, 4½ oz., claret, blown	65.00
Candelabrum, w/two #1503 bobeche & 10		Stem, 4½ oz., claret, pressed	65.00
"A" prisms	180.00	Stem, 4½ oz., oyster cocktail, blown	40.00
Candle block, hurricane type w/globe	200.00	Stem, 6½ oz., sherbet/saucer champagne,	
Candle block, 1-lite	110.00	blown	40.00
Candle holder, 5", ftd., epergne	120.00	Stem, 10 oz., pressed	50.00
Candlestick, 1-lite	100.00	Stem, 10 oz., blown	50.00
Candlestick, 2-lite	80.00	Sugar, ftd.	40.00
Candlestick, 3-lite	110.00	Syrup bottle, w/drip, cut top	140.00
Candy box, w/cover, 7" length, flat bottom	180.00	Tray, 8½", condiment/sugar & creamer	90.00
Candy, w/cover, 5", tall, ftd.	200.00	Tumbler, 5 oz., ftd., juice, pressed	60.00
Cheese, w/cover, 5", ftd.	90.00	Tumbler, 5 oz., ftd., juice, blown	40.00
Cigarette box, w/cover	180.00	Tumbler, 8 oz., water, pressed	125.00
Coaster, 4"	60.00	Tumbler, 10 oz., pressed	90.00
Comport, 5"	50.00	Tumbler, 12 oz., ftd., iced tea, pressed	90.00
Comport, 5", w/cover, deep	100.00	Tumbler, 12 oz., ftd., iced tea, blown	75.00
Creamer, ftd.	40.00	Vase, 5", ftd., flared	90.00
Cup	40.00	Vase, 9", ftd., flared	140.00

Color: crystal

Prelude originated at New Martinsville Glass Company in the mid 1930s; Viking Glass Company continued Prelude production when they took over the New Martinsville Glass factory in 1943. I have included a few pages from an early 1950s Viking Glass catalog. Be sure to notice the shakers on pages 195 and 196. They have only flowers in the pattern. You may also notice that some pieces of Prelude are similar, but diversely shaped. The fancier edged pieces were New Martinsville's production; similar items made at Viking were less detailed to accommodate faster production! Pictured below is a cherub set making use of a Prelude bowl.

	Crystal
Bonbon, 6", hndl.	18.00
Bonbon, 6", 3-ftd.	20.00
Bowl, 7", cupped	25.00
Bowl, 8", crimped	35.00
Bowl, 8", 3-part, shrimp	70.00
Bowl, 9", 3-ftd., crimped	50.00
Bowl, 9½", crimped, ftd.	50.00
Bowl, 10", crimped	45.00
Bowl, 10", 3-ftd.	40.00
Bowl, 10", shallow	35.00
Bowl, 10½", nut, center hndl.	37.50
Bowl, 11", 3 ftd.	50.00
Bowl, 12½", crimped	50.00
Bowl, 13", oval	42.00
Bowl, 13", shallow	45.00
Bowl, 15", 3-ftd.	70.00
Butter dish, 6½", oval w/cover	37.50
Butter dish, 8½", oval w/cover	32.50
Cake salver, 11", 5½" high	55.00
Cake salver, 11" w/metal base	50.00
Candlestick, 4",	17.50
Candlestick, 4½",	20.00
Candlestick, 5", double	35.00
Candlestick, 5½",	25.00
Candlestick, 6", double	40.00
Candy box, 6", w/cover, closed knob	60.00
Candy box, 6½", w/cover, open knob	65.00
Candy box, 7", w/cover, 3-ftd.	65.00
Celery, 10½"	30.00
Cocktail shaker, w/metal lid	185.00
Compote, cheese	15.00
Compote, 5½" diameter, 3" high	30.00
Compote, 6"	22.00
Compote, 7", crimped	32.00
Compote, 7½", flared	32.00
Creamer	12.50
Creamer, 4-ftd.	15.00
Creamer, individual	12.00
Cup	25.00
Ensemble set, 13" bowl w/candle holder	135.00
Ensemble set, 13" bowl w/flower epergne	165.00
Lazy susan, 18", 3-pc. set	165.00
Mayonnaise, 3-pc.	35.00
Mayonnaise, divided, 4-pc.	40.00
Nappy w/pc, 6" for candle	40.00
Oil bottle, 4 oz.	50.00

	Crystal
Pitcher, 78 oz.	250.00
Plate, 6", bread & butter	6.00
Plate, 6½", hndl.	12.50
Plate, 6½", lemon, 3-ftd.	12.50
Plate, 7"	8.00
Plate, 7", lemon, 3-ftd.	13.50
Plate, 8", salad	10.00
Plate, 9"	22.50
Plate, 10", dinner	37.50
Plate, 10", 3-ftd.	22.00
Plate, 11"	27.00
Plate, 11", 3-ftd., cake	35.00
Plate, 11", cracker	22.50
Plate, 13", hndl.	40.00
Plate, 14", flat or turned-up edge	45.00
Plate, 16"	75.00
Plate, 16", 3-ftd.	70.00
Plate, 18"	85.00
Platter, 14½"	65.00
Relish, 6", 2-part	15.00
Relish, 6", 2-part, hndl.	15.00
Relish, 7", 2-part, hndl.	15.00
Relish, 7", 3-part, hndl.	15.00
Relish, 10", 3-part, hndl.	30.00
Relish, 13", 5-part	35.00
Salt and pepper, 3½" pr., 2 styles	40.00
Saucer	5.00

	Crystal
Stem, 1 oz., cordial	40.00
Stem, 1 oz., cordial, ball stem	42.50
Stem, 3 oz., wine	22.00
Stem, 3 oz., wine, ball stem	25.00
Stem, 3½ oz., cocktail	15.00
Stem, 4 oz., cocktail, ball stem	15.00
Stem, 6 oz., low sherbet	12.00
Stem, 6 oz., sherbet, ball stem	12.00
Stem, 6 oz., tall sherbet	15.00
Stem, 9 oz., water	25.00
Sugar	12.50
Sugar, 4-ftd.	15.00
Sugar, individual	12.00
Tidbit, 2 tier, chrome hndl.	40.00
Tray, 11", center hndl.	35.00
Tray, ind. cr./sug.	10.00
Treasure jar, 8", w/cover	100.00
Tumbler, 5 oz., ftd. juice	16.00
Tumbler, 5 oz., juice, ball stem	17.50
Tumbler, 10 oz., water, ball stem	20.00
Tumbler, 12 oz., ftd. tea	20.00
Tumbler, 13 oz., tea, ball stem	25.00
Vase, 8"	40.00
Vase, 10", bud	30.00
Vase, 10", crimped	65.00
Vase, 11", crimped	70.00
Vase, 11", ftd.	75.00

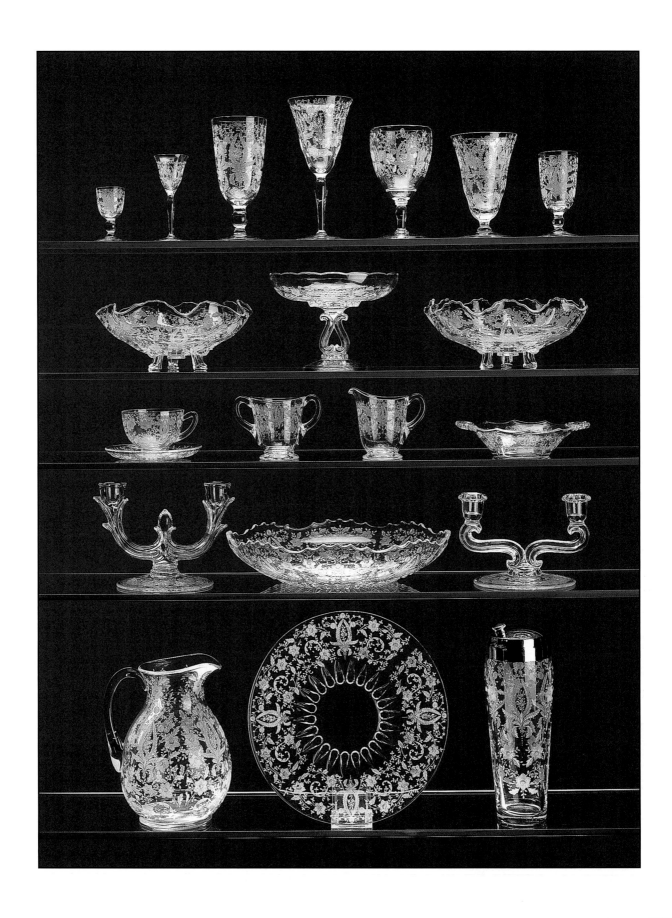

Prelude Etching

Magnificent expression of the designer's art in glass that is timeless and "right", with more than a touch of class.

5217
14" Plate

5201
13" Bowl

7539
8" Vase

5226
11" Cake Salver

5287
13" 5-pt. Relish

5223
13" 2-hdl. Plate

5238
10" 3-pt. Relish

13
Salt & Pepper

5247
Cream & Sugar

PRELUDE

5217
14" RE. PLATE

5249
CELERY TRAY

5247
SUGAR & CREAM

13
3½" SALT & PEPPER
W/CHROME TOP

5226
11" CAKE SALVER

5201
SHALLOW BOWL

7539
8" VASE

1010
LEMON PLATE

1009
BONBON

1091
3 TOED PLATE

1003
10" CRIMPED BOWL

5287
OVAL RELISH

Own PRELUDE and be envied...give PRELUDE and be proud

Choose Viking's beautifully etched Prelude pattern
for your home and your important gift-giving. See your
favorite good store's exciting display.
See the stemware especially.

 Treasured American Glass

Hand made by
VIKING GLASS COMPANY
NEW MARTINSVILLE, WEST VIRGINIA

"PRETZEL," No. 622 INDIANA GLASS COMPANY, LATE 1930s – 1980s

Colors: Crystal, teal, and avocado with recent issues in amber and blue

Indiana's No. 622 is most often referred to by its collector name, "Pretzel." After years of searching, I have finally been able to buy the pitcher and all three sizes of tumblers. Unfortunately, the water tumbler didn't seem to find its way to the photo session; but you can see the pitcher, juice, and iced tea on the next page.

Has anyone found a teal saucer to go with the cup? I found this cup in Seattle which is not exactly the place I would expect to find one. I have now confirmed three such saucer-less cups. This teal is Terrace Green most likely from the Christmas Candy production run in the early 1950s.

Embossed, fruit centered, and frosted crystal items are selling for 25% – 50% more than plain centered pieces. Due to using the blue background, the fruit centered pieces did not show up well and were omitted from this photo. Sorry!

The later made Astrology and advertising pieces are the only colored pieces that are regularly turning up. Astrological bowls are selling in the $3.00 to $6.00 range although some have been found for pennies. I understand Astrological sets of 12 have been discovered for as little as $20.00 and as much as $100.00. Most likely, these were a special order! Notice the Jack Daniel's whiskey advertisement pictured below. I have been told that bars used these to hold peanuts or chips. They wouldn't hold many of either which was probably the idea.

The 4½" fruit cup is being found on a 6" plate that has a 1¼" tab handle. Perhaps this was sold as a small snack set?

I haven't yet received a picture of the calendar plate with side design of "Pretzel" that was promised. It sounded interesting. If you have one, please send some details. Other pieces are being uncovered with dates indicating Indiana used this line to promote special events.

	Crystal
Bowl, 4½", fruit cup	4.50
Bowl, 7½", soup	10.00
Bowl, 9⅜", berry	18.00
Celery, 10¼", tray	1.50
Creamer	4.50
* Cup	6.00
Olive, 7", leaf-shaped	5.00
Pickle, 8½", two hndl.	5.50
Pitcher, 39 oz.	425.00
Plate, 6"	2.50
Plate, 6", tab hndl.	3.00
Plate, 7¼", square, indent	9.00

	Crystal
Plate, 7¼", square, indent 3-part	9.00
Plate, 8⅜", salad	6.00
Plate, 9⅜", dinner	10.00
Plate, 11½", sandwich	11.00
**Saucer	1.00
Sugar	4.50
Tumbler, 5 oz., 3½"	45.00
Tumbler, 9 oz., 4½"	40.00
Tumbler, 12 oz., 5½"	65.00

* Teal - $125.00
**Teal - $35.00

RIPPLE, "CRINOLINE," "PETTICOAT," "PIE CRUST," "LASAGNA"
HAZEL ATLAS GLASS COMPANY, EARLY 1950s

Colors: Platonite white and white w/blue or pink trim

Ripple is the real name of this pattern which was previously listed under the collector name "Crinoline." The names listed above are ones that I have seen or heard for the pattern over the years. All are descriptive and any would work; however, Ripple was the Hazel Atlas name for this pattern. We know this thanks to a lady who wrote and sent a picture of a company box. Her generosity enlightened us all.

We have learned several things about this pattern from selling it over the last three years. First, it displays wonderfully by mixing the colors. We purposely mixed the colors in the picture below to give you an idea of how it looks mingled.

Secondly, cup, creamer, and sugar handles come plain and beaded. The pink cup, white creamer and sugar have beaded handles. All other handles in the photo are plain.

Finally, the small shallow dessert bowl is much more difficult to find than the deeper cereal. I have had numerous collectors say they've never even seen one.

Larger serving plates are few and far between. Those seem to have been used more than other pieces as they are rarely found without scratches and gouges.

Collectors have discovered at least two different pitcher and tumbler designs that can be used with this set. We show a flowered pitcher and banded tumblers. The tumblers come in four sizes. Pictured, also, are a fired-on blue tumbler and mug that Hazel Atlas made to accompany Ripple as accessory pieces. They are also found in pink. Note the white plate with strawberries and the decaled white creamer and sugar. These are unusual. Who knows what else can be found?

	All colors			All colors
Bowl, berry, shallow, 5"	10.00		Saucer, 5⅝"	1.00
Bowl, cereal, deep, 5⅝"	8.00		Sugar	7.50
Creamer	7.50		Tidbit, 3-tier	30.00
Cup	4.00		Tumbler, 5 oz., juice	7.00
Plate, 6⅞", salad	5.00		Tumbler, 6", 16 oz.	8.00
Plate, 8⅞", luncheon	5.00		Tumbler, 6¼", 20 oz.	10.00
Plate, 10½" sandwich	15.00			

ROMANCE Etching #341, Fostoria Glass Company, 1942 – 1986

Color: crystal

Romance is sometimes wrongly identified as Fostoria's June because of the "bow" in the design. Compare the round shapes of Romance to those of June which is found on the Fairfax blank. Romance, found only in crystal, still has allure for collectors. I think some of the charm is in the name itself.

There are extreme geographical pricing differences for Romance. Some dealers have told me my prices are too high and they couldn't give it away; others considered my prices way too low. It really is difficult to please everyone when it comes to pricing. A few dealers submitted pricing information, and I received as varied a range of assessments for Romance as for any pattern in this book! Remember, this pricing is to be taken only as a guide. You alone must decide what any piece is worth, to you!

	Crystal		Crystal
Ash tray, 2⅝", indiv., #2364	15.00	Plate, 11", sandwich, #2364	37.50
Bowl, 6", baked apple #2364	20.00	Plate, 11¼", cracker, #2364	25.00
Bowl, 8", soup, rimmed, #2364	100.00	Plate, 14", torte, #2364	55.00
Bowl, 9", salad, #2364	37.50	Plate, 16", torte, #2364	95.00
Bowl, 9¼", ftd. blown, #6023	150.00	Plate, crescent salad, #2364	42.50
Bowl, 10", 2 hndl., #2594	50.00	Relish, 8", pickle, #2364	22.50
Bowl, 10½", salad, #2364	45.00	Relish, 10", 3-pt., #2364	25.00
Bowl, 11", shallow, oblong, #2596	47.50	Relish, 11", celery, #2364	27.50
Bowl, 12", ftd. #2364	55.00	Salt & pepper, 2⅝", pr., #2364	60.00
Bowl, 12", lily pond, #2364	45.00	Saucer, #2350	5.00
Bowl, 13", fruit, #2364	50.00	Stem, 3⅞", ¾ oz., cordial, #6017	42.50
Bowl, 13½", hndl., oval, #2594	55.00	Stem, 4½", 6 oz., low sherbet, #6017	15.00
Candlestick, 4", #2324	20.00	Stem, 4⅞", 3½ oz., cocktail, #6017	21.50
Candlestick, 5", #2596	30.00	Stem, 5½", 3 oz., wine, #6017	35.00
Candlestick, 5½", #2594	32.00	Stem, 5½", 6 oz., champagne, #6017	17.50
Candlestick, 5½", 2-lite, #6023	40.00	Stem, 5⅞", 4 oz., claret, #6017	35.00
Candlestick, 8", 3-lite, #2594	65.00	Stem, 7⅜", 9 oz., goblet, #6017	25.00
Candy w/lid, rnd., blown, #2364	95.00	Sugar, 3⅛", ftd., #2350½	16.50
Cigarette holder, 2", blown, #2364	37.50	Tray, 11⅛", ctr. hndl., #2364	35.00
Comport, 3¼", cheese, #2364	22.50	Tumbler, 3⅝", 4 oz., ftd., oyster cocktail, #6017	20.00
Comport, 5", #6030	25.00	Tumbler, 4¾", 5 oz., ftd., #6017	17.50
Comport, 8", #2364	45.00	Tumbler, 5½", 9 oz., ftd., #6017	21.00
Creamer, 3¼", ftd., #2350½	17.50	Tumbler, 6", 12 oz., ftd., #6017	27.50
Cup, ftd., #2350½	20.00	Vase, 5", #4121	40.00
Ice tub, 4¾", #4132	70.00	Vase, 6", ftd. bud, #6021	40.00
Ladle, mayonnaise, #2364	5.00	Vase, 6", ftd., #4143	55.00
Mayonnaise, 5", #2364	22.50	Vase, 6", grnd. bottom, #2619½	55.00
Pitcher, 8⅞", 53 oz., ftd., #6011	325.00	Vase, 7½", ftd., #4143	65.00
Plate, 6", #2337	8.00	Vase, 7½", grnd. bottom, #2619½	70.00
Plate, 6¾", mayonnaise liner, #2364	15.00	Vase, 9½", grnd. bottom, #2619½	95.00
Plate, 7", #2337	10.00	Vase, 10", #2614	85.00
Plate, 8", #2337	15.00	Vase, 10", ftd., #2470	115.00
Plate, 9", #2337	47.50		

ROSE, ETCHING #1515 ON WAVERLY BLANK #1519, A.H. HEISEY & CO., 1949 – 1957

Colors: crystal

Heisey Rose oyster cocktails and clarets are rare; buy them when you can! Low sherbets are harder to find than high and the tray for the individual sugar and creamer is harder to find than they are! The 10½" dinner plate has a large center with a small border, while the 10½" service plate has a small center and large border. Those 6" epernettes on the triple candle have turned out to be some of the rarest pieces in Rose.

	Crystal		Crystal
Ash tray, 3"	37.50	Cocktail icer, w/liner, #3304, UNIVERSAL	285.00
Bell, dinner, #5072	150.00	Cocktail shaker, #4225, COBEL	195.00
Bottle, 8 oz., French dressing, blown, #5031	210.00	Comport, 6½", low ft., WAVERLY	65.00
Bowl, finger, #3309	100.00	Comport, 7", oval, ftd., WAVERLY	145.00
Bowl, 5½", ftd., mint	37.50	Creamer, ftd., WAVERLY	35.00
Bowl, 5¾", ftd., mint, CABOCHON	80.00	Creamer, indiv., WAVERLY	40.00
Bowl, 6", ftd., mint, QUEEN ANN	50.00	Cup, WAVERLY	55.00
Bowl, 6", jelly, 2 hndl., ftd., QUEEN ANN	55.00	Decanter, 1-pt., #4036½, #101 stopper	495.00
Bowl, 6", oval, lemon, w/cover, WAVERLY	895.00	Hurricane lamp, w/12" globe, #5080	375.00
Bowl, 6½", 2 pt., oval, dressing, WAVERLY	70.00	Hurricane lamp, w/12" globe,	
Bowl, 6½", ftd., honey/cheese, WAVERLY	60.00	PLANTATION	495.00
Bowl, 6½", ftd., jelly, WAVERLY	45.00	Ice bucket, dolphin ft., QUEEN ANN	325.00
Bowl, 6½", lemon, w/cover, QUEEN ANN	250.00	Ice tub, 2 hndl., WAVERLY	450.00
Bowl, 7", ftd., honey, WAVERLY	60.00	Mayonnaise, 5½", 2 hndl., WAVERLY	55.00
Bowl, 7", ftd., jelly, WAVERLY	45.00	Mayonnaise, 5½", div., 1 hndl., WAVERLY	55.00
Bowl, 7", lily, QUEEN ANN	125.00	Mayonnaise, 5½", ftd., WAVERLY	60.00
Bowl, 7", relish, 3-pt., round, WAVERLY	67.50	Oil, 3 oz., ftd., WAVERLY	185.00
Bowl, 7", salad, WAVERLY	60.00	Pitcher, 73 oz., #4164	575.00
Bowl, 7", salad dressings, QUEEN ANN	60.00	Plate, 7", salad, WAVERLY	20.00
Bowl, 9", ftd., fruit or salad, WAVERLY	195.00	Plate, 7", mayonnaise, WAVERLY	20.00
Bowl, 9", salad, WAVERLY	135.00	Plate, 8", salad, WAVERLY	30.00
Bowl, 9", 4-pt., rnd, relish, WAVERLY	90.00	Plate, 10½", dinner WAVERLY	175.00
Bowl, 9½", crimped, floral, WAVERLY	75.00	Plate, 10½", service, WAVERLY	75.00
Bowl, 10", gardenia, WAVERLY	75.00	Plate, 11", sandwich, WAVERLY	60.00
Bowl, 10", crimped, floral, WAVERLY	75.00	Plate, 11", demi-torte, WAVERLY	70.00
Bowl, 11", 3-pt., relish, WAVERLY	77.50	Plate, 12", ftd., salver, WAVERLY	250.00
Bowl, 11", 3-ftd., floral, WAVERLY	165.00	Plate, 15", ftd., cake, WAVERLY	325.00
Bowl, 11", floral, WAVERLY	70.00	Plate, 14", torte, WAVERLY	90.00
Bowl, 11", oval, 4-ftd., WAVERLY	150.00	Plate, 14", sandwich, WAVERLY	110.00
Bowl, 12", crimped, floral, WAVERLY	70.00	Plate, 14", ctr. hndl., sandwich, WAVERLY	215.00
Bowl, 13", crimped, floral, WAVERLY	110.00	Salt & pepper, ftd., pr., WAVERLY	65.00
Bowl, 13", floral, WAVERLY	100.00	Saucer, WAVERLY	10.00
Bowl, 13", gardenia, WAVERLY	80.00	Stem, #5072, 1 oz., cordial	150.00
Butter, w/cover, 6", WAVERLY	195.00	Stem, #5072, 3 oz., wine	115.00
Butter, w/cover, ¼ lb., CABOCHON	325.00	Stem, #5072, 3½ oz., oyster cocktail, ftd.	60.00
Candlestick, 1-lite, #112	45.00	Stem, #5072, 4 oz., claret	135.00
Candlestick, 2-lite, FLAME	100.00	Stem, #5072, 4 oz., cocktail	45.00
Candlestick, 3-lite, #142, CASCADE	85.00	Stem, #5072, 6 oz., sherbet	30.00
Candlestick, 3-lite, WAVERLY	100.00	Stem, #5072, 6 oz., saucer champagne	33.00
Candlestick, 5", 2-lite, #134, TRIDENT	75.00	Stem, #5072, 9 oz., water	42.00
Candlestick, 6", epergnette, deep,		Sugar, indiv., WAVERLY	40.00
WAVERLY	1,250.00	Sugar, ftd., WAVERLY	35.00
Candy, w/cover, 5", ftd., WAVERLY	195.00	Tumbler, #5072, 5 oz., ftd., juice	55.00
Candy, w/cover, 6", low, bowknot cover	175.00	Tumbler, #5072, 12 oz., ftd., tea	65.00
Candy, w/cover, 6¼", #1951, CABOCHON	175.00	Tray, indiv. creamer/sugar, QUEEN ANN	65.00
Celery tray, 12", WAVERLY	65.00	Vase, 3½", ftd., violet, WAVERLY	110.00
Celery tray, 13", WAVERLY	70.00	Vase, 4", ftd., violet, WAVERLY	120.00
Cheese compote, 4½" & cracker (11" plate),		Vase, 7", ftd., fan, WAVERLY	120.00
WAVERLY	145.00	Vase, 8", #4198	175.00
Cheese compote, 5½" & cracker (12" plate),		Vase, 8", sq., ftd., urn	185.00
QUEEN ANNE	145.00	Vase, 10", #4198	245.00
Chocolate, w/cover, 5", WAVERLY	195.00	Vase, 10", sq., ftd, urn	250.00
Cigarette holder, #4035	125.00	Vase, 12", sq., ftd., urn	295.00

ROYAL RUBY, ANCHOR HOCKING GLASS COMPANY, 1938 – 1960s; 1977

Color: Royal Ruby

Royal Ruby is Anchor Hocking's patented name for their red color. Many dealers and collectors incorrectly call all red glass Royal Ruby. Only red glassware produced by Hocking or Anchor Hocking should be so called. A Royal Ruby sticker was attached to each red piece, no matter what pattern it was. Red "Bubble" or Charm did not mean anything except Royal Ruby at the factory. So, don't be shocked when you see a Royal Ruby sticker on Charm. In this book, Charm and "Bubble" Royal Ruby are covered under those pattern names. Priced below are crystal stems with Royal Ruby tops (Berwick) as well as the stems that go with Royal Ruby "Bubble" (Early American Line). See a complete explanation under "Bubble" on page 14.

Manufacturing of Royal Ruby was begun in 1938, but what collectors usually identify as Royal Ruby was made after 1940. A Royal Ruby section in my thirteenth edition of *Collector's Encyclopedia of Depression Glass* covers the pieces made in patterns of the late 1930s. Royal Ruby will continue to be shown in both books since it can be divided into pre and post 1940 eras.

I found an Anchor Hocking advertising page that shows the 6⅛"x4" "card holder" cataloged as a cigarette box and sold with four Royal Ruby ash trays. The lid is Royal Ruby on a divided crystal bottom. It is one of the pesky pieces to find in Royal Ruby. Either of two styles of quart water bottles (pictured at the bottom of page 206) used to be the most difficult pieces to find in this pattern. Now you have a Royal Ruby globe for a hurricane lamp to pursue. There are fired-on red ones, so don't be fooled. You can see one pictured in my *Anchor Hocking's Fire-King & More*. Those lids on the water bottles are the same. Bottles without a lid fetch about $75.00, but are hard to sell. The lids themselves will not fetch $150.00, but put them together and you can sell the completed bottle for $225.00. The mathematical rule about the sum of its parts does not always work with glassware. Oval vegetable bowls remain elusive in all parts of the country save the Midwest. I've had dealers from that area tell me they have stacks of them and can't sell them. I suspect that advertising in major national papers such as the *Depression Glass Daze* or over the Internet will reach someone looking for one! The punch bowl base and the salad bowl with 13¾" underliner are rarely seen. Once these pieces are absorbed into collections, it usually is years before they are offered for sale again.

There are two styles of sherbets which seem to confuse new collectors. The non-stemmed version is shown in front of the stemmed sherbet on page 206.

Upright pitchers appear to have multiplied and I see less expensive prices on them now when compared to a few years ago.

There were five sizes (7, 8, 12, 16, and 32 ounces) of beer bottles made in several shapes for Schlitz Beer Company in '49, '50, or '63. The date of manufacture is embossed on the bottom of each bottle. Shown is a 7 ounce bottle with the Schlitz label still attached; I have a picture of a 12 ounce throw-away with an Old Milwaukee label. You can see most of the others in the above mentioned Fire-King book. Thousands of these bottles were made, but labeled ones are not often found. Bottle collectors usually find these more charming than Royal Ruby collectors and prices are often higher at bottle shows than at glass shows. The quart size is the most commonly seen. I do not consider these dinnerware items, although some avid beer drinkers would argue that point.

	Red		Red
Ash tray, 4½", leaf	5.00	Punch bowl base	40.00
Beer bottle, 7 oz.	25.00	Punch cup, 5 oz.	3.00
Beer bottle, 12 oz.	75.00	Saucer, round	2.50
Beer bottle, 16 oz.	75.00	Sherbet, ftd.	8.00
Beer bottle, 32 oz.	45.00	Sherbet, stemmed, 6½ oz.	8.00
Bowl, 4¼", round, fruit	5.50	*Stem, 3½ oz., cocktail	10.00
Bowl, 5¼", popcorn	14.00	*Stem, 4 oz., juice	10.00
Bowl, 7½", round, soup	12.50	Stem, 4½ oz., cocktail	10.00
Bowl, 8", oval, vegetable	32.00	Stem, 5½ oz., juice	12.50
Bowl, 8½", round, large berry	17.50	Stem, 6 oz., sherbet	8.00
Bowl, 10", deep, popcorn (same as punch)	40.00	*Stem, 6 oz., sherbet	8.00
Bowl, 11½", salad	33.00	*Stem, 9 oz., goblet	14.00
Cigarette box/card holder, 6⅛" x 4"	60.00	Stem, 9½ oz., goblet	13.00
Creamer, flat	8.00	*Stem, 14 oz., iced tea	20.00
Creamer, ftd.	9.00	Sugar, flat	8.00
Cup, round	6.00	Sugar, ftd.	7.50
Goblet, ball stem	12.00	Sugar, lid	10.00
Ice bucket	35.00	Tumbler, 2½ oz., ftd. wine	14.00
Lamp	35.00	Tumbler, 3½ oz., cocktail	12.50
Pitcher, 3 qt., tilted, swirl	35.00	Tumbler, 5 oz., juice, ftd. or flat	7.50
Pitcher, 3 qt., upright	40.00	Tumbler, 9 oz., water	6.50
Pitcher, 42 oz., tilted or straight	30.00	Tumbler, 10 oz., 5", water, ftd.	6.50
Plate, 6¼", sherbet, round	4.00	Tumbler, 12 oz., 6" ftd., tea	15.00
Plate, 7", salad	5.00	Tumbler, 13 oz., iced tea	13.00
Plate, 7¾", salad, round	6.00	Vase, 4", ivy, ball-shaped	6.00
Plate, 9⅛", dinner, round	11.00	Vase, 6⅜", two styles	9.00
Plate, 13¾"	25.00	Vase, 9", two styles	17.50
Punch bowl	40.00	Water bottle (two styles)	225.00

SANDWICH COLORS, ANCHOR HOCKING GLASS COMPANY, 1939 – 1964

Colors: Desert Gold, 1961 – 1964; Forest Green, 1956 – 1960s; pink, 1939 – 1940; Royal Ruby, 1938 – 1939; White/Ivory (opaque), 1957 – 1960s

Forest Green Sandwich prices have finally slowed down enough for pursuing collectors to catch their breath. The five little pieces that were packed in Crystal Wedding Oats remain easy to find. Literally, thousands of those five pieces (4⁵⁄₁₆" bowl, custard cup, custard liner, water and juice tumblers) are available today. Everyone had hot oats for breakfast; thus these pieces accumulated very fast. Prices for other Forest Green pieces have risen due to demand! All known pieces of Forest Green Sandwich are shown in the photograph. That rolled edge custard cup shown in the front has never been accounted for in any quantity. It is rarer than the pitchers!

Forest Green pitchers are scarce. Everyone obtained the juice and water tumblers free in oats as explained above. Juice and water sets were offered for sale with a pitcher and six tumblers. Most everyone already had enough tumblers, so they did not buy sets. Most of these pitcher sets were returned to Anchor Hocking for credit.

Lids for Forest Green Sandwich sugar and cookie jars have never surfaced. Anchor Hocking employees remembered selling lidless cookie jars as vases. They must have sold well!

New collectors seem to be attracted to Forest Green Sandwich more than any other Sandwich color. Dinner plates are now selling above $100.00, and I sell any I can unearth!

Cups are apparently more available than saucers; accordingly, the price of saucers is about to surpass the price of cups.

I have priced Royal Ruby Sandwich here, but it is also found in *Collector's Encyclopedia of Depression Glass* in the Royal Ruby section of that book.

I had thought only bowls were made in pink. A very light pink pitcher was found a few years ago. It is not a vivid pink, but none of the pink is!

New collectors are starting to look at amber Sandwich. However, few are finding footed amber tumblers. The rest of the set can be completed with some work and luck. There are no pitchers to find in amber.

Ivory punch sets were first offered in 1957, both plain and trimmed in 22K gold. There is little price distinction today; that set trimmed in gold seems to be less in demand because the gold has a tendency to erode when used! In 1964 and 1965 Marathon gas stations in Ohio and Kentucky sold Ivory (with gold trim) punch bowl sets for $2.89 with an oil change and lubrication. Many of these are still being found in their original boxes. One collector told me he had amassed ten of these.

	Desert Gold	Royal Ruby	Forest Green	Pink	Ivory/White
Bowl, 4⁵⁄₁₆", smooth			6.00		
Bowl, 4⅞", smooth	3.00	16.00		4.00	
Bowl, 5¼", scalloped	6.00	20.00		7.00	
Bowl, 5¼", smooth				7.00	
Bowl, 6½", smooth	6.00				
Bowl, 6½", scalloped		27.50	50.00		
Bowl, 6¾", cereal	12.00				
Bowl, 7⅝", salad			70.00		
Bowl, 8¼", scalloped		40.00	85.00	27.50	
Bowl, 9", salad	30.00				
Cookie jar and cover	37.50		*25.00		
Creamer			35.00		
Cup, tea or coffee	3.50		22.50		
Custard cup			3.50		
Custard cup, rolled edge			45.00		
Custard cup liner			2.50		
Pitcher, 6", juice			195.00	300.00	
Pitcher, ½ gal., ice lip			495.00		
Plate, 9", dinner	10.00		120.00		
Plate, 12", sandwich	15.00				
Punch bowl, 9¾"					15.00
Punch bowl stand					15.00
Punch cup					2.00
Saucer	3.00		22.50		
Sugar			*40.00		
Tumbler, 3⁹⁄₁₆", 5 oz., juice			4.00		
Tumbler, 9 oz., water			5.00		
Tumbler, 9 oz., footed	250.00				

* no cover

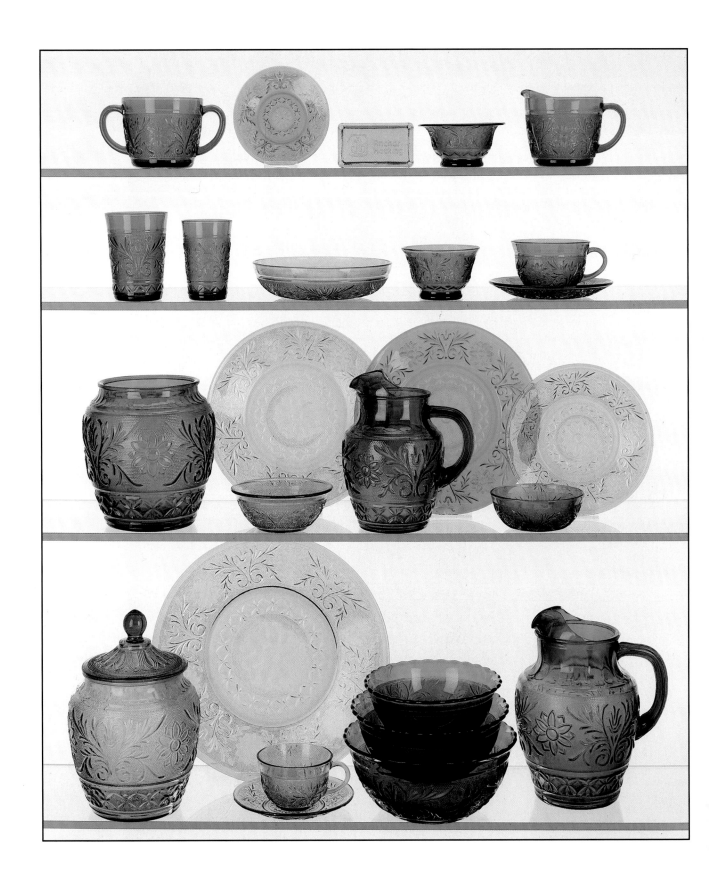

I have separated Anchor Hocking's crystal Sandwich from the colors to simplify writing about each.

There are four sizes of tumblers found in crystal. The footed tumbler has never been easy to find, but the 3⅜", 3 ounce juice is missing in many collections. These juice tumblers are found in the New England area — or they used to be. One dealer from there, from whom I have bought several hundred of these over the last twenty-five years, tells me they have disappeared from the market place in his area, too. Collectors say they are not being offered for sale in any of the antique publications or over the Internet. Don't pass these by if you see them for sale!

A recently discovered piece is the scalloped top, 6¾" cereal bowl which has settled into a price range of $125. Not every collector wants these and they are so rarely found that not every Sandwich collector could own one if they so wished. Apparently, these scalloped edge pieces were a special order or a trial issue. It is interesting that heretofore unknown pieces continue to appear. Who knows what else will surface as more and more people enter the collecting world?

I was informed by an avid collector that the 9" salad bowl and the punch bowl are not the same bowls. He says the true salad bowl will fit inside the punch bowl and the reason that there is a shortage of punch bowl bases is that there are too many salad bowls posing as punch bowls. The salad bowl was listed at 9" in the catalogs and the punch bowl 9¾"; so, he probably is right.

Other crystal pieces that are seldom found are the regular cereal, 5" crimped dessert bowl, and unblemished 12" plates. That 12" plate has made the biggest jump in price in this pattern. A 5" crimped dessert listed by Anchor Hocking only measures 4⅞". Mould variation makes size listings a major problem! Both this and the crimped sherbets are listed as occasional Sandwich pieces only in the 1956 catalog. "Crimped" is their word used to describe these pieces. Listings in only one catalog normally means pieces are in short supply today.

Collecting Anchor Hocking's Sandwich continues to flourish. Indiana's Sandwich does not do as well. Hocking went to some trouble to maintain the collectibility of their older glassware while Indiana did not. Prices continue to increase in this popular Hocking pattern. Surprisingly, this Sandwich may be the most collected crystal pattern in this book except for Iris.

Remember that Anchor Hocking reintroduced a crystal cookie jar in the late 1970s that was larger than the old. For a comparison of these cookie jars, see measurements below. The newer one now sells in the $15.00 range. These are beginning to be seen in quantities at flea markets and even antique malls. Unfortunately, they are approaching a quarter of a century in age — nearing collectibility themselves. Cups, saucers, and 8" plates were premiums for buying $3.00 (about ten gallons) of gas at Marathon stations in the mid 1960s. The promotion took at least four weeks for cups, saucers, and plates. You could have gotten the crystal punch bowl set for only $2.89 with an oil change and lube! Ah, the good old days! Most of these crystal punch sets were gold trimmed as were the Ivory ones and many of these can still be found in their original boxes.

	Crystal
Bowl, 4⁵⁄₁₆", smooth	5.00
Bowl, 4⅞"/5", crimped dessert	18.00
Bowl, 4⅞", smooth	6.00
Bowl, 5¼", scalloped	7.50
Bowl, 6½", smooth	7.50
Bowl, 6½", scalloped, deep	7.50
Bowl, 6¾", cereal	45.00
Bowl, 7", salad	7.00
Bowl, 7⅝", scalloped	8.00
Bowl, 8¼", scalloped	10.00
Bowl, 8¼", oval	7.00
Bowl, 9", salad	23.00
Butter dish, low	45.00
Butter dish bottom	25.00
Butter dish top	20.00
Cookie jar and cover	40.00
Creamer	6.00
Cup, tea or coffee	2.50
Custard cup	3.50
Custard cup, crimped, 5 oz.	14.00
Custard cup liner	18.50
Pitcher, 6", juice	65.00
Pitcher, ½ gal., ice lip	85.00
Plate, 7", dessert	11.00
Plate, 8"	6.00
Plate, 9", dinner	20.00
Plate, 9", indent for punch cup	5.00
Plate, 12", sandwich	37.50
Punch bowl, 9¾"	20.00
Punch bowl stand	30.00
Punch cup	2.25
Saucer	1.50
Sherbet, footed	8.00
Sugar	8.50

COOKIE JARS	NEW	OLD
Height	10¼"	9¾"
Opening width	5½"	4⅞"
Circumference/largest part	22"	19"

	Crystal
Sugar cover	15.00
Tumbler, 3⅜", 3 oz., juice	20.00
Tumbler, 3⁹⁄₁₆", 5 oz., juice	6.50
Tumbler, 9 oz., water	8.00
Tumbler, 9 oz., footed	33.00

SANDWICH, INDIANA GLASS COMPANY, 1920s – 1980s

Colors: crystal late 1920s – 1980s; teal blue 1950s – 1980s; milk white, mid 1950s; amber, late 1920s – 1980s;
Red, 1933/1969 – early 1970s; Smokey Blue, 1976 – 1977

Indiana's Sandwich pattern is highly thought of by some collectors; it is a pretty pattern with a historical basis. However, many dealers and collectors view it with skepticism for investment purposes due to this company's history for reissuing their glass patterns in older glass colors. This process never allows the older glassware to gain the status that other companies' glassware has. Pink and green Sandwich is priced in the *Collector's Encyclopedia of Depression Glass* since they were made in the 1930s; and although green (called Chantilly) has been made again, it is a different shade than the original. You can see examples of both greens in the Depression book. The older green Indiana Sandwich will glow under an ultraviolet (black) light while the newer will not. Do not use this as a blanket test for all old glass. Newer glass will glow, too, especially yellow or vaseline using the proper chemical formula; and that is a favorite trick of unscrupulous dealers who portray their new glass as old. Chantilly green was made in dinnerware sets whereas the original green was made only in occasional pieces. No dinner plates, cups, saucers, creamers, sugars, or water goblets were made in green until the 1980s. I actually don't care who told you how old these dinnerware items are; they were never made until the early 1980s. I say that because I received a letter from a lady who had taken her green Chantilly pieces to a popular television antiques show, and they explained to her they were from the 1930s; everybody, even the experts make some mistakes!

Tiara Exclusives took over Sandwich production by Indiana with an issue of red in 1969, amber in 1970, Smokey Blue in 1976 and crystal in 1978. Amber, Chantilly green, and crystal were made into the late 1980s.

Basically, the list below incorporates the original Sandwich line from the 1920s and the original Tiara listings from the late 1960s and early 1970s. Eventually, I may be forced to add all the Tiara listings throughout the 1970s and 1980s, but only if they become more collectible. So far, I've seen little evidence of that. You can probably stock up on Tiara sandwich pieces at a reasonable price if you have a friend who used to sponsor Tiara parties.

The mould for the old wine broke and a new one was designed. All the wines made in the last few years are fatter (amber middle row, next page) than the earlier ones that were shaped like the red one next to the amber. Older wines are 4½" tall and hold 3 ounces. The newer wines are shown in Tiara catalogs, but no measurements or capacities are given. Sorry, I didn't measure the one shown; but it appears to be about an eighth of an inch taller looking at the picture. I suspect it holds at least 4 ounces. All green wines shaped like the amber one are new and will not glow under a black light.

Teal blue (bottom row) and milk glass (white in middle row)) are colors distributed in the 1950s; but Tiara remade a teal Sandwich butter dish as an exclusive hostess gift that unconditionally destroyed the $200.00 price tag on the 1950s butter dish. This new Tiara one originally sold for approximately $15.00. "New" Sandwich has been heralded to prospective customers as glass that's going to be valuable based on its past performance; but the company eroded the collectability of their older glassware by selling new glass copies!

Six items in red Sandwich date from 1933, i.e., cups, saucers, luncheon plates, water goblets, creamers, and sugars. A few red pieces were made for the 1933 Chicago World's Fair. In 1969, Tiara Home Products produced red pitchers, 9 oz. goblets, cups, saucers, wines, wine decanters, 13" serving trays, creamers, sugars, salad, and dinner plates. There is virtually no difference in pricing unless you have some red Sandwich marked 1933 Chicago World's Fair. This older, inscribed glass will fetch more by virtue of its being a World's Fair collectible.

Amber and crystal prices are shown, but you must realize that most of the crystal and all the amber have been made since 1970. Prices below reflect the small amounts of these colors that I see at flea markets and malls.

	Amber Crystal	Teal Blue	Red		Amber Crystal	Teal Blue	Red
Ash trays (club, spade,				Goblet, 9 oz.	13.00		45.00
heart, dmd. shapes, ea.)	3.50			Mayonnaise, ftd.	13.00		
Basket, 10", high	32.50			Pitcher, 68 oz.	22.50		165.00
Bowl, 4¼", berry	3.50			Plate, 6", sherbet	3.00	7.00	
Bowl, 6"	4.00			Plate, 7", bread and butter	4.00		
Bowl, 6", hexagonal	5.00	14.00		Plate, 8", oval, indent for sherbet		6.00	12.00
Bowl, 8½"	11.00			Plate, 8⅜", luncheon	5.00		20.00
Bowl, 9", console	16.00			Plate, 10½", dinner	8.00		
Bowl, 11½", console	19.00			Plate, 13", sandwich	13.00	25.00	35.00
Butter dish and cover, domed	22.50	*155.00		Puff box	16.50		
Butter dish bottom	6.00	42.50		Salt and pepper, pr.	16.50		
Butter dish top	16.50	112.50		Sandwich server, center handle	18.00		47.50
Candlesticks, 3½", pr.	17.50			Saucer	2.25	6.00	7.00
Candlesticks 7", pr.	25.00			Sherbet, 3¼"	5.50	12.00	
Creamer	9.00		45.00	Sugar, large	9.00		45.00
Celery, 10½"	16.00			Sugar lid for large size	13.00		
Creamer and sugar on				Tumbler, 3 oz., footed cocktail	7.50		
diamond-shaped tray	16.00	32.00		Tumbler, 8 oz., footed water	9.00		
Cruet, 6½ oz. and stopper		135.00		Tumbler, 12 oz., footed tea	10.00		
Cup	3.50	8.00	30.00	Wine, 3", 4 oz.	6.00		12.50
Decanter and stopper	22.50		85.00				

*Beware, recent vintage sells for $25.00

SEASCAPE #2685 LINE, FOSTORIA GLASS COMPANY, 1954 – 1958

Color: blue, green, and pink Opalescent

Seascape is found with Fostoria's Contour (#2666) shapes, but the company gave them separate line numbers. Pictured with the pink Seascape on the top of the next page are three pink Contour line stems. These are not opalescent, just pink. You can use these with pink, but there are no blue ones available.

Seascape comes in green opalescent according to all the information I can find; but in three years of buying, I have seen only blue and pink. Too, I don't believe I have ever seen a more divergent range of prices on any other pattern that I have tried to add to the book. Few pieces are advertised for sale; when you see it out at markets, more times than not, it is labeled Duncan and Miller and priced out the kazoo. Duncan opalescent is hard enough to sell without adding a "pseudo" Duncan pattern to the mix. Actually, the more reasonably priced pieces have been bought from knowledgeable dealers who knew what Seascape was, who manufactured it, and when.

Cathy likes this pattern, thinks it apropos for a time when people were thinking about space travel and going to the moon someday. She has doggedly hunted it for these pictures. Once I have enough pieces for a decent picture, I tend to get conservative in my buying, whereas she believes if we don't have it, we should. You have more pieces to view due to her persistence. By the way, the 12" footed salver is called a cake stand by many. Notice the blue one in the bottom row has an ivy type design. I have not been able to find any information on this; if you can enlighten me, please do.

	Opalescent		Opalescent
Bowl, 4½", pansy	35.00	Mint tray, 7½", ftd.	30.00
Bowl, 8", shallow	50.00	Plate, 14", buffet	65.00
Bowl, 8¾", ftd.	75.00	Preserve, 6½", handled	50.00
Bowl, 8¾", square, scalloped	65.00	Relish, 9" x 6", two-part	40.00
Bowl, 10", salad	65.00	Relish, 11¾" x 8½", three-part	50.00
Bowl, 11½", shallow	65.00	Salver, 12", ftd.	125.00
Candleholder, 2" high, 4½" diameter	25.00	Sugar, 2⅝"	25.00
Cream, 3⅜"	25.00	Sugar, individual	25.00
Creamer, individual	25.00	Tray, 7½", oval, ftd.	50.00
Mayonnaise, 3-pc. set	50.00	Tray, individual sug/cr	25.00

SHELL PINK MILK GLASS, JEANNETTE GLASS CO., 1957 – 1959

Color: opaque pink

Those formerly skyrocketing price increases for Shell Pink have steadied. All pieces that were exorbitantly priced, still are; but there are new collectors buying the pattern! The Lazy Susan and heavy bottomed National vase are continuing to surpass all regularly found pieces in price. This fashionable Jeannette pattern was made for only a brief time in the late 1950s. It was called Shell Pink and included pieces from several standard Jeannette lines (Anniversary, Baltimore Pear, Floragold, Harp, Holiday, National, and Windsor). It was promoted as "a delicate coloring that blends perfectly with all kinds of flowers. Its smooth satiny finish goes all the way through the glass - is not a spray or surface coating."

The excerpt above is from a four page catalog from Jeannette. These pages also state the "Shell Pink Milk Glass's lovely color and design make women admire it — and buy it!" Today, there may be more male collectors searching for this colored glassware than women. My grammar dictionary on the computer frowns upon gender specific references; it keeps annoying me on this paragraph!

There are a couple of rarely seen Shell Pink pieces at the bottom of page 220, the Shell Pink ash tray and the bird candle holder, which evidently was sold for a short time with the three-footed pheasant bowl. I assume the tail feathers were a problem and this mould was discontinued. A lone Anniversary cake plate was unearthed; no others have appeared at present. Anniversary pin-up vases are being found, but not by me to photograph. You can see a duck powder jar in *Very Rare Glassware of the Depression Years, Sixth Series*. I recently bought a Shell Pink "Genie" bottle that came from the same factory worker's relative's home in which the rare duck powder jars were found. Also, I recently photographed a collector's large Shell Pink plate with the same pattern as the punch bowl pictured on the top of page 220. It may have been designed as a liner for the punch bowl, but the pattern was underneath where it didn't show. Was it experimental and rejected for some reason or another? In any case, it was the first one of those I have seen. Speaking of the punch bowl reminds me that the original ladle was pink plastic and not crystal. New pieces in Shell Pink just keep showing up. Keep your eyes peeled!

Watch for the Butterfly cigarette box and ash trays. They have become very popular with collectors. Be sure to check those butterfly wings. Pieces of those wings have a tendency to "fly off". The price below is for mint condition butterfly boxes. The oval, four-footed Lombardi bowls turn up regularly, but those with an embossed design on the inside are not being discovered nearly enough to supply collectors' desires. The difference in price should be much greater; but some collectors feel one oval bowl is enough, so why buy the higher priced one if you have one that looks nearly the same. The honey jar is easy to spot with its beehive shape, but it is not found as regularly as it once was.

That Harp tray is hard to find; but the greater demand for the Harp cake stand almost makes these two comparable in price. Most of you will recognize the large, three-footed Holiday bowl; the footed, oval bowl with a pattern similar to Holiday was called Florentine. The Gondola fruit bowl is the long (17½"), two-handled bowl and the Venetian tray (16½") is the six-part one. There is also a four-part (12") Vineyard (grapes) relish. I'm speculating that someone in the design department made a trip to Italy right before these pieces were christened. The five-part, two-handled oval tray is beginning to show up on most every collector's want list.

Shell pink was sold to the florist industry and other pieces were made for "Napco Ceramics, Cleveland, Ohio." Each piece is marked thus with numbers (quoted in the price list) except for the piece with a sawtooth edge that only has "Napco, Cleveland." The National Shell Pink candy bottom was promoted as a vase with no lid. It could have been rejected as a candy since you wouldn't have been able to see the candy inside it.

	Opaque Pink		Opaque Pink
Ash tray, butterfly shape	28.00	"Napco" #2250, ftd. bowl w/berries	15.00
Base, for Lazy Susan, w/ball bearings	160.00	"Napco" #2255, ftd. bowl w/saw tooth top	25.00
Bowl, 6½", wedding, w/cover	22.50	"Napco" #2256, square comport	12.50
Bowl, 8", Pheasant, ftd.	37.50	"National" candy bottom	10.00
Bowl, 8", wedding, w/cover	27.50	Pitcher, 24 oz., ftd., Thumbprint	27.50
Bowl, 9", ftd., fruit stand, Floragold	27.50	Powder jar, 4¾", w/cover	45.00
Bowl, 10", Florentine, ftd.	30.00	Punch base, 3½", tall	35.00
Bowl, 10½", ftd., Holiday	45.00	Punch bowl, 7½ qt.	60.00
Bowl, 10⅞", 4-ftd., Lombardi, designed center	42.00	Punch cup, 5 oz. (also fits snack tray)	6.00
Bowl, 10⅞", 4-ftd., Lombardi, plain center	27.00	Punch ladle, pink plastic	20.00
Bowl, 17½", Gondola fruit	40.00	Punch set, 15-pc. (bowl, base, 12 cups, ladle)	225.00
Cake plate, Anniversary	225.00	Relish, 12", 4-part, octagonal, Vineyard design	42.00
Cake stand, 10", Harp	45.00	Stem, 5 oz., sherbet, Thumbprint	10.00
Candle holder, 2-lite, pr.	45.00	Stem, 8 oz., water goblet, Thumbprint	12.50
Candle holder, Eagle, 3-ftd., pr.	85.00	Sugar cover	17.50
Candy dish w/cover, 6½" high, square	30.00	Sugar, ftd., Baltimore Pear design	11.00
Candy dish, 4-ftd., 5¼", Floragold	20.00	Tray, 7¾" x 10", snack w/cup indent	9.00
Candy jar, 5½", 4-ftd., w/cover, grapes	20.00	Tray, 12½" x 9¾", 2 hndl., Harp	60.00
Celery and relish, 12½", 3-part	45.00	Tray, 13½", Lazy Susan, 5-part	55.00
Cigarette box, butterfly finial	235.00	Tray, 15¾", 5-part, 2 hndl.	85.00
Compote, 6", Windsor	20.00	Tray, 16½", 6-part, Venetian	40.00
Cookie jar w/cover, 6½" high	100.00	Tray, Lazy Susan complete w/base	235.00
Creamer, Baltimore Pear design	15.00	Tumbler, 5 oz., juice, ftd., Thumbprint	8.00
Honey jar, beehive shape, notched cover	40.00	Vase, 5", cornucopia	15.00
"Napco" #2249, cross hatch design pot	15.00	Vase, 7"	30.00
		Vase, 9", heavy bottom, National	135.00

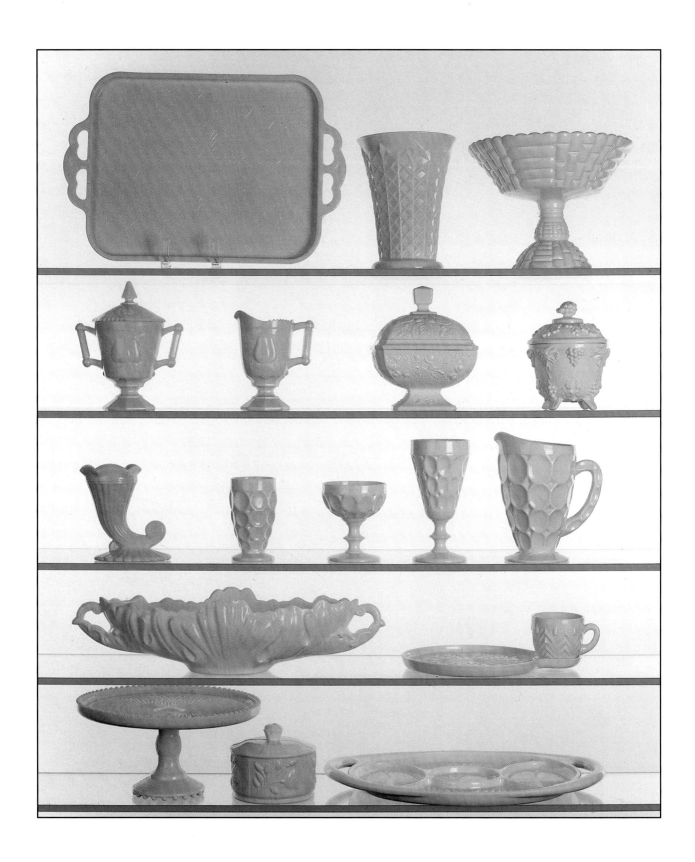

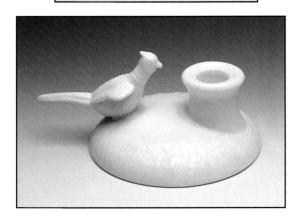

SILVER CREST, FENTON ART GLASS COMPANY, 1943 – PRESENT

Color: white with crystal edge

Silver Crest is one of Fenton's patterns long in production. Every time they have discontinued it, requests and/or other concerns coerce them into reissuing it. There are several ways to guide you in dating your pieces. Before 1958, the white was called opal and had an opalescence to it when held up to the light. In 1958, a formula change to milk glass made the glass look very white without "fire" in the white. All pieces reinstated after 1973 will be signed Fenton. Fenton began marking carnival pieces in 1971, and in 1973 they continued this practice with all pieces. If you acquire items that have white edging encompassing crystal, this is called Crystal Crest and dates from 1942.

The pitcher, punch bowl set, and hurricane lamps are very hard to acquire, but delightful when found in spite of the price tag. Tumbler prices are edging upward at a leisurely pace; latch on to a few before they become too expensive. As with Fenton's Emerald Crest, you will encounter several styles of tidbits using bowls and plates or a blending of both.

Some pieces of Silver Crest are assigned two different line numbers. Initially, this line was #36 and all pieces carried that classification. In July 1952, Fenton began issuing a Ware Number for individual pieces. That is why you see two distinct numbers for many of the items below.

See page 56 for prices of Emerald Crest. Aqua Crest has a blue edge around the white and prices for it track between those of Silver Crest and Emerald Crest. Remember, demand for Silver Crest is making it one of Fenton's most recognized line.

	White		White
Basket, 5" hndl. (top hat) #1924	65.00	Chip and dip (low bowl w/mayo in center) #7303	65.00
Basket, 5", hndl. #680	40.00	Comport, ftd. #7228	11.00
Basket, 6½", hndl. #7336	40.00	Comport, ftd., low #7329	18.00
Basket, 7" #7237	35.00	Creamer, reeded hndl. #680	22.50
Basket, 12" #7234	100.00	Creamer, reeded hndl. (same as #680) #7201	22.50
Basket, 13" #7233	150.00	Creamer, ruffled top	50.00
Basket, hndl. #7339	65.00	Creamer, straight side #1924	32.50
Bon bon, 5½" #7225	12.00	Creamer, threaded hndl. #680	17.50
Bon bon, 8" #7428	12.00	Cup, reeded hndl. #680	29.50
Bonbon, 5½" #36	12.00	Cup, threaded look hndl. #7209	22.50
Bowl, 5", finger or deep dessert #680	22.50	Epergne set, 2-pc. (vase in ftd. bowl) #7202	75.00
Bowl, 5½", soup #680	35.00	Epergne set, 3-pc. #7200	125.00
Bowl, 7" #7227	18.00	Epergne, 2-pc. set #7301	110.00
Bowl, 8½" #7338	30.00	Epergne, 4-pc. bowl w/3 horn epergnes #7308	140.00
Bowl, 8½" flared #680	30.00	Epergne, 5-pc. bowl w/4 horn epergnes #7305	175.00
Bowl, 9½" #682	40.00	Lamp, hurricane #7398	185.00
Bowl, 10" #7224	50.00	Mayonnaise bowl #7203	11.00
Bowl, 10" salad #680	50.00	Mayonnaise ladle #7203	5.00
Bowl, 11" #5823	50.00	Mayonnaise liner #7203	27.50
Bowl, 13" #7223	65.00	Mayonnaise set, 3-pc. #7203	45.00
Bowl, 14" #7323	80.00	Nut, ftd. #7229	15.00
Bowl, banana, high ft. w/upturned sides #7324	65.00	Nut, ftd. (flattened sherbet) #680	15.00
Bowl, banana, low ftd. #5824	45.00	Oil bottle #680	85.00
Bowl, deep dessert #7221	32.50	Pitcher, 70 oz. jug #7467	225.00
Bowl, dessert, shallow #680	22.50	Plate, 5½" #680	6.00
Bowl, finger or dessert #202	18.00	Plate, 5½", finger bowl liner #7218	6.00
Bowl, ftd. (like large, tall comport) #7427	67.50	Plate, 6½" #680, #7219	6.50
Bowl, ftd., tall, square #7330	67.50	Plate, 8½" #680, #7217	15.00
Bowl, low dessert #7222	22.50	Plate, 10" #680	37.50
Bowl, shallow #7316	46.00	Plate, 10½" #7210	55.00
Cake plate, 13" high, ftd. #7213	45.00	Plate, 11½" #7212	37.50
Cake plate, low ftd. #5813	40.00	Plate, 12" #680	47.50
Candle holder, 6" tall w/crest on bottom, pr. #7474	45.00	Plate, 12" #682	35.00
Candle holder, bulbous base, pr. #1523	30.00	Plate, 12½" #7211	40.00
Candle holder, cornucopia, pr. #951	60.00	Plate, 16", torte 7216	60.00
Candle holder, cornucopia (same as #951), pr. #7274	50.00	Punch bowl #7306	350.00
Candle holder, flat saucer base, pr. #680	25.00	Punch bowl base #7306	90.00
Candle holder, low, ruffled, pr. #7271	25.00	Punch cup #7306	15.00
Candle holder, ruffled comport style, pr. #7272	55.00	Punch ladle (clear) #7306	22.50
Candy box #7280	70.00	Punch set, 15-pc. #7306	625.00
Candy box, ftd., tall stem #7274	125.00	Relish, divided #7334	32.50
		Relish, heart, hndl. #7333	22.50
		Saucer #680, #7209	5.00

	White
Shaker, pr. #7206	110.00
Shaker, pr. (bowling pin shape)	175.00
Shaker, pr. #7406	225.00
Sherbet #680	10.00
Sherbet #7226	10.00
Sugar, reeded hndl. #680	22.50
Sugar, reeded hndl. (same as #680) #7201	22.50
Sugar, ruffled top	45.00
Sugar, sans hndls. #680	35.00
Tidbit, 2-tier (luncheon/dessert plates) #7296	47.50
Tidbit, 2-tier (luncheon/dinner plates) #7294	47.50
Tidbit, 2-tier plates #680	47.50
Tidbit, 2-tier, ruffled bowl #7394	75.00
Tidbit, 3-tier (luncheon/dinner/dessert plates) #7295	47.50
Tidbit, 3-tier plates #680	47.50
Tidbit, 3-tier, ruffled bowl #7397	85.00
Top hat, 5" #1924	125.00
Tray, sandwich #7291	35.00
Tumbler, ftd. #7342	57.50

	White
Vase, 4½" #203	12.50
Vase, 4½" #7254	12.50
Vase, 4½", double crimped #36, #7354	15.00
Vase, 4½", fan #36	11.00
Vase, 5" (top hat) #1924	125.00
Vase, 6" #7451	16.00
Vase, 6", doubled crimped #7156	19.00
Vase, 6¼", double crimped #36, #7356	17.50
Vase, 6¼", fan #36	20.00
Vase, 7" #7455	30.00
Vase, 8" #7453	25.00
Vase, 8", bulbous base #186	40.00
Vase, 8", doubled crimped #7258	22.00
Vase, 8", wheat #5859	42.50
Vase, 8½" #7458	55.00
Vase, 9" #7454	47.50
Vase, 9" #7459	47.50
Vase, 10" #7450	115.00
Vase, 12" (fan topped) #7262	110.00

SQUARE, NO. 3797, CAMBRIDGE GLASS COMPANY, 1949 – MID 1950s

Colors: crystal, some red and black

Cambridge Square was initially illustrated in the 1949 Cambridge catalog but was shown as "patent pending." You will find unused Square pieces that still have "patent pending" as well as Cambridge labels. In the past, I pictured a cordial with both stickers. This is one of the few Cambridge patterns that totally falls into the time frame of this book.

The punch bowl set seems to be one of the more difficult pieces to find in crystal. The icers with inserts are also missing from many collections. Square is reasonably priced for a Cambridge pattern; but there are not as many seeking Square as there are other Cambridge patterns such as Rose Point or Gloria. Square was made during the financially troubled last years of Cambridge which may mean items are limited more than we know. It will take a few years and more collectors buying it to determine that.

Some Square was made in color, Carmen and Ebony; however, Ruby (Imperial's name) pieces were also made from Cambridge moulds at Imperial in the late 1960s. Carmen pieces by Cambridge are rarely seen; Ruby can be found with some searching. I've been told that the "old timers" can tell the difference; personally, I can't!

	Crystal		Crystal
Ash tray, 3½" #3797/151	8.00	Plate, 9½", tidbit #3797/24	20.00
Ash tray, 6½" #3797/150	11.00	Plate, 11½" #3797/26	25.00
Bon bon, 7" #3797/164	13.50	Plate, 13½" #3797/28	30.00
Bon bon, 8" #3797/47	24.00	Relish, 6½", 2-part #3797/120	17.50
Bowl, 4½", dessert #3797/16	11.00	Relish, 8", 3-part #3797/125	22.50
Bowl, 6½", individual salad #3797/27	13.50	Relish, 10", 3-part #3797/126	25.00
Bowl, 9", salad #3797/49	22.50	Salt and pepper, pr. #3797/76	22.50
Bowl, 10", oval #3797/48	25.00	Saucer, coffee #3797/17	5.00
Bowl, 10", shallow #3797/81	30.00	Saucer, tea #3797/15	5.00
Bowl, 11", salad #3797/57	40.00	Stem, #3798, 5 oz., juice	10.00
Bowl, 12", oval #3797/65	30.00	Stem, #3798, 12 oz., iced tea	12.00
Bowl, 12", shallow #3797/82	35.00	Stem, #3798, cocktail	17.50
Buffet set, 4-pc. (plate, div. bowl, 2 ladles)		Stem, #3798, cordial	25.00
#3797/29	55.00	Stem, #3798, sherbet	11.00
Candle holder, 1¾", block #3797/492, pr.	25.00	Stem, #3798, water goblet	12.00
Candle holder, 2¾", block #3797/493, pr.	27.50	Stem, #3798, wine	20.00
Candle holder, 3¾", block #3797/495, pr.	27.50	Sugar #3797/41	10.00
Candle holder, cupped #3797/67, pr.	27.50	Sugar, individual #3797/40	10.00
Candy box and cover #3797/165	30.00	Tray, 8", oval, for individual sug/cr #3797/37	17.50
Celery, 11" #3797/103	23.00	Tumbler, #3797, 5 oz., juice	12.50
Comport, 6" #3797/54	25.00	Tumbler, #3797, 14 oz., iced tea	17.50
Creamer #3797/41	10.00	Tumbler, #3797, low cocktail	12.00
Creamer, individual #3797/40	10.00	Tumbler, #3797, low cordial	20.00
Cup, coffee, open handle #3797/17	10.00	Tumbler, #3797, low sherbet	10.00
Cup, tea, open handle #3797/15	10.00	Tumbler, #3797, low wine	15.00
Decanter, 32 oz. #3797/85	90.00	Tumbler, #3797, water goblet	13.50
Ice tub, 7½" #3797/34	37.50	Vase, 5", belled #3797/92	22.50
Icer, cocktail w/liner #3797/18	40.00	Vase, 5½", belled #3797/91	25.00
Lamp, hurricane, 2-pc. #3797/68	50.00	Vase, 6" #3797/90	22.50
Mayonnaise set, 3-pc. (bowl, plate, ladle)		Vase, 7½", ftd. #3797/77	22.50
#3797/129	30.00	Vase, 7½", rose bowl #3797/35	35.00
Oil bottle, 4½ oz. #3797/100	22.00	Vase, 8", ftd. #3797/80	20.00
Plate, 6", bread and butter #3797/20	8.00	Vase, 9½", ftd. #3797/78	27.50
Plate, 7", dessert or salad #3797/23	12.00	Vase, 9½", rose bowl #3797/36	45.00
Plate, 7", salad #3797/27	11.00	Vase, 11", ftd. #3797/79	40.00
Plate, 9½", dinner or luncheon #3797/25	28.00		

STAR, FEDERAL GLASS COMPANY, LATE 1950s – EARLY 1960s

Colors: amber, crystal, and crystal w/gold trim

The good news about Federal's Star pattern is that there are cup and saucer sets in the pattern; the bad news is that I didn't get one pictured. While checking out the strawberries in Plant City last year, I saw a set of amber Star at a flea market. I had to buy the six-piece setting to get one cup and saucer. The saucers are like the 6³⁄₁₆" plate, but with an indented cup ring. Cups will escape your eye unless you find them in a set as I did. They are plain with no hint of the "star" design on them. Without a catalog listing for this pattern (except for the pitchers and tumblers), the only way to add pieces is through unearthing them. Now there is a large, round platter added to that listing.

Amber Star sells well when we put the pieces out at a show. There are more collectors of amber than crystal at the present time. Star is found in two different shades of amber, much like Hocking's Princess pattern. Mostly, I see the lighter shade; there are darker amber pieces being found.

Although there were only a few different pieces made, you can put together a small set rather inexpensively. Notice the "star" shaped design on each piece (except the cup). Cathy remembers the pitchers being marketed with small colored soaps for the bath. Colored soaps weren't a priority with me when I was young! Star pitchers were also acquired in a set with Park Avenue tumblers.

You will find frosted, decorated juice pitchers with several designs and matching tumblers. Watch for a similar pitcher with painted flowers matching the red trimmed, Mountain Flowers Petalware (Depression glass book). The one I saw was frosted, but alas, not for sale. I would like to find one to photograph!

That whisky (sic) tumbler is found with labels showing jelly was packaged in them. Does anyone remember if these were samples or individual servings in gift packs?

	Amber	Crystal
Bowl, 4⅝", dessert	7.00	4.00
Bowl, 8⅜", vegetable	15.00	10.00
Creamer	9.00	6.00
Cup	10.00	5.00
Pitcher, 5¾", 36 oz., juice		9.00
Pitcher, 7", 60 oz.		12.00
Pitcher, 9¼", 85 oz., ice lip		15.00
Plate, 6³⁄₁₆", salad	5.00	3.00
Plate, 9⅜", dinner	9.00	5.00
Platter 11", round	15.00	12.00
Saucer	3.00	2.00
Sugar	9.00	5.00
Sugar lid	10.00	5.00
Tumbler, 2¼", 1½ oz., whisky		3.00
Tumbler, 3⅜", 4½ oz., juice	10.00	4.00
Tumbler, 3⅞", 9 oz., water	12.00	5.50
Tumbler, 5⅛", 12 oz., iced tea	15.00	8.00

STAR

PRESSED TUMBLERS

1123 — 1½ oz.
STAR WHISKY
Ht. 2¼"
Pkd. 12 doz. ctn. Wt. 17 lbs.

1123 — 4½ oz.
STAR JUICE TUMBLER
Ht. 3⅜"
Pkd. 12 doz. ctn. Wt. 37 lbs.

1123 — 9 oz.
STAR TUMBLER
Ht. 3⅞"
Pkd. 12 doz. ctn. Wt. 56 lbs.

1123 — 12 oz.
STAR ICED TEA
Ht. 5⅛"
Pkd. 6 doz. ctn. Wt. 42 lbs.

2844 — 36 oz.
STAR JUICE JUG
Ht. 5¾"
Pkd. 2 doz. ctn. Wt. 37 lbs.

(Also available — **2845-60 oz. JUG**
Ht. 7" Pkd. 1 doz. ctn. Wt. 26 lbs.)

2846 — 85 oz.
STAR ICE LIP JUG
Ht. 9¼"
Pkd. 1 doz. ctn. Wt. 38 lbs.

1116 — 5 oz.
PANEL JUICE TUMBLER
Ht. 3⅜"
Pkd. 12 doz. ctn. Wt. 38 lbs.

1116 — 9 oz.
PANEL TUMBLER
Ht. 4"
Pkd. 12 doz. ctn. Wt. 59 lbs.

1116 — 12 oz.
PANEL ICED TEA
Ht. 5⅜"
Pkd. 6 doz. ctn. Wt. 43 lbs.

1131 — 9 oz.
CATHEDRAL TUMBLER
Ht. 4"
Pkd. 12 doz. ctn. Wt. 58 lbs.

STARS and STRIPES, ANCHOR HOCKING GLASS GLASS COMPANY, 1942

Color: crystal

Collectors are drawn to Stars and Stripes even though it only has three items. With so few pieces I figured there were limited ways of displaying them for the book. As it happens, fate put me in front of a table of glassware with the red and gold plate pictured. Cathy convinced me I had to buy it. I doubt it was factory decorated; but it shows wear and the coloring suggests the "patriotic" theme the pattern was created for during World War II. It was a new find for the book. Do you suppose there is a sherbet or tumbler to match?

While writing about Stars and Stripes in the first edition of *Collectible Glassware of the 40s, 50s, 60s...*, we were in the middle of Desert Storm and this 40s pattern seemed to still fit the nationalistic passion of that time, too.

Tumblers appear to be almost non-existent while sherbets are fairly common. Plates cost twice as much as other pieces originally; that has certainly changed in today's market.

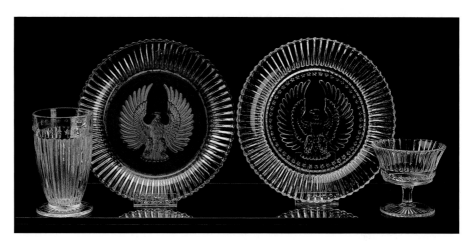

	Crystal
Plate, 8"	15.00
Sherbet	18.00
Tumbler, 5", 10 oz.	40.00

SWANKY SWIGS, 1930s – 1950s

Swanky Swigs were initially sold as Kraft® cheese containers. Illustrated here are the Swigs sold from the late 1930s into the 1950s with a collectible 1976 Bicentennial also displayed. Smaller size glasses (3¼") and the larger (4½") seem to have been distributed exclusively in Canada. The limited distribution of these sizes in the States makes their prices increase more than those regularly found here! Tulip No. 2 was sold only on the West Coast and prices are somewhat lower there. Earlier Swanky Swigs can be found in *The Collector's Encyclopedia of Depression Glass* if you become addicted to collecting these as many have. The two jars on row 2 of page 231 are store display Swankys (painted to look full of cheese). Some original lids from these Swigs are shown on page 234. Lids sell for $8.00 up, depending upon condition and the advertisement! Those with Kraft® caramels, Miracle Whip®, and TV show ads run $15.00 up. The most sought lid is pictured at the bottom of page 234. Bing was a popular guy and his Swanky lid will fetch $20.00 to $25.00 depending upon condition!

Page 231:

Row 1: Tulip No. 1

black, blue, red, green	3½"	3.00 – 4.00
black w/label	3½"	10.00 – 12.00
Blue, red, green	4½"	15.00 – 17.50
green	3¼"	15.00 – 17.50

Row 2: Tulip No. 3

lt. blue, yellow display jars	3¾"	25.00 – 30.00
lt. blue, red, yellow	3¾"	2.50 – 3.50
lt. blue, yellow	3¼"	15.00 – 17.50
red	4½"	15.00 – 17.50

Cornflower No. 1

lt. blue	4½"	15.00 – 17.50
lt. blue	3½"	4.00 – 5.00
lt. blue	3¼"	15.00 – 17.50

Row 3: Tulip No. 2

black, green, red	3½"	27.50 – 30.00
Carnival blue, green, red, yellow	3½"	6.00 – 8.00

Tulip No. 3

dk. blue	4½"	15.00 – 17.50
dk. blue	3¾"	2.50 – 3.50
Dk. blue	3¼"	15.00 – 17.50

Row 4: Posy Jonquil

yellow	4½"	17.50 – 20.00
yellow	3½"	6.00 – 7.00
yellow	3¼"	17.50 – 20.00

Posy: Tulip

red	4½"	15.00 – 17.50
red	3½"	5.00 – 6.00
red	3¼"	15.00 – 17.50

Posy: Violet

purple	4½"	17.50 – 20.00
purple	3½"	6.00 – 7.00
purple	3¼"	15.00 – 17.50

Row 5: Cornflower No. 2

dk. blue, lt. blue, red, yellow	3½"	2.50 – 3.50
dk. blue, lt. blue, yellow	3¼"	15.00 – 17.50

Forget-Me-Not

dk. blue,	3½"	2.50 – 3.50
dk. blue or yellow w/label (yel p 220)	3½"	10.00 – 12.50
dk. blue	3¼"	15.00 – 17.50

Page 232:

Row 1: Forget-Me-Not

lt. blue, red, yellow	3½"	2.50 – 3.50
lt. blue, red, yellow	3¼"	15.00 – 17.50

Daisy

red & white	3¾"	25.00 – 30.00
red & white	3¼"	35.00 – 40.00

Rows 2 – 5: Daisy

red, white & green	4½"	15.00 – 17.50
red, white & green	3¾"	2.00 – 3.00
red, white & green	3¼"	15.00 – 17.50

Bustling Betsy:

all colors	3¼"	15.00 – 17.50
all colors	3¾"	4.00 – 5.00

Antique Pattern:

all designs	3¼"	15.00 – 17.50
all designs	3¾"	4.00 – 500

clock & coal scuttle brown;
lamp & kettle blue;
coffee grinder & plate green;
spinning wheel & bellows red;
coffee pot & trivet black;
churn & cradle orange

Kiddie Cup:

all designs	4½"	20.00 – 25.00
	3¾"	4.00 – 5.00
	3¼"	15.00 – 17.50

bird & elephant red;
bear & pig blue;
squirrel & deer brown;
duck & horse black;
dog & rooster orange,
cat and rabbit green

bird & elephant w/label	3¾"	10.00 – 12.50
dog & rooster w/cheese	3¾"	25.00 – 30.00

Bicentennial issued in 1975;

yellow, red, green	3¾"	3.00 – 5.00

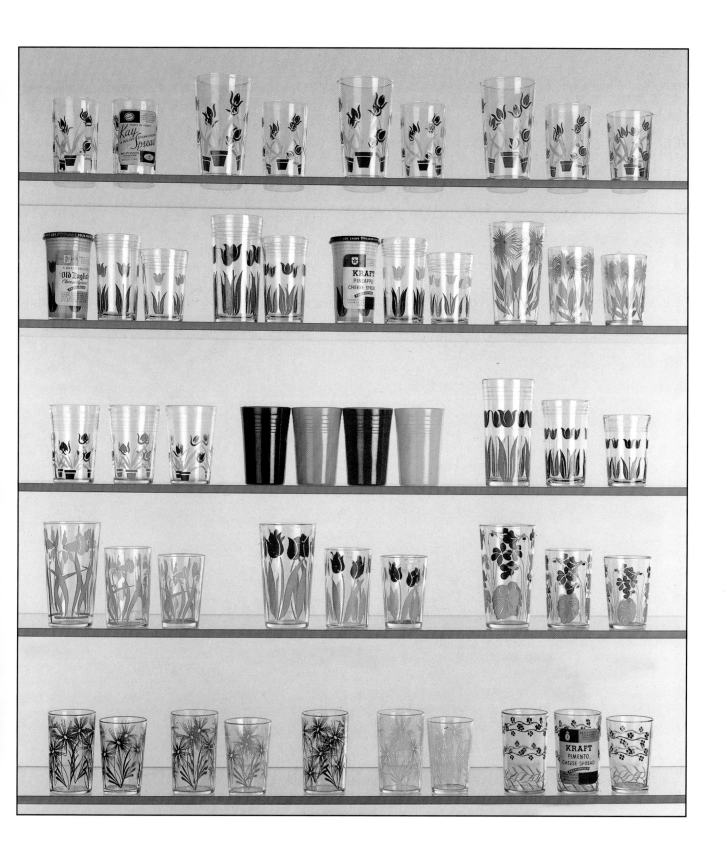

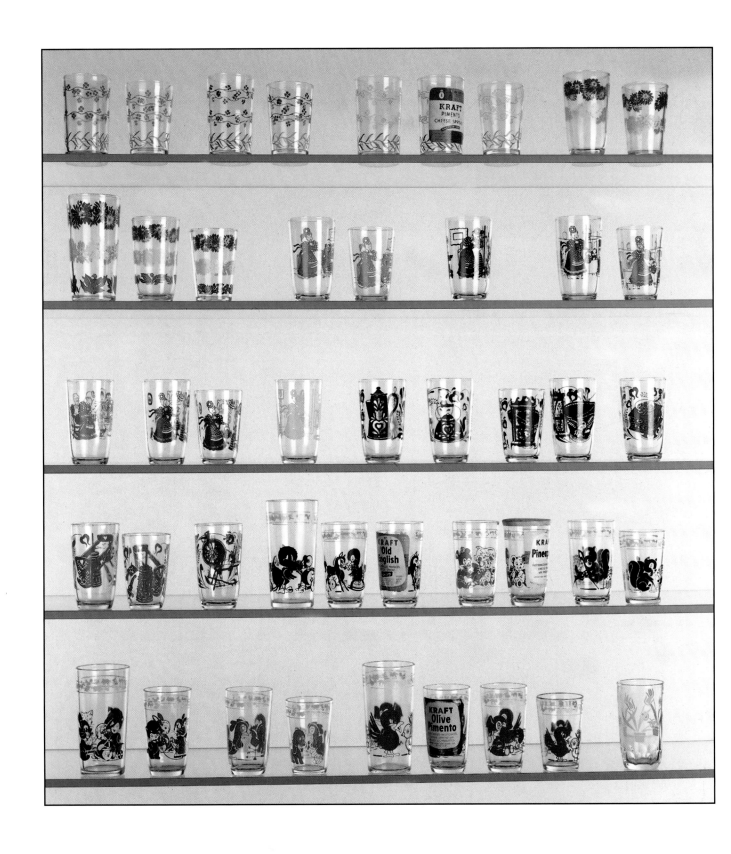

Thousand Line "Stars & Bars," ANCHOR HOCKING GLASS COMPANY, 1941-1960s

Colors: crystal, satinized green

This smaller Hocking line is beginning to be noticed by collectors of Fire-King and Early American Prescut. All Early American Prescut pieces have line numbers in the 700s, but this "Stars and Bars" line has nearly all pieces numbered in the 1000s. Many collectors buy the large salad bowl and tray — to use for salads! These may be accompanied by a glass fork and spoon. It was a popular gift item to new brides during WWII. You can find these more reasonably priced than buying newly made glassware items!

That luncheon plate may be the hardest item to find in this pattern.

You will find some satinized pieces in Thousand Line, and many of these will be color decorated. I'm not sure the bit of color adds anything to the appearance; you should be able to find these Thousand Line pieces with a little searching. I see some item from the line at nearly every market I visit. Sugar and creamers abound. They must have marketed them to restaurants who used one set per table!

	Crystal		Crystal
Bowl, 6", handled	10.00	Plate, 8", lunch	10.00
Bowl, 7½" deep	10.00	Relish, 12", six-part	13.00
Bowl, 8", vegetable	12.00	Relish, three-part, round	8.00
Bowl, 10½", salad, flat base, 7" ctr.	25.00	Relish, 10", two-handled, oval	6.00
Bowl, 10⅞", vegetable, rim base, 5½", ctr.	15.00	Spoon	7.50
Candle, 4"	3.00	Sugar, 2½"	4.00
Candy w/lid	17.00	Tray, 12½", sandwich	12.00
Creamer, 2½"	4.00	Vase, bud	12.00
Fork	7.50		

WILD ROSE WITH LEAVES & BERRIES, INDIANA GLASS COMPANY, EARLY 1950s – 1980s

Colors: crystal, crystal satinized, iridescent, milk glass, multi-colored blue, green, pink, and yellow; satinized green, pink, and yellow; sprayed green, lavender, and pink

    Wild Rose with Leaves and Berries is a small pattern that collectors in increasing numbers are noticing. Bowls especially can be utilized with many different patterns. I had mistakenly thought Cathy was the only person enamored with Wild Rose. Then I started getting letters and pictures from collectors. I began to pay attention when I saw it. A rather wide range of colors is available in Wild Rose. I have also encountered a multitude of prices, some exorbitant on the multi-colored pieces. I admit they are nicely colored, but it is not Victorian Pattern glass as I once saw it marked. Find a piece or two to use or go for all eight pieces. We have enjoyed our multi-colored sherbet dishes at many family meals! Those we hand wash lest the color fade in the dishwasher. Using crystal presents no such problem.

	Crystal Milk Glass Crystal Satinized	Sprayed & Satinized Colors Iridescent	Multi-colored
Bowl, handled sauce	4.00	6.00	10.00
Bowl, large vegetable	10.00	12.00	40.00
Candle	5.00	8.00	20.00
Plate, sherbet	2.00	3.00	10.00
Relish, handled	7.00	10.00	25.00
Relish, two-part, handled	7.00	10.00	25.00
Sherbet	4.00	6.00	10.00
Tray, two-handled	15.00	18.00	35.00

YORKTOWN, FEDERAL GLASS COMPANY, MID 1950s

Colors: amber, crystal, white, iridized, and smoke

Federal's Yorktown was a contemporary of Heritage and Golden Glory, but dispersal of Yorktown seems to have surpassed those two patterns combined. I added this pattern to the book to try to eliminate some of the letters I receive each year proclaiming that Heisey's Provincial has been found in yellow (Sahara). Provincial was not made in yellow; so readers assume that they have found rare pieces of Heisey. I can now refer them to this book. Rare pieces and colors do show up occasionally; but if you find a set priced very cheaply, the seller probably knows more than you do; you need to study more.

Crystal Yorktown can be collected within a short time if you pursue it. The punch set is inexpensive and could be used without fear of breaking it and spending hundreds of dollars to replace it. There is enough amber around to collect a set, also, but it will take a bit longer to piece together. I am pricing both colors the same for now, based strictly upon what I have paid or seen priced. Personally, I have not paid any more for amber than crystal; time will inform us if there is to be a difference. I see only a few pieces of the iridized, mostly the punch bowl set.

	Crystal/amber		Crystal/amber
Bowl, 5½", berry #2905	4.00	Plate, 11½" #2904	8.50
Bowl, 9½", large berry #2906	10.00	Punch set, 7 qt., base, 12 cups	40.00
Bowl, 10", ftd., fruit #2902	17.50	Saucer #2911	.50
Celery tray, 10" #2907	9.00	Sherbet, 2½", 7 oz. #1744	3.00
Creamer #2908	4.00	Sugar w/lid #2909	7.50
Cup #2910	3.00	Tumbler, 3⅞", 6 oz., juice #1741	4.00
Cup, snack/punch, 6 oz.	2.00	Tumbler, 4¾", 10 oz., water #1742	5.50
Mug, 5¹⁄₁₆"	15.00	Tumbler, 5¼", 13 oz., iced tea #1743	7.00
Plate, 8¼" #2903	4.00	Vase, 8"	16.00
Plate, 10½" x 6¾", snack w/indent	3.00		

A Publication I recommend:

DEPRESSION GLASS **DAZE**

The Original National Depression glass newspaper

Depression Glass Daze, the original, national monthly newspaper dedicated to the buying, selling and collecting of colored glassware of the 20s and 30s. We average 60 pages each month, filled with feature articles by top-notch columnists, readers' "finds," club happenings, show news, a china corner, a current listing of new glass issues to be aware of and a multitude of ads! You can find it in the DAZE! Keep up with what's happening in the dee gee world with a subscription to the DAZE. Buy, sell or trade from the convenience of your easy chair.

Name_____
Street_____
City_____ State_____ Zip_____
☐ 1 Year - $21.00   ☐ Check Enclosed   ☐ Please bill me
☐ Mastercard   ☐ Visa
    (Foreign subscribers - Please add $1.00 per year)

Card No. _____ Exp. Date_____
Signature_____

Send to: D.G.D., Box 57GF, Otisville, MI 48463-0008
Please allow 30 days

WHY SURF THE INTERNET?

ONE STOP SHOPPING

Depression Era Glassware
glassshow.com
Elegant Glassware, China & Pottery
www.glassshow.com

MegaShow
Glass Dealers Galore

OTHER BOOKS BY GENE FLORENCE

Anchor Hocking's Fire-King & More $24.95
Kitchen Glassware of the Depression Years, 5th Edition...............$19.95
Pocket Guide to Depression Glass, 11th Edition $9.95
Collector's Encyclopedia of Depression Glass, 14th Edition $19.95
Collector's Encyclopedia of Occupied Japan I................................$14.95
Collector's Encyclopedia of Occupied Japan II $14.95
Collector's Encyclopedia of Occupied Japan III.............................$14.95
Collector's Encyclopedia of Occupied Japan IV $14.95
Collector's Encyclopedia of Occupied Japan V...............................$14.95
Collector's Encyclopedia of Occupied Japan Price Guide I – V........$9.95
Elegant Glassware of the Depression Era, VIII $19.95
Glass Candlesticks of the Depression Era....................................$24.95
Pattern Identification Guide...$18.95
Very Rare Glassware of the Depression Years, 3rd Series $24.95
Very Rare Glassware of the Depression Years, 5th Series $24.95
Very Rare Glassware of the Depression Years, 6th Series $24.95
Stemware Identification $24.95

Collector's Encyclopedia of DEPRESSION GLASS, Fourteenth Edition

Gene Florence

Since the first edition of *Collector's Encyclopedia of Depression Glass* was released in 1972, it has been America's number one best-selling glass book. Gene Florence now presents the completely revised 14th edition, introducing newly discovered pieces to the 116 popular patterns and adding seven additional patterns to make this the most complete reference to date. With the assistance of several nationally-known dealers, this book illustrates, as well as realistically prices, items in demand. Dealing primarily with the glass made from the 1920s through the end of the 1930s, this beautiful reference book contains stunning color photographs, vintage catalog pages, updated values, and a special section on reissues and fakes. This dependable information comes from years of research, experience, fellow dealers and collectors, and millions of miles of travel by full-time glass dealer, Gene Florence.

ISBN: 1-57432-140-4
#5358 • 8½ x 11 • 240 pgs. • HB • $19.95

Florence's Glassware PATTERN IDENTIFICATION Guide

Gene Florence

Gene Florence's *Glassware Pattern Identification Guide* is a great companion for his other books. It includes most every pattern featured in his other price guides, as well as many more — over 400 patterns in all. A gorgeous close-up photograph of a representative piece of each pattern shows great detail to make identification easy. Florence provides the names, the company which made the glass, dates of production, and even colors available. This new guide is the ideal reference for all glass collectors and dealers, as well as the novice, and will be a great resource for years to come. No values.

ISBN: 1-57432-045-9
#5042 • 8½ x 11 • 176 Pgs. • PB • $18.95

Schroeder's ANTIQUES Price Guide

OUR #1 BEST-SELLER!

...is the #1 bestselling antiques & collectibles value guide on the market today, and here's why...

• *More than 450 advisors, well-known dealers, and top-notch collectors work together with our editors to bring you accurate information regarding pricing and identification.*

• *More than 45,000 items in almost 500 categories are listed along with hundreds of sharp original photos that illustrate not only the rare and unusual, but the common, popular collectibles as well.*

• *Each large close-up shot shows important details clearly. Every subject is represented with histories and background information, a feature not found in any of our competitors' publications.*

• *Our editors keep abreast of newly developing trends, often adding several new categories a year as the need arises.*

8½" x 11"
608 pages
$12.95

If it merits the interest of today's collector, you'll find it in *Schroeder's*. And you can feel confident that the information we publish is up-to-date and accurate. Our advisors thoroughly check each category to spot inconsistencies, listings that may not be entirely reflective of market dealings, and lines too vague to be of merit. Only the best of the lot remains for publication.

COLLECTOR BOOKS
A Division of Schroeder Publishing Co., Inc.

Without doubt, you'll find
Schroeder's Antiques Price Guide
the only one to buy for
reliable information and values.

COLLECTOR BOOKS
P.O. Box 3009 • Paducah, KY 42002–3009